The
Talmud

by Arthur Kurzweil

A Wiley Brand

The Talmud For Dummies®

Contents at a Glance

Table of Contents

Introduction

Maybe you heard someone say, "The Talmud says . . ." and you wonder just what the Talmud is. Well, the Talmud isn't so easy to define. The word itself literally means *learning*, but the text by that name has a more complex true definition. The best way to understand what it is, as I explain in this book, is to jump right into it and swim around a little.

Think of studying the Talmud kind of like kissing. You can read about kissing, you can watch people kiss, you can understand the physiology of how to kiss, but if you want to learn about kissing, the best thing to do is to experience some kissing!

The phrase "the Sea of Talmud" has been used for many centuries to describe the Talmud, and the metaphor of a sea is apt. The Talmud, like a sea

>> Has no real beginning. Just jump in.

>> Is deep and vast. (The Talmud consists of 63 books, 517 chapters, 2,711 double-sided pages, and 1,860,131 words.)

>> Needs an experienced captain to navigate through its waters.

>> Can be dangerous; you might drown in it.

The Talmud presents a number of challenges to the reader:

>> Written in a mixture of Hebrew and Aramaic

>> Contains no vowels, just consonants

>> Has incredibly complex text

>> Jumps from subject to subject without warning

>> Contains a lot of text that may seem irrelevant to modern life

>> Much more interested in questions than in answers

Discouraged already? Please don't be. Translations of the Talmud into modern English use punctuation, and you can find commentaries that go word by word, phrase by phrase, to help even the absolute beginner navigate the Sea of Talmud. And I'm here to act as your guide while we explore the Talmud together.

Talmudic scholars say that the Talmud is written in the language of thought. In the same way that your thoughts can be all over the place almost simultaneously, the Talmud goes from topic to topic by free association.

Someone seeking spiritual enlightenment often has trouble with the Talmud. Why? Because the Talmud has a unique quality that probably no other religious text has: It requires the student to object to it! That's right. In fact, if you're not arguing with the text, you're probably not really studying the Talmud correctly. Although the Talmud is a sacred book of the Jewish people, it encourages — no, it demands — that you question it.

The Inuit, indigenous people native to the Artic and Subarctic regions of North America, have a lot of words for snow in all its varieties. Although people often exaggerate exactly how many words they have, you can understand why they might have more words for snow than people who live in the tropics, for example. Exposure to and constant contact with something makes all its variations clear.

Well, the Talmud doesn't have too many words for snow, but it has a lot of different words for questions. In fact, the sages who first recorded the Talmud built it on questions. While you study the Talmud, if you don't ask questions, you can't really participate in the process of Talmud study. The student of Talmud must eagerly question and re-examine accepted views.

The Talmud was originally compiled over 2,000 years ago, but it serves as the repository of thousands of years of Jewish wisdom.

Another unique aspect of the Talmud is that it treats both familiar topics and imaginary topics with the same degree of seriousness. In other words, to test an idea, the Talmud often invents an impossible situation in order to see the implications of the idea. For example, even though no flying machines existed when the Talmud was compiled, the Talmud doesn't hesitate to say, "Well, what if we had a flying machine? What would that mean?"

The Talmud is filled with wisdom on almost every subject that you can imagine, but the text of the Talmud is more interested in the discussions that lead to the piece of wisdom, rather than merely the conclusion. When a Jewish child comes home from school, the appropriate question their parent asks isn't, "What did you learn today?" Instead, they ask, "Did you ask a good question today?"

The writers and compilers of the Talmud never imagined a final, written work, but rather an open-ended text in which new questions and points of view are constantly asked. Talmudic scholars consider it a great achievement when a student of the Talmud comes up with an angle that no one had considered before.

About This Book

The Talmud is Judaism's most important spiritual text, after the Bible. In fact, when students study a sacred Jewish text, they almost always study the Talmud. In *The Talmud for Dummies*, I aim to acquaint you with its key elements.

One of those elements is the great sages (wise rabbis) whose thoughts, ideas, and points of view appear in the pages of the Talmud. Probably a thousand different personalities have their words represented in the Talmud. Some of those sages appear only once in the entire text, while others appear hundreds of times. I introduce you to many of the key sages whose wisdom is laid out in the dialogues and debates in the Talmud.

The Talmud, unfortunately, has had a rough history, much like the Jewish people, who have had to face *antisemites* (people who are hostile to or prejudiced against Jews) since ancient times. Groups that have wanted to destroy the Jewish people over the centuries attacked and burned the Talmud because it's such a vital text for Jews.

The Talmud also faces attack because of a widespread misunderstanding of its contents and intentions. When the sages debate a certain subject, the pages of the Talmud record all sides of the debate, even the points of view ultimately rejected by the debaters. When someone quotes from the Talmud, that quote may reflect an idea that the overall text fiercely rejects. But someone can say, "The Talmud says . . ." even if the sages in the Talmud condemn the statement that they quote. This quoting out of context has happened many times throughout history, with horrible results.

The Talmud has a fascinating history, but it also has a tragic side because of the ways in which those opposed to the Jews have manipulated and distorted its purpose. In this book, I take you through some of the highlights and lowlights of the Talmud's story.

You can't get around the fact that the Talmud has been something of a men's club. The Talmud's personalities are 99 percent male, so their points of view are, not surprisingly, male-oriented. Additionally, only men have studied the Talmud over the centuries (for the most part), so men have also written the commentaries. In *The Talmud for Dummies*, I confront this fact head-on and describe some of the efforts being made in our generation to change that situation.

The Talmud deals with every topic under the sun in its 63 volumes and countless commentaries. I often challenge people to name a topic, and I can show them where in the Talmud they can find a discussion relevant to the topic. I've never lost that challenge. The topics in the Talmud include subjects and situations limited only by the imagination. In *The Talmud for Dummies*, I select and explore a number of topics discussed in the pages of the Talmud that I hope interest you. Those topics include sex, the courts, marriage and divorce, eating, celebrating holy days, and humor.

Conventions Used in This Book

To help you navigate this introduction to the Sea of Talmud, I use the following conventions:

>> **Definitions:** I define each Hebrew term the first time I use it, and I provide you with a pronunciation guide. I don't use a standard pronunciation system, but rather an easy-to-use system based on plain-spoken English.

>> **Dates:** When I provide a date, I use the secular abbreviations CE (Common Era), rather than AD (Anno Domini) and

BCE (Before the Common Era) rather than BC (Before Christ). The year numbers are the same (meaning 500 CE is the same as 500 AD). I use a reference point that's not Christian-oriented in fairness to our topic.

Foolish Assumptions

While I wrote this book, I had to make some assumptions about you. If you fit into *any* of these assumptions, this book is for you:

>> You feel pretty educated as a Jewish person, but you never really understood what the Talmud is all about.

>> You've heard about the Talmud but have no idea what it is.

>> You've heard the word *Talmudic* used in a negative way, implying overly complex or hair-splitting arguments.

>> You know nothing about the Talmud, or you're aware of some common misconceptions about the Talmud that you want to clear up.

>> You've seen accusations online that the Talmud is somehow against non-Jews.

>> You've read some horrible quotations supposedly from the Talmud and you want to know the truth.

>> You want to learn about the Talmud, but you don't want to struggle through an academic book about it. Instead, you want a friendly, informal, but accurate treatment of the subject.

>> You know some people who study the Talmud, and you want to try it, too.

Icons Used in This Book

You don't have to read this book cover to cover (though you certainly can). Think of it as your guide to understanding the Talmud. You can jump straight to the topics that interest you most — like how debates between sages shaped Jewish law or what the structure of a Talmudic discussion looks like — or you can read it in order to build your knowledge step by step.

Keep an eye out for some special icons to help you navigate the book:

Look for this icon to find quick, practical insights that can help make sense of Talmudic study.

This icon highlights key concepts and ideas that you need to know in order to properly understand the text of the Talmud.

This icon points you to deeper discussions or background information if you want to explore further; but don't feel obligated to read these paragraphs.

You can find common misunderstandings or tricky concepts that might lead to confusion pointed out with this icon.

Beyond the Book

In addition to the pages that you're reading right now, this book comes with a free, access-anywhere online Cheat Sheet that summarizes some of our key advice at a glance. There are also two additional chapters — one on marriage and divorce in the Talmud and one that explores my personal **minyan**, the quorum of ten Jewish adults required for certain communal prayers. These chapters are available online, along with a glossary of key figures in the Talmud. To access this material, go to www.dummies.com/go/talmudfd.

Where to Go from Here

You might want to purchase a Steinsaltz Talmud volume (Koren Publishers). Out of the 42 volumes available, I recommend you start with *Volume 1: Berakhot* (pronunciation; Blessings). Just roll up your sleeves and chip away at it slowly. Take advantage of all of the notes provided by Rabbi Adin Steinsaltz. You can also try *The Essential Talmud* (Basic Books) by Rabbi Steinsaltz. It's not an easy book, but it's worth the effort. I suggest additional further reading in Chapter 17.

Also, see whether you can find a Talmud class in a local synagogue. You can also watch some YouTube videos on the Talmud to introduce yourself to some ideas of this important Jewish text.

1

Introducing the Talmud

Discover what the Talmud is and why it holds such a central place in Jewish thought.

Trace the fascinating history of how the Talmud was compiled, preserved, and studied.

See how people engage with the Talmud today and why it continues to be relevant.

Explore historical attacks on the Talmud and efforts to suppress it.

Get familiar with essential legal terms used throughout Talmudic discussions.

IN THIS CHAPTER

» **Defining the Talmud and its importance**

» **Navigating a page of the Talmud**

» **Understanding the topics the Talmud discusses**

» **Getting to know the rabbis — and where are the women?**

» **Preparing to start studying the Talmud**

Chapter **1**

What is the Talmud?

The Talmud (TAL-muhd) is unlike any book you've ever seen. In fact, the Talmud isn't a singular book at all; it's a set of books — 63 in all — and each contains five books on almost every page! You don't open the Talmud at the beginning and start reading from front to back. When I describe the Talmud to you, you may begin to get a sense of its unique structure. (The word *Talmud* means "study" or "learning.")

In this chapter, I provide an overview of the Talmud in broad strokes and point you to where, in the rest of the book, you can read about everything in deeper detail.

Defining the Talmud

In a nutshell, the Talmud is the heart of Jewish learning — a sprawling, multi-layered conversation that has been unfolding for a few thousand years. It's a collection of teachings, debates, and stories, centered on Jewish law and ethics, while touching on nearly every aspect of human life. At its core are the *Mishna* (MISH-nah), a concise compilation of legal principles, and the *Gemara* ("G" as in goat gehm-AH-rah), a vast commentary and exploration of those principles, written in the lively and questioning spirit of ancient Jewish scholars. Together, these texts create a dialogue that spans generations, inviting readers not just to learn, but to engage, question, and contribute. Far from being a dry legal code, the Talmud is dynamic, thought-provoking, and deeply human — a living testament to the power of study and the pursuit of wisdom.

If this topic sounds overwhelming, don't worry. The Talmud might feel intimidating at first glance, but it's one of the most fascinating and enriching works you'll ever encounter. For centuries, it's been a cornerstone of Jewish thought, shaping not only religious practices, but also a way of approaching life itself.

For me, the Talmud is deeply personal. It has challenged, inspired, and guided me in ways I never imagined. And for the Jewish people as a whole, it's a treasure — an ongoing conversation that spans millennia. That's why I'm writing this book: to help more people understand and appreciate the Talmud's timeless wisdom and remarkable structure. Whether you're curious, skeptical, or just eager to learn, this journey into the Talmud is one I'm thrilled to take with you.

The Talmud: The Central Pillar of Judaism

Many people who don't know much about the Talmud think it's the law book of Judaism, but that's an over-simplification. One of the most concise descriptions of the Talmud I know comes from Rabbi Adin Steinsaltz, who died in 2020 at the age of 83 and is considered by many to be the greatest Talmud scholar of the last century, if not the last 1,000 years. (I was a private student of his for over 35 years, and I wrote a book about him called *On the Road with Rabbi Steinsaltz* [Jossey-Bass, Inc.].)

Rabbi Steinsaltz once wrote, "If the Bible is the cornerstone of Judaism, then the Talmud is the central pillar, soaring up from the foundations and supporting the entire spiritual and intellectual edifice." He called the Talmud the most important book in Jewish culture and described it as a repository of thousands of years of Jewish wisdom. He wrote, "(The Talmud) is a conglomerate of law, legend, and philosophy, a blend of unique logic and shrewd pragmatism, of history and science, anecdotes and humor."

By the "Bible" Rabbi Steinsaltz is referring to the "Holy Scriptures" of Judaism: the Five books of Moses, the Prophets, and the Writings. Christians refer to this as the "Old Testament."

You may find it strange to hear the Talmud, such a serious-looking and important text, described as full of anecdotes and humor; but I assure you, the Talmud is full of humorous stories.

REMEMBER

The Talmud has also been a target of *antisemitism* (prejudice and hatred against Jews), which I discuss in Chapter 4. The Talmud has been slandered, vilified, and burned by antisemites who don't know the first thing about the Talmud, what it is, or how it works. Popes, Nazis, and Jews who left the religion have all had a hand in the burning and destruction of volumes of the Talmud over the centuries.

Jewish tradition teaches that when God gave the Written Torah (also known as the Five Books of Moses) to Moses, God also gave him, orally, a detailed explanation of how to apply its teachings to life.

TIP

I discuss the history of the Talmud and its evolution from oral tradition to printed text in detail in Chapter 2.

The Talmud was never meant to be a completed document. Individual students add new commentaries and insights to the Talmud daily in the form of their own margin notes. More significantly, new editions of the Talmud have been published in our day, containing new contemporary commentaries. One excellent example of this is the Steinsaltz Talmud, also known as the Koren Talmud Bavli (see Chapter 17). Rabbi Adin Steinsaltz published an edition of the Talmud that includes his own commentary to help the modern student understand the text and participate in its discussions.

REMEMBER

Rabbi Steinsaltz described the Talmud as a "photograph of a fountain," where the photo captures just one frozen moment. At its best, the Talmud inspires the student to get involved in the discussion, having an active dialogue with the rabbis and sages whose teachings are recorded in the Talmud. Jewish scholarship permits and even encourages the student of Talmud to object to a text and demand further explanation and even justification. A person doesn't read the Talmud passively.

The Layout of the Talmud: What Are You Looking At?

When you first open a page of the Talmud, you probably notice that it doesn't look like any book you've seen — Figure 1-1 is an example of a page (I talk about the layout of the Talmud in Chapter 6). A portion of two books appears in the middle of each page. One is called the *Mishna,* and the other is called the *Gemara.* The *Mishna* is in Hebrew, and the *Gemara* is in Aramaic (the language spoken by people in Israel 2,000 years ago). The word *Mishna* means "instruction." The word *Gemara* means "to finish" or "to complete."

The *Mishna* provides the laws of the Oral Torah. But, like any book of law, many elements need explanation. What do certain words mean? How, more precisely, does a person perform or follow or understand those laws? That's where the *Gemara* comes in. The *Gemara* (which is almost always longer than the accompanying *Mishna*) explains the laws in that *Mishna*; along the way, it also contains thousands of years of Jewish wisdom. The *Gemara*, if gathered together, also adds up to a book — or more accurately, to the size of many books.

A *Gemara* is almost always longer than its *Mishna*, which is usually rather short. The *Gemara* can sometimes go on for pages before a new *Mishna* appears. Together, the *Mishna* and the *Gemara* form the Talmud. With some exceptions, the Talmud generally contains a *Mishna* and its *Gemara*, another *Mishna* and another *Gemara*, for a total of 63 volumes, running down the middle of each page.

Just like the *Mishna* needs the commentary of the *Gemara* to help make it understandable, the *Gemara* needs a commentary that provides its explanation. A rabbi called Rashi (RAH-she), born in 1040 CE, wrote this commentary. Rashi's commentary appears on almost every page of the Talmud and seeks to elucidate the *Gemara*. But much of Rashi's commentary also needed explanations, and often objections and clarifications, and that part of a page of the Talmud is called *Tosafot* (TOE-sah-foat; addition) which includes Rashi's grandsons. (For a lot more about Rashi, see Chapter 2.)

So, in a nutshell, the *Mishna* needs the *Gemara*, the *Gemara* needs Rashi's commentary, and Rashi's commentary needs the *Tosafot*. These elements appear throughout the volumes of the Talmud, page by page, and additional commentaries and references by important scholars over the centuries surround the text of the Talmud on each page to help the reader grasp its meaning and intention. Five things occur on each page, so you see five different texts simultaneously when you look at a single page. The Talmud is essentially a written record of discussions and debates on the part of at least 1,000 rabbis.

Are you dizzy yet? Just take it in slowly. It's worth the effort. Because it is a unique document, the Talmud's structure is not so easy to master.

Let's imagine that the Mishna states a law that a cigarette is bad for your health. Then the *Gemara* might ask, "What's a cigarette?" Then someone will try to define what a cigarette is. Someone else will say, "That sounds more like a cigar."

Then, a discussion will occur, with several rabbis each weighing in on the difference between a cigarette and a cigar. After a while someone will ask, "What does the Mishna mean by "health"? Mental health, physical health?

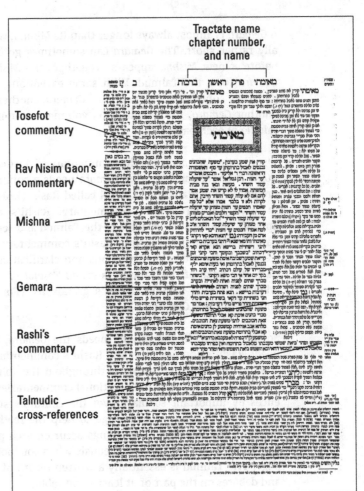

Tractate name
chapter number,
and name

Tosefot commentary

Rav Nisim Gaon's commentary

Mishna

Gemara

Rashi's commentary

Talmudic cross-references

FIGURE 1-1.
A page of the Talmud, showing the Mishna, the *Gemara*, Rashi's commentary, and the Tosafot.

Then someone will say, "Rabbi so-and-so smoked cigarettes for 90 years." Someone will then tell a story about that same rabbi which has little if anything to do with cigarettes.

In the meantime, Rashi will suggest that the Mishna used the word "cigarette" to mean anything that one smokes. Then one of Rashi's grandsons will insist that it said "cigarette" and it means "cigarette."

It is the task of the student of Talmud to sort out the various points of view and join in the discussion.

Do you get the idea?

THE REVERENCE OF TALMUD SCHOLARS

Before you open the Talmud to see what's inside, you first need to know how to treat a volume of the Talmud and how a student of the Talmud needs to behave. The Talmud isn't just another book to grab or toss around. It's not unusual, for example, to see a Talmud student pick up a volume or take it off a shelf and kiss it gently before opening it as a sign of respect and reverence. Before beginning to study from its pages, students recite a blessing of gratitude. Everyone exerts great effort to ensure that no volume of the Talmud ever drops to the floor. In preparation for studying the Talmud, students often wash their hands, not with soap and water, but in a ritualized way as dictated by Jewish tradition as described in the *Shulkhan Arukh, the Code of Jewish Law*. It's almost like a baptism of the hands, a spiritual cleansing. There is no English translation of *the Code of Jewish Law*, but there is an abridged version called the *Kitzur Shulkhan Arukh* (kit-tzur shool-khan ah-rukh; abridged *Shulkhan Arukh)* which will explain the handwashing ritual.

The great sages of the past recommend that students of the Talmud set aside time every day to study. Like working out at the gym, studying for 15 minutes a day is better than studying for 5 hours once a month. It's the routine, sustained practice that is valuable. The great Jewish sages recommend regular study as part of a person's daily routine. The sages also recommend that you find a regular study partner, called your khevrusa (khev-roo-sa). Not only does such a commitment keep a student on track. It also avoids the ease of fooling yourself into thinking that you understand what you're studying. A perspective by someone else will challenge your understanding of the text.

What's It All About? Everything!

In its vastness, the Talmud contains discussions about just about every topic under the sun — and above it, too! And the Talmud itself makes the point that the best subjects to study are the subjects that you want to study. For example, if you're interested in child-rearing, look for texts in the Talmud about child-rearing. The Talmud deals, for example, with agriculture, dream interpretation, etiquette, theology, faith, mathematics, lavatory behavior, obesity, astronomy, medicine and medical advice, medical remedies, folklore, science, heresy, human habits, ethical problems, sexual life, astronomy, astrology, and business ethics.

If you want to study human sexuality, you can find plenty of material on that subject, too (See Chapter 13 for an exploration of this topic in the Talmud.) You can locate texts by subject in the Talmud in several ways, and I offer some suggestions about how to find what you're looking for in Chapter 17.

In this book, I offer several chapters that deal with specific topics. I have pored over the Talmud, looking for texts that deal with the same general subject. Many Talmudic students and scholars perform this kind of research. Although many students of the Talmud study page by page, others want to locate the points of view of the rabbis on particular subjects, and so their research takes them all over the Talmud.

In *The Talmud for Dummies*, I discuss topics that I selected based on my own interests and those that I think would be general interests. These topics include marriage and divorce (Chapter 12), Jewish holidays (Chapter 10), the Jewish court system (Chapter 14), human sexuality (Chapter 13), eating (Chapter 11), and praying (Chapter 11).

Because the Talmud doesn't have a Volume 1, you can really jump in anywhere. Start with a *Mishna* and try to understand it. The Steinsaltz edition (which I talk about in Chapter 17) helps you to do that. Then, start to study the *Gemara* immediately following that *Mishna*, and work on it word by word, phrase by phrase, and sentence by sentence.

Again, a commentary such as what appears in the Steinsaltz edition not only helps you understand the text you are reading. I suggest you begin with one of these *masekhtot* (mah-**sekh**-toat; tractates, an organizational unit within the Talmud that examines a specific subject):

» *Berakhot* (beh-rah-**khoat**; Blessings): About prayers and blessings

» *Pesakhim* (peh-**sah**-kheem): About the holiday of Passover

» *Bava Metzia* (bah-vah met see-ah: The Middle Gate): About buying and selling, lost and found objects, and other down-to-earth topics

The *masekhtot* in the preceding list are far less technical than so many other sections of the Talmud.

The Great (and Not So Great) Rabbis of the Talmud

When you study the Talmud you need to know who said what because knowing who represented a certain point of view or action has an impact on understanding what is being said. (For example, if a poor man gives charity of a dollar it is more significant than if a millionaire gives a dollar to charity. Also "attribution" is an important principle in the Talmud. In other words, give credit where credit is due. Knowing who said what also gives greater insight into what is being said. In Chapter 7 and in the additional appendix, found at www.dummies.com/go/talmudfd, I introduce you to many of the rabbis and other personalities in the Talmud. An important thing to remember, however, is that the rabbis in the Talmud are people, not plastic saints. Judaism assumes that even the greatest rabbis are only human. They make mistakes and can express wrong opinions about things. Jews don't make people into gods. Keep an open mind.

Some rabbis described in the Talmud have great authority and sterling reputations, so you interpret a remark made by one of them far differently than a statement made by a heretic, for example. In principle, the Talmud teaches that the wise person is the one who learns from everyone.

The words of a rabbi quoted in the Talmud just once or twice in the entire 63 volumes might have something profoundly important to teach. After a while, students of the Talmud get to know many of the rabbis who are quoted or described in the text, and you develop favorites. Two of my favorites are Rabbi Akiva and Nachum ish Gamzu (see Chapter 7 for details on these two sages and others).

Some of my favorite quotes are such because they challenge my thinking. Both Rabbi Akiva and Nachum ish Gamzu are quoted in the Talmud as saying essentially the same thing: "This too is for good." This reflects a theological stance that assumes anything that the Almighty allows to happen to you is ultimately for good. Nachum ish Gamzu would always say, "This is also for good," while Rabbi Akiva would say, "All that the Merciful One does, He does for good." The idea seems outrageous. Is the suffering of an innocent child in any way good? Was the Holocaust in any way good?

In the first place, one never says "Everything is for good" to someone else, only to oneself. Also, this attitude is probably the most difficult approach to life in all of Judaism and other religions. Do I really believe that everything is for the best? My rational mind does not allow for such an approach to life. But I appreciate the teaching of these two sages because they challenge me spiritually. Could it be that in some inexplicable way, everything leads to something good? I can't deny that these two great sages in the Talmud represent this attitude. And I would be dishonest if I did not confess that I strive for an unwavering faith and optimism, even in the face of adversity.

Women in the Talmud

In Chapter 8, I make no bones about it: an apology — and more — is necessary regarding women and the Talmud. Few women are quoted in the text, and throughout history, few women have studied the Talmud. The good news is this: In our generation, more women than ever are studying the Talmud. And I predict that, in time, reputable Jewish publishers will issue Talmudic commentaries written by women.

I'm not the first person to suggest that if women had participated in Talmud study over the centuries, many of the issues dealt within the pages of the text would be treated quite differently. I'm not suggesting that the Talmud would always contain something called *a woman's voice. All people are, of course, unique.* But I would contend that women's voices in the text and commentary of the Talmud would make it a much different document. Chapter 8 deals with the important topic of the role (and lack thereof) for women in the Talmud in greater detail.

Studying the Talmud — Some Things to Keep in Mind

One of the complexities of the Talmud is that, although its 63 volumes are organized by topic (see Appendix for a list of all 63 Tractates of the Talmud), the Talmud is continually free-associating. Like conversations in real life, Talmudic discussions jump from topic to topic, at times returning to the original subject and sometimes not. Of course, two topics can seem to discuss two different issues when actually, at the heart of things, they deal with the same issue. The Talmud often quotes a particular rabbi on a certain topic, followed by, "Speaking of Rabbi So-and-So, he also said . . ." and then go to an entirely different subject.

Also, keep in mind that when studying the Talmud the best way to do it is to crack open the text and locate the eternal ideas embedded within it.

For example, a somewhat long passage in the Talmud discusses brides and how they look. You can easily judge this passage to be sexist. After all, the text doesn't discuss how grooms look! But when you crack open the text and try to locate the eternal idea embedded within it, you can understand that the discussion is really about the permissibility to tell white lies. (I go into more detail about the discussion on flattering brides in the additional chapter on marriage and divorce, available on www.dummies.com/go/talmudfd.)

Rather than reject the discussion outright, the text can become a springboard toward a deep discussion about when you can tell a lie in good conscience. For example, I wouldn't visit my grandmother in the hospital and say, "Grandma, you look worse than you did yesterday." Although the Torah teaches you to tell the truth, sometimes a white lie, particularly not to hurt a person's feelings, is what the situation calls for.

When you start exploring the Talmud, stay with it — you can find knowledge and inspiration on every page. Words of wisdom pop up in the Talmud often when you least expect it. And if you are reading a book or essay that quotes the Talmud and gives a page number from the Talmud, you might want to go to that page and read around it. Sometimes I get caught in a string of references from different tractates of the Talmud and I begin to explore an entirely different topic. I jump into the "sea of Talmud" and start to swim.

You can swim in the sea of Talmud, too.

Chapter **2**

Tracing the History of the Talmud

The history of the Talmud (TAL-muhd; to study/to learn) is deeply intertwined with the broader history of Judaism because the Talmud represents the transmission and evolution of Jewish thought from ancient times to today. Before the Talmud, Judaism was primarily defined by the Written Torah (also known as the Five Books of Moses) and the Oral Torah, an accompanying body of interpretation and practice that was passed down orally.

Jews relied on these teachings to apply the laws of the Torah to daily life; but without a formal record, they risked losing or understanding those teachings over time. So, at one point, the Oral Torah was written down. Without commentary, a person might find the Torah difficult, if not impossible, to fully understand. For example, take a look at the very first sentence in the Written Torah, "In the beginning, God created the heaven and the earth." The very first word in Hebrew, *Berayshit* (buh-ray-SHEET), actually has more than one interpretation. It could mean

>> "In the beginning" (In the beginning, God created)

>> "In the beginning of" (In the beginning of God's creation)

>> "(God created) the beginning"

>> "With *reishit* (Ray-sheet), "God created with wisdom" (in the book of Psalms, Psalm 111:10, the word *reishit* refers to wisdom. This in turn refers to Torah as in a statement in a mystical Jewish text the *Zohar*, ZOWE-hahr) "God looked into the Torah and created the world"

>> Or it could even be a contraction of two words, *barah* (bah-RAH; created) and *shis* (shaysh; six), referring to six dimensions of being: Above, Below, Right (South), Left (North), In front (East), Behind (West).

And this is just the first word! For the Children of Israel to understand and grasp the Written Torah, they needed help.

This chapter delves into the Talmud's history, beginning with the essential contributions of Rashi, one of its most influential commentators, whose work connects ancient traditions to future generations. I also present a condensed explanation of key events in the history of Judaism and, therefore, the Talmud.

The history of the Talmud begins at Mount Sinai, when God dictated the Written Torah to Moses. At that same time, God also gave Moses the Oral Torah. The written version of the Oral Torah is called the Talmud.

Compare the situation to the United States Constitution and the decisions of the Supreme Court. The Court interprets the words of the Constitution and shows how to apply them to reality.

Introducing Rashi: The Great Commentator of the Talmud

If you want to study Talmud, you need to get familiar with Rashi (1040–1105 CE). The name Rashi is actually an acronym for his full name, RAbbi SHlomo Itzchaki (SHLOW-mow Itz-KHAH-Kee). The shorter form is more convenient to say and write. (See the sidebar "Important Rabbis from History Known by Acronyms," in this chapter, for more abbreviated names in Jewish culture.)

In the standard edition of the Talmud, Rashi's commentary has appeared on every page since the 16th century. Rashi's Talmud commentary reflects his ability to explain complexities in simple, straightforward, concise language. His commentary made Talmud study far more accessible and reached many people. In addition to his Talmud commentary, Rashi also provided a well-known commentary on the Torah.

REMEMBER

The word *commentator* in this context simply means someone who helps to explain what the text means. If Rashi thinks that the reader might need some clarification, he makes a comment. In a Talmud class, the teacher often says, "What's bothering Rashi?" This question refers to a comment by Rashi that offers some explanation of the Talmud's text.

Scholar, rabbi, and vintner

Rashi was born in 1040 in Troyes, France. His father, Yitzchok (YITZ-khahk; Isaac), was a great rabbinical scholar. In addition to being a rabbi, Yitzchok was a vintner; Rashi also worked as a vintner.

In Jewish custom, you begin your Torah studies at the age of 5; and legend says that, at that young age, Rashi was already beginning to show evidence of great scholarship. In his teens Rashi left his home to study in Germany's famous *yeshivas* (yeh-SHEE-vahz; Jewish schools), in both Mainz and Worms.

One of the most illustrious rabbis in all of Jewish history was known as *Rabbeinu* Gershom ("our teacher Gershom, Rah-BAY-new GUHR-shum) known as "the Light of the Exile"). Two of his disciples, Rabbi Yitzchok ben Yehuda and Rabbi Yaakov ben Yakar acted as Rashi's main teachers.

After studying in Germany for eight years, Rashi returned to Troyes. At about 25, he was appointed to the community's rabbinical court. When he was about 30, he established his own *yeshiva* in Troyes. The finest students from all over Europe came to study there, and Rashi became known as a superb teacher and authority on Jewish law. Rashi's work earned him the title (Rabban Shel Yisrael, RAH-bahn shell yis-row-ale, the Teacher of the Jewish People.

Rashi was the senior rabbi in Troyes, but he didn't receive a salary for his work. Rather, his work as a *vintner* (a wine merchant) provided his livelihood. His knowledge of winemaking appears occasionally in his Talmudic commentary. Rashi died at the age of 65 in 1105.

Could Rashi read Rashi?

If you know how Hebrew looks, you may notice that the commentary by Rashi often doesn't really look much like Hebrew. The typeface of Rashi's writing and Hebrew have some similarities, but a person who can read Hebrew can't automatically read Rashi's commentary.

Rashi could not read "Rashi script." Rashi likely never saw, knew or would have even been able to read the script that bears his name. The script now known as "Rashi script" was developed long after Rashi's death. The script we now call "Rashi script" was actually created by early printers in the late 15th century, nearly 400 years after Rashi's death. The script was named after him due to its common use for printing his widely-studied commentaries, not because he created or used it himself.

His commentaries are essential for beginners and advanced students. Modern translations of the Talmud (some wonderful examples of which I talk about in Chapter 3) have incorporated Rashi's commentary into the translated text.

TECHNICAL STUFF

Scholars of the French language have also used Rashi's commentaries in their work. Sometimes, the earliest examples of French language usage appear within Rashi's Torah or Talmud commentaries. When Rashi wanted to clarify or translate something, he sometimes found he could best make his point by using a French word or phrase. Rashi's commentaries have preserved about 3,000 Old French words, to the delight of the French and Francophiles.

Post-Rashi: The Tosafot Period

In addition to Rashi's commentary on each page of the Talmud, another commentary called *Tosafot* (toe-sah-fote, Addition) appears there, too. The commentaries of the *Tosafot* were originally written by students in their *yeshivas*, Jewish educational institutions that focused on the study of traditional religious texts.

These notes were edited and were placed in various parts of the text surrounding the Talmud. They appear on every page, with Rashi's commentary always on the inside margin and *Tosafot* always on the outside margin.

The *Tosafot* period began when Rashi finished his Talmud commentary in the late 11th century. The very first commentators of the *Tosafot* period were Rashi's sons-in-law and his grandsons.

Rashi's legacy through his daughters and their families

Rashi had three daughters: Yocheved, Miriam, and Rachel. Each of them married scholars. Those husbands became illustrious rabbis and scholars, and their writing appears on just about every page of the standard edition of the Talmud.

Legend has it that Rashi taught his daughters Talmud, an unusual practice for women in medieval Europe. His three daughters are sometimes credited with helping to preserve and pass on Rashi's teachings. They not only upheld his legacy, but became part of an enduring chain of scholarship:

>> **Yocheved:** Rashi's eldest daughter married Meir ben Samuel. They had four sons, two of whom became illustrious commentators, known as the *Rashbam* (Rabbi Samuel ben Meir) and *Rabbenu* Tam (Rabbi Jacob ben Meir).

>> **Miriam:** Rashi's second daughter married Rabbi Judah ben Nathan, also a great commentator.

>> **Rachel:** Rashi's third daughter married Rabbi Eliezer. They divorced, an uncommon occurrence in Jewish communities at the time. Unlike her sisters, who married men who became renowned Talmudic scholars and commentators, Rachel's life took a different path. No one knows much about her because few records of her life and contributions exist.

Rashi's most accomplished grandson

From the early 12th century until the 14th century, the *Tosafot* were active with their commentaries. The leading *Tosafist* (toe-sah-fist) was Rashi's grandson, *Rabbenu* Tam (Rabbi Jacob ben Meir).

Rashi and his *Tosafot* grandsons often disagreed, and you can plainly see those disagreements in the Talmud. One of the most famous of these disputes was one regarding *tefillin* (teh-FILL-in; two small black leather boxes containing Hebrew parchment). Observant Jewish men wear *tefillin* on an arm and on their forehead, usually during weekday morning prayers. Four scriptural passages appear on the parchment placed in *tefillin*. The dispute between grandfather (Rashi) and grandson (*Rabbenu* Tam) concerns itself with the order in which you should place the four parchments in the *tefillin*. Their disagreement actually prompts some people today to put on two sets of *tefillin* each morning out of respect for both grandfather and grandson.

IMPORTANT RABBIS FROM HISTORY KNOWN BY ACRONYMS

Jewish history often remembers many influential rabbis by acronyms derived from their names. These acronyms honor their contributions to Torah, Talmud, philosophy, and mysticism, while making it easier for students to refer to them in study and conversation. Here are a few of the most celebrated:

- **Rashi** (Rah-she): Rabbi Shlomo Yitzchaki, the renowned medieval Torah and Talmud commentator

- **Rambam** (RAHM-bahm): Rabbi Moshe ben Maimon, also known as Maimonides

- **Ramban** (Rahm-BAHM): Rabbi Moshe ben Nachman, also known as Nachmanides

- **Rashbam** (RAHSH-Bahm: Rabbi Shmuel ben Meir, grandson of Rashi and notable Torah commentator

- **Maharal** (Mah-ha-RAHL): Rabbi Judah Loew ben Bezalel, famous for his works on Jewish philosophy and mysticism

- **Besht** (BEHSHT Rabbi Israel ben Eliezer, also known as the *Baal Shem Tov (*Bah-ahl shehm-tove_; Master of the Good Name), founder of Hasidism, a mystical religious revival movement within Judaism that originated in the 18th century, emphasizing emotional spiritual expression, devotion, and the omnipresence of God.

- **Ramchal** (Rahm-KHAL): Rabbi Moshe Chaim Luzzatto, prominent Italian rabbi and kabbalist

- **Radak** (Rah-DAHK): Rabbi David Kimhi, medieval rabbi and grammarian known for his biblical commentaries

- **Malbim** (MAHL-Bihm): Rabbi Meir Leibush ben Yechiel Michel Wisser, 19th-century rabbi and Torah commentator

Key Milestones in Jewish History

In the following section I have not given you a comprehensive timeline of Jewish history. Rather, I've selected some important dates that had a significant impact on the decision to write down the Oral Torah.

70 CE: Destruction of the Second Temple

The destruction of the Second Temple by the Romans in 70 CE was cataclysmic for the Jewish people and Judaism. Essentially, the Jews needed to design a new form of Judaism because the Temple was such an important part of Jewish life.

While the Holy Temple stood, the sacrificial system was a central aspect of Jewish life. It had several functions. It provided

>> A means of atonement for sins that individual Jews committed

>> A means to express gratitude for and seek purification from God

>> Reaffirmation of their commitment to God and God's laws

>> Symbolic acts that stressed the seriousness of sin

>> Reinforcement of Jewish identity, particularly when pilgrims gathered at the Temple three times a year on days of major festivals

The Book of Leviticus in the Written Torah details the system of sacrifices. These laws ensured that priests performed these rituals properly within the Temple's sacred space.

The destruction of the Temple shifted the focus from Temple rituals to Rabbinic Judaism and Torah study, which you can see throughout the Talmud.

70 CE: The establishment of the Yavneh school

Rabbi Yochanan ben Zakkai established a center for Jewish learning at the city of Yavneh, which was crucial for the development of Rabbinic Judaism. It was a true watershed moment. As you will see in the paragraphs below, a group of Jews led by Rabbi Yochanan be Zakkai, chose to negotiate with the Romans and to establish a center for Torah study. Rather than fight to the death against the Romans, as many Jews did, the sensible path was to establish a center for Jewish learning.

General Vespasian led the Roman siege of Jerusalem and was replaced by his son Titus, who was successful in destroying whatever remained of the Temple.

Many legends exist about Rabbi Yochanan Ben Zakkai. Jewish legend says that he studied Scripture, the *Mishna* (MISH-NAH; Study by Repetition; the first written compilation of Jewish oral traditions, known as the Oral Torah), *Gemara* (geh-MAR-ah; learning, the second part of the Talmud, providing commentary on the first part the Mishna), *halakhah* (ha-la-khah; laws), *gematria* (geh-MAT-ree-ah; a method of interpreting Hebrew text by calculating the numerical value of letters, words, or phrases. Each Hebrew letter corresponds to a specific number, allowing for the conversion of text into numerical values), parables, fox fables, and Kabbalah; (kah-bah-LA; Jewish mysticism aimed at understanding the nature of God, the universe, and the human soul).

In the most famous story about him, he arranged a secret escape from the city of Jerusalem to meet with Vespasian, who was then a Roman general. He asked Vespasian for permission to establish a center of Jewish learning in the city of Yavneh. He taught, "If you have learned much Torah, do not ascribe any merit to yourself because this is what you were created for."

I don't exaggerate when I say that all students of Torah owe a debt of gratitude for his establishing his school. Every Jewish school from the time of Yochanan ben Zakkai until today is his heir.

132 CE: Roman Emperor Hadrian enacts oppressive laws

Realizing that the Torah and *mitzvot* (mitz-vote; command-ments to connect with God) were the key to Jewish survival, Roman Emperor Hadrian instituted laws banning *mitzvah* (mitz-vah; singular of *mitzvot*) observance; specifically, Shabbat and circumcision. Many Jews found the situation under Hadrian's rule intolerable, and the harsh restrictions led to widespread unrest within the Jewish community.

The Roman authorities imposed severe punishments for those who defied the new laws, leading to increased tension and resentment. This period marked the beginning of a series of revolts, with Jews resisting Roman rule in desperate attempts to preserve their religious practices and cultural identity. Hadrian sought to transform Jerusalem into a Roman metropolis, and aimed to quell Jewish nationalism and prevent further uprisings following the Bar Kokhba revolt of 132-135 CE (see below). In addition, his affinity for Greek culture and pagan theology con-flicted with Jewish religious practices.

135 CE: The Bar Kokhba revolt

In the face of Roman Emperor Hadrian's intolerable conditions and oppression (see the preceding section), Bar Kokhba, a Jew-ish military leader, led a rebellion against the Romans. It failed, with an estimated half million Jews killed in the fighting. Large numbers also died from hunger or disease, or were sold into slavery. After the revolt, Hadrian increased the laws against Torah observance. Among the *mitzvot* outlawed by Hadrian were *tefillin* (leather cases holding prayers on parchment), matzah (matz-ah; unleavened bread), *lulav* (loo-lav), palm fronds used in a ritual on the Jewish holy days of Succot (sew-COAT), and reading the Torah in public.

The leading rabbinic figure at that time was Rabbi Akiva (flip to Chapter 15 for more about this rabbi), whom the Romans ulti-mately tortured and murdered.

138 CE: Hadrian and his laws die

When Hadrian died in 138, his successor, Antonius Pius, revoked the most oppressive anti-Jewish laws. The *Sanhedrin*, the Jewish Supreme Court, reconvened. (See more about the Sanhedrin in Chapter 13).

Key Events in Talmudic History

The following sections provide a timeline of the Talmud's evolution and various editions, tracing its development from 200 CE to the modern day. Beginning with the compilation of the *Mishna* (the first major written collection of Jewish oral traditions, known as the Oral Torah, that serves as the basis for all subsequent rabbinic literature, and was the foundation of the entire Talmud), Jewish scholars began shaping the foundational text of Jewish law. Those same scholars also then created the *Gemara* (geh-mar ah; an extensive rabbinical analysis and commentary on the Mishnah, a major part of the Talmud) in two distinct regions — scholars in Palestine created the Jerusalem Talmud in the 4th century, and scholars in Babylonia wrote the Babylonian Talmud, which became the more influential and widely studied version of the two by the 6th century.

Over the centuries, the Talmud went through numerous editions and commentaries, reflecting shifts in Jewish scholarship and practice. This timeline highlights the key moments in the Talmud's history, from its early stages of compilation to its ongoing study and influence in contemporary Jewish life.

200 CE: The compilation of the Mishna

Rabbi Yehudah HaNasi (also called Judah the Prince; I discuss this rabbi in detail in Chapter 7) and his colleagues decided that they needed to write down what, up until then, Jewish scholars had always transmitted orally from generation to generation. They feared that if they didn't write it down, the Jewish people would lose and forget the Oral Torah received by Moses at Mount

Sinai. The *Mishna* (Study by repetition) is a written collection of those oral laws and traditions. The rabbis and sages quoted in the *Mishna* are known as *Tannaim* (tah-NAH-yeem; to teach/to repeat). The *Mishna* is the collection of teachings, traditions, and laws.

200 CE: The Amoraic Period begins

In their efforts to understand the meaning of the contents of the *Mishna*, the rabbis and sages began to produce a body of teachings dedicated to explaining the *Mishna*, adding their own recollections of the Oral Torah that they heard. When compiled, these teachings became known as the *Gemara* (geh-MAH-rah; to complete/to finish).

The rabbis and sages are quoted in the *Gemara* to interpret and expand upon the *Mishna*. They are known as the Amariam (ah-ma-rye-eem; speakers or interpreters). The *Mishna* and the *Gemara* combined is called the Talmud. The word "Talmud" derives from the Hebrew verb meaning "to teach" or "to learn." The term "Talmud" in its current sense, refers to the compilation of the Mishnah and *Gemara,* and became more widely used after the completion of the Babylonian Talmud. It likely came into use as a term for the body of rabbinic teachings sometime after the compilation of the Mishnah around 200 CE. This compilation is traditionally dated to around 500 CE.

219 CE: The Sura academy opens

The Sura school (established in the ancient Babylonian city of Sura, on the banks of the Euphrates River) played a pivotal part in developing the Babylonian Talmud (which I talk about in the section "3rd–6th Centuries CE: The Babylonian Talmud," later in this chapter) by serving as a major center of Jewish learning and scholarship in Babylonia. Founded by Abba Arikha, known as Rav, the Sura academy became a center of Torah study, attracting scholars from across the Jewish world. Rav was a disciple of Rabbi Yehudah HaNasi, the compiler of the *Mishna* (discussed in the section "200 CE: The complication of the Mishna." In addition to Rav Ashi and Ravina (see the section "4th–5th Centuries CE: Rav Ashi and Ravina," later in this chapter), other notable scholars associated with Sura include Rav Huna, Rav Chisda, and Saadia Gaon.

259 CE: The Pumbedita academy opens

Judah bar Ezekiel founded the Pumbedita school in 259 CE in Pumbedita, a city in ancient Babylonia. Students of the Sura academy (see the preceding section) sometimes criticized the Pumbedita academy as being overly intricate or hair-splitting in its analyses of the Mishna. But despite their differences, both schools were essential to the preservation and evolution of Jewish law and tradition. Like Sura, Pumbedita was responsible for the development and preservation of the Babylonian Talmud. (See the section "3rd–6th Centuries CE: The Babylonian Talmud," later in this chapter.)

3rd–5th centuries CE: The Jerusalem Talmud

Known as the *Yerushalmi* (Yeh-roo-SHAHL-mi) the Jerusalem Talmud is the written Oral Torah that uses the same *Mishna* that the Babylonian Talmud does (see the following section for talk about the Babylonian Talmud). But the *Yerushalmi* generally contains a different *Gemara* than the Babylonian Talmud, reflecting the opinions and interpretations of the rabbis and sages living in Palestine at the time.

When most Jews study Talmud today, they study the Babylonian Talmud, not the Jerusalem Talmud. The less polished Jerusalem Talmud can't compare to the Babylonian Talmud, which was carefully and systematically edited. In addition, after Jerusalem's Second Temple was destroyed (see the section "70 CE: Destruction of the Second Temple," earlier in this chapter), Jewish life shifted to Babylonia. Also, because Rashi completed his commentary on almost the entire Babylonian Talmud (but not the Jerusalem Talmud), we have his authoritative voice to help us understand it. (Flip back to the section "Introducing Rashi: The Great Commentator of the Talmud," earlier in this chapter, for more information about this great rabbi.)

3rd–6th centuries CE: The Babylonian Talmud

The Babylonian Talmud, or Talmud *Bavli* (bahv-lee), was compiled in Babylonia and became more comprehensive than the Jerusalem Talmud (discussed in the preceding section). Talk about the Talmud today refers to the Babylonian Talmud. (The *Mishna* is the same in both Talmuds; the *Gemara* is different.)

The Babylonian Talmud is considered more authoritative and influential than the Jerusalem Talmud because of its more extensive discussions and deeper analysis of Jewish law and tradition. It reflects the unique conditions and intellectual climate of the Babylonian Jewish community, which allowed for a broader interpretation of the teachings in the *Mishna*. This Talmudic version has a huge impact on Jewish scholarship and continues to be the central text for religious study and legal decision-making in Jewish communities worldwide.

224 to 651 CE: Influence of Sasanian Culture

The Sasanian Empire (also called the Iranian Empire; 224–651 CE) influenced the Babylonian Talmud (see the preceding section) through the socio-political and cultural context of its rule over Babylonia. The rabbis who compiled the Talmud didn't do so in isolation from their surroundings; instead, they engaged with a diverse cultural milieu that included Zoroastrianism, an ancient Persian religion that was the dominant religion of the Sasanian Empire. The Babylonian Talmud contains over 300 Persian words. Also, discussions in the Talmud often reflect familiarity with Persian customs and social norms.

4th–5th centuries CE: Rav Ashi and Ravina

Two sages, Rav Ashi and Ravina, compiled and edited the Babylonian Talmud. Ravina's work came after Rav Ashi's initial compilation and organization. Rav Ashi is generally considered the first major editor of the Babylonian Talmud. He spent over fifty years collecting and organizing the material for the Talmud. Ravina is often regarded as the one who completed the work begun by Rav Ashi. He is credited with the final revision and editing of the Talmud, around 500 CE. Ravina died seven years before Rav Ashi.

Rav Ashi (b. 352) played a crucial role in the development of Jewish scholarship. He collected and organized discussions and teachings from Babylonian schools, and he promoted the school at Sura (see the section "219 CE: The Sura academy opens," earlier in this chapter), which developed into a major academy for the study of the Torah.

Rav Ashi headed the school in Sura for 56 years. Without his scholarship, the Talmud wouldn't exist. He essentially assembled and arranged the Babylonian Talmud, as well as editing it, a pursuit to which he dedicated his life. He worked with his students to compile teachings that had been taught orally for centuries. Many Talmudic scholars regard Ravina as the scholar who finished the work that Rav Ashi began, taking over the editing process upon the death of Rav Ashi in 420 CE.

11th century CE: Medieval commentaries

Scholars such as Rashi wrote extensive commentaries on the Talmud, making it more accessible to students and scholars alike, during the Middle Ages. (See "Introducing Rashi: The Great Commentator of the Talmud" later in this chapter.)

12th–13th centuries CE: The Tosafot

A group of medieval rabbis known as the *Tosafot* (Additions) expanded on Rashi's commentaries, further elaborating on Talmudic discussions. (For more about the *Tosafot*, see the section "Post-Rashi: the Tosafot Period," earlier in this chapter.)

1240 CE: Disputation of Paris

A public debate in 1235 was held at the instigation of Nicholas Donin, a Jewish convert to Christianity who was excommunicated from the Jewish community in Paris around 1225. He accused the Talmud of containing blasphemous content against Christianity. The debate, called the Disputation of Paris, led to the Talmud's censorship and actual burning in France. (See Chapter 4 for more about the Disputation of Paris, as well as other historical burnings of the Talmud.)

16th century CE: Printing of the Talmud

The invention of the printing press allowed for wider dissemination of the Talmud. The first complete printed edition of the Talmud was produced by Daniel Bomberg, a Christian printer from Antwerp, who established his press in Venice. Bomberg began printing the Talmud in 1519, using the relatively new technology of movable type, which revolutionized the production of books. His edition was notable for setting the standard layout still used today, with the Talmudic text in the center of the page, and with Rashi's commentary on one side and *Tosafot* on the other. (Flip to Chapter 1 for more on the layout of the Talmud's pages.)

19th Century CE: The Vilna Edition

The Vilna edition of the Talmud was first published in the 1870s and again in the 1880s in Vilna, Lithuania. The publisher was a non-Jewish family, The Widow and Brothers Romm. In 1836, Russian Czar Nicholas I closed all printing houses of Jewish text except for two, one of which was the Romm House. They produced what became the definitive edition of the Talmud. The Romm family did have some illegal competition in publishing, but it didn't prevent their great power in the world of Jewish publications.

The Vilna edition includes the text of the *Mishna* and the *Gemara*, as well as Rashi's commentary on the inner margin and *Tosafot* on the outer margin. Remarkably, traditional Jews still consider the Vilna edition the standard edition of the Talmud, and many students and scholars use it today. Digital reproductions make it accessible worldwide, and although publishers have reproduced the text exactly as it was over a century ago, some have also made improvements by clearing up the text and correcting errors.

20th–21st centuries CE: The Steinsaltz Talmud Bavli

In 1965, Rabbi Adin Steinsaltz began a project that took him 45 years to complete. It was a translation from the Talmud's original Aramaic (the language spoken by Jews at the time of the Talmud's compilation) into modern Hebrew. Because Hebrew often doesn't use vowels, Rabbi Steinsaltz's addition of vowels to the text, along with his brilliant commentary, made the Talmud accessible, for the first time, to the masses. Hebrew has a *consonantal alphabet* (made up only of consonants, no vowels) that contains 22 letters, but it uses a system called *nikud* (nee-COOD; vowels), in which you place marks either under or within consonants to signify vowel sounds. These marks help with pronunciation.

Rabbi Steinsaltz's Hebrew edition of the Talmud includes his own commentary, as well as margin notes that provide short biographies of major personalities in the Talmud, background information, and other remarks by Rabbi Steinsaltz, helping the student of Talmud to better understand the text. Steinsaltz's Talmud editions also uses many color illustrations to help in explaining a topic in the Talmud. Koren, a leading Israeli publisher, has issued a complete English translation (in 42 volumes) of the Steinsaltz Talmud, making Talmud study accessible to English speakers everywhere.

20th–21st centuries CE: Schottenstein Talmud

Mesorah Publications, located in New Jersey, followed Rabbi Steinsaltz's example (see the preceding section) and published its own English translation of the Talmud. Unlike the Steinsaltz edition, which Rabbi Steinsaltz himself wrote, Mesorah's Schott-stein edition was the result of the efforts of many scholars. The Steinsaltz Talmud and the Schottenstein Talmud have several differences. For example, the Steinsaltz edition offers a modern translation, whereas the Schottstein edition is more literal.

TIP

The most significant development for any student of Torah is the online resource Sefaria (www.sefaria.org). Sefaria offers a growing library of Jewish literature for free. On this website, you can find the entire Babylonian Talmud in the William Davidson edition, which is based on the Steinsaltz English edition but without Rabbi Steinsaltz's margin notes.

Chapter **3**

Tackling the Talmud Today

I n this chapter, I discuss the nitty-gritty of modern Talmud study, including how scholars of the Talmud treat their books, what blessings they say before a Talmud study session, how they prepare to study, the spiritual meaning of studying Talmud, how scholars celebrate their study progress, how tens of thousands of people are studying the exact same page of Talmud every day around the world, and more.

I'll begin with an exploration of Torah, focusing on the blessings to say before studying it (including the Talmud). From the Five Books of Moses to the broader spectrum of Jewish teachings, Torah is a living tradition that encompasses sacred texts, including the Talmud.

Blessings for Studying Torah (Including the Talmud)

First, a note on the word *Torah*. The term can refer to any Jewish sacred text that you read or learn from. So, when you dive into the Talmud, you're engaging with Torah.

In the same way, studying any classic Jewish text, whether in Hebrew, English, or any language, is all part of what we call Torah. As I share in my book *The Torah for Dummies* (Wiley), Torah beautifully encompasses the whole spectrum of Jewish teachings.

In Jewish tradition, people recite blessings of gratitude before many of the commandments and pleasures of life — including Torah study. In the Talmud's *Masekhta Berachot* (Beh-rah-KHOAT; Tractate Blessings), the sages teach us blessings for many of life's activities.

WHY NOT RECITE BLESSINGS FOR EVERY COMMANDMENT?

Not all commandments requite a blessing. Some mitzvot Divine Commandments, such as giving charity (tzedakah) or honoring parents, depend on the participation or acceptance of another person. The Rashba (Rabbi Solomon ben Abraham Adret, 1235–1310) explains that no blessing is recited for these mitzvot because if the recipient refuses, the blessing would be in vain.

Mitzvot based on common sense or logic, which are also performed by non-Jews (like charity), do not require a blessing. This is because the purpose of the mitzvot is to sanctify us and elevate our lives, which is not evident when performing universally recognized good deeds.

Mitzvot which are constant obligations, such as belief in God or loving one's neighbor, do not have blessings because they are ongoing and not performed at specific times. Some mitzvot, like fasting on Yom Kippur, do not have blessings because they could potentially cause harm if performed improperly.

The practice of reciting blessings before studying Torah holds deep significance in Jewish tradition. The Talmud establishes that you should say a blessing before performing many *mitzvot* (*mitz-VOTE. Plural of mitzvah*; Divine Commandment), including Torah study. This commandment is rooted in the Torah itself, as derived from the verse "When I proclaim the name of the Lord, ascribe greatness to our God." The Jerusalem Talmud (which I talk about in Chapter 2) confirms that Torah study necessitates a blessing, emphasizing its sanctity and the intentionality with which you have to approach such study.

Blessings before a study session

Before I share the blessings themselves, let me offer a few guidelines for how to say a blessing before studying Torah (including the Talmud):

>> You may say the blessings in Hebrew or English. (A person should recite blessings and prayers in a language that they can understand.)

>> You may say the blessing standing or sitting.

>> You recite blessings on Torah study only once a day because Torah study is a constant obligation and should always be in your mind.

Here's a translation of the first blessing:

Blessed are You, Hashem our God, King of the universe, who has sanctified us with His commandments and has commanded us to engross ourselves in the words of Torah.

I translate the Hebrew word *la'asok* (la-ah-SOKH) as "engross ourselves." The Hebrew word includes the English sound "soak," which can remind the student that they want to soak — as though they're marinating themselves — in Torah.

Here's the transliteration of the Hebrew blessing so that you can make out the pronunciation:

Bah-RUKH ah-TAH Ah-doe-NAI, Eh-low-HAY-new MEH-lekh ha-owe-LAHM ah-SHARE kid-dish-AH-new bu-mitz-voe-TAHV vih-tzee-VAH-new la-ah-SOAK buh-DEEV-ray TOE-rah.

You also recite the following two blessings when you prepare for Torah study:

> Please, Hashem, our God, sweeten the words of Torah in our mouth and in the mouths of Your people, the family of Israel. May we and our offspring and the offspring of Your people, the House of Israel — all of us — know Your Name and study Your Torah for its own sake. Blessed are You, Hashem, who teaches Torah to His people Israel.

> Blessed are You, Hashem our God, King of the universe, who selected us from all the peoples and gave us His Torah. Blessed are You, Hashem, giver of the Torah.

The three blessings above are included in the morning prayers found in a prayerbook. The Talmud teaches that if you rise early, before the morning service, say the blessings before you study the Written Torah or the Oral Torah (the Talmud).

Blessing for after Torah study

Talmudic scholars recite a traditional blessing at the conclusion of a Torah study session. This blessing expresses gratitude for the opportunity to engage in Torah study and reflects on the value and sanctity of the learning process. The translation of the blessing is

> Blessed are You, Lord our God, King of the universe, who has given us a Torah of truth and has planted eternal life in our midst. Blessed are You, Lord, giver of the Torah.

This blessing stresses Torah's eternal nature and acknowledges God's role in providing these teachings to humankind. It provides a fitting conclusion to a period of study, reinforcing the spiritual significance of engaging with sacred texts.

Rituals for Studying Torah

Rituals and traditions play a significant role in enhancing the experience of studying Torah — including the Talmud. Beyond blessings (which you can read about in the section "Blessings for

Studying Torah [Including the Talmud]," earlier in this chapter), these practices help create a sense of reverence and intentionality, connecting the physical act of study with deeper spiritual meaning. The following sections describe some of these practices.

Washing your hands

In Judaism, students customarily wash their hands before studying Torah. I am not talking about washing hands with soap and water. The act is seen as a form of spiritual cleansing, like a mini-*mikvah*. (A *mikvah* (MIK-vah) is a ritual bath used to achieve purity.) The handwashing helps individuals focus and rededicate themselves to the study of Torah. Washing before Torah study prepares one spiritually for engaging with sacred texts.

Washing hands signifies the removal of impurities and distractions, allowing an individual to engage with sacred texts in a pure state. This symbolic cleansing mirrors the broader Jewish tradition of ritual purity, where physical acts denote spiritual readiness.

To ritually wash your hands before studying Torah, follow these steps:

1. Fill a cup with water.

2. Hold the cup in your right hand and pour water over your left hand, covering the entire hand up to the wrist.

3. Transfer the cup to your left hand and pour water over your right hand in the same manner.

4. Repeat steps 2 and 3, pouring water over each hand twice more, for a total of three times on each hand.

5. Recite the following blessing:

   Blessed are You, Lord our God, King of the universe, who has sanctified us with His commandments and commanded us concerning the washing of hands.

6. Dry your hands thoroughly.

You are now ready to study Torah, beginning with the three blessings described in "Blessings before a study session" earlier in this chapter.

WEARING A HEAD COVERING DURING TORAH STUDY

The custom of males wearing a head covering during Torah study has evolved over time.

Although the Torah doesn't explicitly require a person to cover their head with a *kippah* (KEEP-ah; skullcap) or hat, this practice originated during the Talmudic Period (70m CE to 500 CE). It spread from Babylon to various Jewish communities, including those in Spain and eventually across Europe.

During the Middle Ages, Jewish legal authorities commonly agreed that everyone should speak sacred words, including Torah study, with their head covered. This practice became linked to reverence and humility before God, symbolizing acknowledgment of Divine authority.

In Jewish mystical tradition, covering your head carries *kabbalistic* significance (concepts, practices, or interpretations related to Kabbalah — the mystical tradition within Judaism). It represents a constant awareness of God's presence. Over time, this practice acquired the weight of religious law.

The expulsion of the Jews from Spain led to a mass migration to many parts of Europe, including France, Italy, and other regions around the Mediterranean Sea. They brought with them cultural and religious practices, including the custom of head coverings.

The Jews who emigrated from Spain carried with them customs that had evolved over centuries. The respect that the entire Jewish world had for Babylonian Jewish scholarship contributed to the acceptance of these traditions, including head covering.

Although historically, only men have participated in the custom of covering their heads, more and more women are adopting the custom, too.

Kissing the books

Individuals kiss the Torah scroll when removing it from or returning it to the *ark* (aron kodesh, AH-ron KOH-desh), frequently using an intermediary such as the edge of a *tallit* (Tah-LEET): a fringed prayer shawl) to avoid direct hand contact with the scroll. In the same way, observant Jews may kiss prayer books and other sacred texts, such as the Talmud, when they take those texts out for use and before storing them, or if they accidentally drop the text.

Traditionally, if someone accidentally drops a sacred book, they kiss the book as a sign of respect and atonement for the mishap. This gesture acknowledges the sanctity of the text and serves as an immediate corrective action.

Although it's not mandatory, kissing religious texts is a cherished tradition that underscores the significance of those texts in Jewish spiritual practice. In Judaism, this gesture of kissing a holy object is a heartfelt way to show reverence and deep devotion. It reflects a person's commitment to Judaism and unwavering loyalty to God. Moreover, it serves as a physical expression of love for the *mitzvot* (mitz-VOTE; Divine Commandments) and the sacred texts that represent them.

Stacking sacred Jewish books

In Judaism, books have an interesting hierarchy when it comes to stacking them, especially those that hold significant meaning. This thoughtful ordering reflects the importance and sanctity of various texts, rooted in the principle of "increasing in holiness, and not decreasing," as described in the Talmud. This hierarchy honors the sacred texts, ensuring they are treated with the deep respect they deserve within Jewish tradition.

The hierarchy for stacking Jewish sacred texts, from top to bottom, is as follows: 1) Torah (Five Books of Moses); 2) Nevi'im (Prophets); 3) Ketuvim (Writings); 4) Talmud; 5) Siddur (prayer book) 6) other holy books.

The Torah, containing the Five Books of Moses (Genesis, Exodus, Leviticus, Numbers, and Deuteronomy), is considered the holiest and most important text. It always goes on top of other books.

After the Torah, the books of the Prophets (Nevi'im, neh-vee-EEM, Prophets) are placed, followed by the Writings (Ketuvim, keh-too-VEEM, writings). Together with the Torah, these form the Hebrew Bible.

Following the biblical texts, rabbinic literature such as the Talmud is placed. This includes the Mishnah and its commentaries. Prayer books (siddurim, sid-duhr-EEM, Jewish prayer books) and other holy texts come next in the hierarchy. Secular books should always be placed below Torah-based books.

Handling Torah scrolls with care

If a Torah scroll falls to the ground, Jewish tradition views this event as an extremely unfortunate occurrence. Jews commonly kiss a religious text after dropping that text. (I talk about that practice in the section "Kissing the books," earlier in this chapter.) The faithful might perform additional acts if a Torah scroll falls, such as fasting or giving charity, in hopes of restoring spiritual balance.

Jews have observed the practice of fasting after dropping the Torah scroll for many centuries (even though you can't find it in the Talmud). In some communities, this fasting extends to those who were present during the incident, although not everyone follows this custom. Many people think that if you accidentally drop a Torah scroll, you have to fast for 40 days. This is a myth.

WRITING IN YOUR TALMUD — WOW!

Many years ago, when I first began to study Talmud, I asked my teacher a question. He walked over to his bookshelves and pulled out a volume. He brought it to the table where we sat, and he turned to the page where he thought we could find a response to my question. "This is going to be good," he said. "There are five 'Wows' on this page."

"Wows? What's a Wow?" I asked. I thought it was some Talmudic phrase or term that I didn't know.

"What's a Wow? What's a Wow?" he repeated. "You know — Wow!"

I then looked at the page he had turned to, and I saw what he was referring to: In the margins, five words appeared, all of them the same. The word was "Wow."

He then explained, "I've studied this page before, and it contains several amazing passages. With each one that I originally read, I said, 'Wow.' So I wrote it in the margin of the page. Wow. Wow. Wow. Wow. Wow." It was his way of underlining.

That's when I learned that people write in their Talmud volumes!

As a newcomer to the Sea of Talmud, I was more than a bit intimidated by the large volumes. And I never imagined that people write in holy books. But they do. Now, many years later, I know that the Talmud demands that the student argue with the text, get involved, roll up their sleeves and jump in.

Around the same time, I wandered into a used Jewish bookstore in downtown Manhattan. It had two floors, and on the second floor, they kept the used Talmud volumes. I looked at several of them, and in every case, there was writing on the pages. The writing consisted of notes, questions, summaries, great passages, and more.

You can definitely write in a Talmud volume but do so with thoughtfulness and respect. Remember, this text holds a sacred place and plays a key role in Jewish learning. Choosing to write in a Talmud volume can often come down to personal preference and the traditions of your community or study group. Some folks or communities might feel that keeping their volumes unmarked is a way to honor the text's sanctity.

Throughout history, scholars have annotated their Talmudic texts. These thoughtful annotations have blossomed into valuable commentaries, enriching our understanding of the text as a whole.

If you decide to write in a volume of Talmud, keep the original text clear and unchanged. Make sure that your annotations don't cover up or harm the printed words.

Finding a Study Partner

A *khevruta* (khev-ROO-ta, a traditional way of studying texts together in pairs) highlights the beauty of collaborative learning and dialogue, letting two individuals dive deeply into Jewish texts, such as the Talmud or Torah, by sharing and debating their interpretations.

The term *khevruta* comes from the Hebrew word for "friendship" or "companionship," emphasizing the importance of partnership in this dynamic study method. Partners read texts aloud, engage in lively discussions, and challenge each other's interpretations, fostering deeper understanding and multiple perspectives. Traditionally not the main mode of study in Jewish education (which is classroom style, with the teacher up front and the student sitting facing him), *khevruta* learning now holds a central place in *yeshivot* (yeh-SHE-vote; traditional Jewish schools), promoting active engagement, better memory retention, and a supportive atmosphere. Pairing students who have similar skill levels enhances the experience, encouraging collaboration and the exploration of sacred texts through dialogue.

Selecting a khevruta partner

When selecting a *khevruta* partner for Torah study, consider several key factors for a productive experience. When students take these criteria into consideration, they can find *khevruta* partners who really enhance their learning journey and help them connect more deeply with the texts that they explore together.

Partners who have similar knowledge and skills foster balanced discussions, while partners who have complementary strengths, such as analytical thinking and verbal skills, enhance learning by supplementing their knowledge and skills with their partner's knowledge and skills. You must match learning styles and personalities to maintain harmony and mutual respect between *khevruta* partners. Both partners need to have a commitment to regular study sessions, a shared interests in texts, an effective method of communication, and open-mindedness. Although friendships can enrich the experience, the partners must maintain focus on study to have a successful and engaging *khevruta* partnership.

Giving tzedakah each time you study

In Judaism, a student traditionally gives *tzedakah* (tze-DUCK-ah; charity) whenever they study Torah or engage in learning. This practice comes from the belief that diving into sacred texts enriches not just our spiritual journey, but also uplifts the entire community and supports those in need.

Some people I know give donations to the website Sefaria.com, because of its amazing and free online Jewish library — including a complete English translation of the Talmud. Others give to their favorite non-profit organizations.

Many people keep a tzedakah box on their desk. A tzedakah box, also known as a *pushke* (PUSH-keh) in Yiddish, is a receptacle used in Judaism for collecting charitable donations. The word *tzedakah* comes from the Hebrew root *tzedek*, which means justice or righteousness, emphasizing that giving to those in need is considered an act of justice rather than mere charity. Giving tzedakah is considered a religious imperative in Judaism, even for those who have little to give. Its primary function is to collect money for various charitable causes.

The amount a student contributes may change, but it usually represents a thoughtful, symbolic gesture that showcases the student's willingness to help. Regularly giving *tzedakah* during study sessions encourages a habit of generosity and mindfulness.

Here are some key points about this beautiful custom:

>> Contributing *tzedakah* before or after learning can tie together the pursuit of knowledge with the meaningful values of charity and supporting the community. It emphasizes that our understanding should inspire us to take action and show responsibility for those around us.

>> Many sources highlight the notion that giving *tzedakah* can truly enrich a person's learning journey because it brings a sense of purpose and intention to the study. It reminds the student that learning is most fulfilling when they pair it with actions that uplift others.

>> In *yeshivot* (traditional Jewish schools), synagogues and study groups, students often feel inspired to give *tzedakah* each time they dive into their learning journey.

Participating in Daf Yomi

Daf Yomi (dahf YO-me; page of the day) offers a wonderful way to dive into the rich teachings of the Talmud. Each day, all participants engage with the same page, or *daf*, which makes the journey so much more manageable and enjoyable because it not only helps its students connect with Jewish law and tradition, it also creates a sense of unity and shared experience across diverse communities.

The program has made Talmud study accessible to Jews who are not Torah scholars, democratizing this form of learning. By providing a structured, communal approach to Talmud study, Daf Yomi offers both intellectual stimulation and a sense of connection to Jewish tradition and community, making it a valuable practice for many participants. By following this method, you can complete the entire Talmud, consisting of 2,711 double-sided pages, in about seven and a half years.

You can study *Daf Yomi* on your own or enjoy it with friends in groups. You can find many great resources available, such as classes led by friendly rabbis, online lectures, and audio recordings to suit all kinds and levels of learning styles.

Try putting "Dafi Yomi" into a search engine like Google. You will find websites and apps like Sefaria that offer digital versions of the Talmud with translations, commentaries, and audio lessons. Many sites provide daily audio or video classes as well as study guides and summaries. Resources like Daf Yomi Advancement Forum offer outlines, insights, and review materials. Various websites provide Daf Yomi calendars to help learners stay on schedule. There are also platforms where Daf Yomi participants can connect and discuss the daily learning.

DAF REACTIONS: COMEDIC AND INSIGHTFUL COMMENTARY

One of the more unusual and often irreverent online offerings on pages of the Talmud is created by Miriam Anzovin, a visual artist, writer, and content creator known for her engaging approach to Jewish themes, particularly through her popular series of videos called Daf Reactions. These videos, which she shares on platforms like TikTok and Instagram and YouTube provide comedic and insightful commentary on passages from the Talmud, reflecting her journey as a formerly Orthodox, now secular Jewish woman. Through these platforms, Miriam Anzovin invites others to engage with Jewish teachings in a humorous and accessible manner, fostering a sense of community among her followers. I enjoy Anzovin's take on the Talmud immensely.

The first *Daf Yomi* cycle kicked off on Rosh Hashanah in 1923, thanks to Rabbi Meir Shapiro, who introduced this idea at a conference in Vienna. He wanted to make Talmud study welcoming and accessible to every Jew, no matter their level of scholarly background.

Here are the key features: Every day, students dive into a particular daf, exploring both sides of a page from the Talmud. Hundreds of thousands of Jews worldwide join together in Daf Yomi. This shared journey can make the students feel like they're part of a welcoming global classroom.

Completing each *masekhta* (mah-SEKH-tah, tractate) is often a joyful occasion celebrated with a gathering called a *siyum* (SEE-um; completion). (The following section gives the details of a *siyum*.) When a whole cycle draws to a close, it culminates in a wonderful celebration known as the *Siyum Hashas* (SEE-um ha-SHAS, completion of the Talmud), attracting hundreds of thousands of excited participants.

For example, for the 9th Siyum HaShas in 1990, Agudath Israel of America made the bold decision to book Madison Square

Garden in New York City. Despite initial skepticism about filling the 20,000-seat arena, the event was a resounding success, with tickets selling out weeks in advance. For the 10th Siyum HaShas in 1997, this venue in New York hosted 20,000 participants alongside. The 13th Siyum HaShas, held on January 1, 2020, took place at MetLife Stadium in East Rutherford, New Jersey. This event drew a sellout crowd of over 90,000 participants.

KEEPING TRACK OF THE PAGE OF THE DAY

Before the Internet, people learned about and participated in Daf Yomi through various traditional methods. Many synagogues and yeshivas offered daily Daf Yomi classes led by rabbis or experienced teachers. Jewish organizations published and distributed calendars showing which page was to be studied each day. Special editions of the Talmud were printed with the Daf Yomi schedule, making it easier for participants to follow along. In some areas, Daf Yomi lessons were broadcast on Jewish radio stations. The program's popularity spread through personal recommendations and community discussions, especially after its introduction in 1923.

Today, people learning Daf Yomi have several convenient ways to keep track of the current page of the day:

Online calendars: Websites like MyJewishLearning.com provide comprehensive Daf Yomi calendars that show which tractate and page is studied on any given date.

Apps: Many Daf Yomi apps, such as the Sefaria app, include built-in calendars that automatically display the current day's page.

Email subscriptions: Services like MyJewishLearning's "A Daily Dose of Talmud" send daily emails with insights from the current page, effectively informing subscribers of the day's page.

Social media: Some Daf Yomi learners follow accounts on platforms like Twitter (for example, @TweetTheDaf) that post about the daily page.

The Steinsaltz Daily Study App is my favorite app for Talmud study. It is a digital platform designed to make Jewish texts and learning accessible to a wide audience. Launched by the Steinsaltz Center, this app embodies Rabbi Adin Even-Israel Steinsaltz's vision of "Let My People Know" by providing easy access to foundational Jewish texts and commentaries. The app includes a vast collection of Jewish texts. Texts are available in both Hebrew and English, with Rabbi Steinsaltz's commentary. Users can engage in various daily learning programs, including Daf Yomi. The app represents a significant step in making Jewish knowledge universally accessible, allowing users to study Torah anytime and anywhere, continuing Rabbi Steinsaltz's legacy of removing barriers to Torah learning.

Enjoying a siyum

A *siyum*, which means "completion," is a joyful occasion in Judaism. This event celebrates the end of a unit of Torah study, especially when finishing a *masekhta* (tractate) of the Talmud. These are the key aspects of a *siyum* in the context of Talmud study:

>> Participants usually share insights from the last topic they studied, highlighting the key points and takeaways from the *masekhta* (tractate) with enthusiasm.

>> Students of Talmud recite together the *Hadran* (ha-DRAHN prayer (discussed in the section "Saying the Hadran," later in this chapter), which expresses students' commitment to returning to their studies.

>> Students of Talmud also recite the *Kaddish D'Rabanan* (KAH-dish dih-rahb-ah-NAHN; Rabbis' Holy Prayer), which holds a special place in Jewish tradition. (See the following section.)

>> The event includes a unique passage that prays for the well-being of Jewish teachers, their students, and all those who engage in Torah study. By combining praise for God, honor for Torah scholars, and the elevation of Torah study, Kaddish D'Rabanan encapsulates core values of Jewish tradition, making it a uniquely significant prayer in Jewish practice.

Reciting the Kaddish D'Rabbanan

Kaddish D'Rabbanan (KAH-dish Duh RAH-bah-NAHN, Rabbis' Holy Prayer) is a special version of the Kaddish prayer which is a central Jewish prayer that praises and sanctifies God's name. It is written primarily in Aramaic and recited during various parts of Jewish prayer services. While it is most commonly associated with mourning, the Kaddish has a broader liturgical role and exists in multiple forms, each serving different purposes.

Here are the key features of the Kaddish D'Rabbanan:

» Honors the teachings of the Torah and shows the students' gratitude for the opportunity to learn together, acknowledging the preciousness of the knowledge that they gain.

» Praises God while sharing a heartfelt longing for peace and redemption. It also includes blessings for the Jewish community and all who embrace the study of Torah.

» A minyan (min-YAHN a gathering of ten Jews) recites the Kaddish D'Rabbanan, highlighting the importance of coming together as a community to learn.

Saying the Hadran

After completing the study of a masekhta (tractate) of the Talmud, a student recites the Hadran (Ha-DRAHN; from the Aramaic word meaning "we have returned"). Here are the key aspects of the Hadran in Talmud study:

» Expresses the student's commitment to revisiting the text that they just completed. It captures a connection to and fondness for the material.

» Typically recited during a siyum, the celebratory event marking the completion of a masekhta (see the section "Enjoying a siyum," earlier in this chapter, for an explanation of this celebration.)

» Represents students' commitment to continuous study and the bright journey of intellectual growth within the Jewish community.

The individual or group completing the study reads a small portion of that section of the Talmud aloud before reciting the *Hadran* three times together, which serves to establish and reinforce the learner's commitment to returning to the text. It reflects the Jewish concept that repeating something three times solidifies its importance and establishes it as a firm intention. Reciting the *Hadran* three times is considered a *segulah* (seh-GOO-lah, propitious remedy) for remembering what one has learned. This repetition is believed to help imprint the knowledge more deeply in the learner's mind.

The number three also holds special significance in Jewish thought. It represents the establishment or reinforcement of a particular aspect. In this case, it establishes the learner's desire to return to further study of the completed tractate in the future. This practice has become a well-established custom in Jewish learning, passed down through generations. While its exact origins may not be explicitly stated, it has become an integral part of the siyum (completion ceremony) tradition.

The text of the *Hadran*, translated into English, is:

> We have returned to you, Tractate [*Name of tractate*], and you have returned to us; our mind is on you, Tractate [*Name of tractate*], and your mind is on us; we will not forget you, Tractate [*Name of tractate*], and you will not forget us — not in this world and not in the World to Come.

Chapter 4

The Antisemitic War Against the Talmud

The Talmud, like Judaism itself, has long faced waves of repression and prejudice. Throughout history, religious and political forces have targeted this sacred text, which forms the foundation of Jewish law and thought, seeking to diminish Jewish identity.

In the 13th century, Europe was gripped by a climate of intense religious intolerance, fueled in large part by the Catholic Church's desire for control and its self-styled mission to eradicate what it viewed as heresy. Jews, who were seen as obstinate in their refusal to convert to Christianity, became scapegoats for broader societal tensions. Central to the Church's opposition was the Talmud, which it believed not only reinforced Jewish identity, but also stood in opposition to Christian teachings.

Knowing this unsavory history when you study the Talmud can shed light on the enduring challenges this text has faced and continues to face in the modern world.

In this chapter, you will explore how antisemitism manifested historically, from the 13th century to modern times, and how the Talmud's role within this history shaped its legacy for generations to come.

Falsehoods that Fueled the War Against the Talmud

Throughout history, the Talmud has been the subject of widespread misrepresentation and baseless accusations, many of which have contributed to the hostility and persecution it faced. These falsehoods — often propagated by those seeking to undermine Judaism — have painted the Talmud as everything from a tool of anti-Christian propaganda to a dangerous and blasphemous text. In reality, these misconceptions have no foundation in the text itself. To understand the true nature of the Talmud and dispel these myths, first examine some of the most prevalent *false claims* that have fueled the war against it:

>> **The Talmud is anti-Christian.** Nothing in the Talmud makes it anti-Christian. All accusations are based on fabricated quotations supposedly from the Talmud. In fact, neither the Talmud nor Judaism, in general, represent any desire to criticize other religious traditions. In addition, Jews don't try to convert non-Jews to Judaism. If anything, Judaism represents the belief that Judaism is the religion of the Jews.

>> **The Talmud replaced the Torah.** The Torah is also known as the Written Torah, and the Talmud is called the Oral Torah. Both are essential parts of Jewish scripture.

>> **Jews expect everyone to follow the teachings of the Talmud.** The Talmud records the discussions and debates about Jewish law by the rabbis and sages over the centuries. It's not a code of law, and it actually expresses differences of opinion throughout. No one is bound by the Talmud, and surely not non-Jews.

>> **Non-Jews can't study the Talmud.** Non-Jews can certainly study the Talmud. It's not a secret document of any kind.

The Talmud has recently been translated into English making it more accessible than ever to non-Jews and those who can't read the original Hebrew and Aramaic.

>> **The Talmud contains blasphemous teachings.** The Talmud is a holy book of the Jews and doesn't contain blasphemous teachings from the Jewish perspective. Some theological positions might appear blasphemous to some non-Jews, but no different than non-Jewish books of theology can appear blasphemous to Jews.

Fabricated quotes and false statements about the Talmud

I have mixed feelings about including the following quotations in this book. Why repeat ideas that are absurd and antisemitic? But I include them not only to show you how far antisemites go in their baseless hatred, but also to inform you to watch out for these hate-inspired ideas, particularly on the Internet.

Social media has spread false accusations about the Talmud. The quotes are often fabricated or taken out of context, yet they reach large audiences and perpetuate antisemitic stereotypes.

To combat misleading or fabricated quotes attributed to the Talmud, you can take several important steps to verify a quote's accuracy:

>> **Look it up.** Check the alleged quote against authentic Talmudic texts. With the Talmud now available online, comparing the supposed quote with the actual text can often reveal discrepancies.

>> **Ask the experts.** Engage with knowledgeable scholars and rabbis who are familiar with the Talmud. These experts can help verify the authenticity of a quote and offer insights into the context and meaning of specific passages. Many false quotes arise from taking statements out of context, so you must understand the broader discussion within the Talmud. The Talmud offers a complex dialogue among rabbis over centuries, and you have to grasp the full scope of a conversation to accurately interpret its teachings.

Additionally, some quotes may be based on real Talmudic discussions but are misinterpreted to appear malicious or offensive. Scholars frequently highlight these misinterpretations by providing accurate translations and clarifications.

>> **Confirm the sources.** Fabricated quotes often cite non-existent sources, such as *Gad Shas* or *Libbre David*, which don't appear in any recognized Jewish texts.

Identifying these red flags can help distinguish falsehoods from the true content of the Talmud.

TECHNICAL
STUFF

These complete fabrications float around on the Internet. All these statements have no basis whatsoever in the Talmud or any recognized Jewish text:

>> "The Jews are called human beings, but goyim [non-Jews] are not humans."

The word "goy,"(plural is goyim) which means "nation," is not an insult, although many people think it is. It simply refers to people who are not Jewish.

>> "A pregnant goy is no better than a pregnant animal."

>> "Although the goy has the same body structure as the Jew, they compare with the Jew like a monkey to a human."

>> "If a Jew is called upon to explain any part of the Rabbinic books, he ought to give only a false explanation."

>> "Jews are allowed to violate (but not marry) non-Jewish girls."

>> "Jews may lie to goyim if it benefits them."

>> "Goyim are created solely to serve Jews."

>> "Jews can cheat goyim during business transactions."

>> "Even the best of goyim should be killed."

>> "All children of goyim are animals."

>> "Goys are not human, they are beasts."

>> "If you eat with a goy, it's the same as eating with a dog."

>> "Goys prefer sex with cows."

You may also see some gross misinterpretations presented as fact:

>> "The Talmud permits sexual relations with a girl under the age of three or a boy under the age of nine."

This claim is based on a gross misinterpretation of a discussion in the Talmud and doesn't reflect any legal or moral stance in Judaism. The discussion in Tractate Niddah (44b) on which this gross misinterpretation is based is part of a complex legal discussion that an ignorant person would easily misinterpret. The Talmud and Jewish law explicitly forbids in absolute terms any sexual contact with a child of any age.

>> "Jews need not return lost objects to goyim."

IS JESUS MENTIONED IN THE TALMUD?

In Tractate Sanhedrin 43a, the Talmud refers to "Jesus the Nazarene." However, as Rabbi Adin Steinsaltz notes in his Talmud commentary, "From the historical context of that passage, it is clear that it is not referring to Jesus, the founder of Christianity. Nevertheless, as the incident recounted here resulted in the persecution of the Jews throughout history, it was often subject to censorship and is not found in most published editions of the Talmud." The Steinsaltz edition provides students with the complete text, while the Schottenstein edition omits it, explaining that since the Vilna edition of the Talmud excludes the passage, their edition will follow suit.

There are several other instances in the Talmud where a man named Yeshu — a common name during Talmudic times — was mistakenly thought by non-Jewish censors to refer to Jesus. In some cases, non-Jewish censors also believed that certain personalities in the Talmud were Jesus disguised under a different name. It is important to note, however, that the dates associated with these so-called references to Jesus do not align with the historical timeline of his life.

Tragically, these misinterpretations of the Talmud's text have fueled antisemitism throughout history.

Major culprits who spread lies about the Talmud

Several people throughout history perpetuated lies about the Talmud, often exploiting their positions of power or scholarly authority to lend credibility to their false claims. By framing these fabrications as academic or religious critiques, they could spread misinformation that seemed plausible to many.

The individuals I discuss in the following list played major roles in spreading misinformation about the Talmud. They often used their positions or scholarly appearances to lend credibility to their false claims. Their works have had a lasting impact on antisemitic narratives throughout history:

» **Nicholas Donin** (circa 1240): A Jewish convert to Christianity who played a pivotal role in the 13th century. He presented 35 charges against the Talmud to Pope Gregory IX, claiming it contained blasphemous content against Christianity. His actions led to the public disputation and subsequent burning of numerous Talmudic texts.

» **Johannes Pfefferkorn** (1469–1524): A Jewish convert to Christianity who became an anti-Talmud campaigner in the early 16th century, Pfefferkorn advocated for the confiscation and destruction of Jewish books, including the Talmud, under Holy Roman Emperor Maximilian I.

» **Johann Andreas Eisenmenger** (1654–1704): A German scholar educated in Hebrew and Semitic languages. In 1700, he published *Entdecktes Judenthum* (Judaism Unmasked), one of the first major works to claim that the Talmud contained anti-Christian sentiments. His work included many misinterpretations, lies and fabrications.

» **August Rohling** (1839–1931): A Professor of Hebrew Antiquities in Prague, active in the late 19th century. Rohling wrote *Der Talmudjude* (The Talmud Jew), heavily plagiarizing Eisenmenger's work. He propagated falsified quotes, lies and interpretations of the Talmud, claiming it endorsed unethical behaviors against non-Jews.

» **Justinas Pranaitis** (1861–1917): Catholic priest and professor of Hebrew in Saint Petersburg. In 1892, Pranaitis published "The Christian in the Jewish Talmud," which falsely attributed derogatory statements about Christians to the Talmud. His work relied heavily on previous falsifications and out and out lies by Eisenmenger and others.

Religious Intolerance through History

The history of religious persecution against the Jews, particularly during the medieval and early modern periods, is deeply intertwined with the treatment of the Talmud. As a cornerstone of Jewish religious and cultural life, the Talmud became a target for hostility from Christian authorities who viewed it as a barrier to conversion and a source of alleged heretical teachings. This hostility often led to censorship, public disputations, and the mass destruction of Jewish texts. Beginning in the 13th century and extending into the modern era, Christian leaders used the Talmud as a focal point for their efforts to suppress Judaism and assert dominance.

The following sections describe pivotal moments of persecution, highlighting how the attacks on the Talmud reflected a broader campaign of religious intolerance aimed at undermining Jewish identity and instilling fear within Jewish communities.

Debating in the Disputation of Paris

In the 13th century, a wave of religious intolerance pervaded Europe, primarily motivated by a desire for power and control by the Catholic Church, which represented itself as combating heresy. This climate contributed to an environment of anti-Jewish sentiment. The church was eager to convert Jews to Catholicism, and it believed the Talmud reinforced Jewish identity, which made it, in the eyes of the Church, a major factor to contend with.

A Jewish convert to Christianity named Nicholas Donin played an important role in the Christian war against the Talmud.

(I talk about Nicholas Donin in the section "Major culprits who spread lies about the Talmud," earlier in this chapter.)

Donin's accusations prompted Pope Gregory IX to issue a papal bull in 1239, which ordered the confiscation of Jewish books, including all copies of the Talmud across Europe. On March 3rd, 1240, Jewish texts were confiscated from synagogues across Paris during the first Sabbath of the Christian observance of Lent.

The Disputation of Paris was held in Paris from June 25th to June 27th, 1240. Nicholas Donin and other Christian theologians, who argued against a group of prominent rabbis led by Rabbi Yechiel of Paris had already decided the result of the disputation before the debate even began. Rabbi Yechiel's arguments made no difference. The Talmud was found guilty of heresy.

After the disputation, King Louis IX condemned the Talmud and ordered the books to be burned. On June 6, 1242, 24 wagon loads of Talmudic manuscripts in Paris were publicly burned. Thousands of volumes copied by hand over generations were destroyed. In addition to the physical destruction of the Talmud, the burning became a symbol of the Christian assault on Jewish life. It also set a precedent for more anti-Jewish persecution and book burnings throughout Europe.

In 1264, Pope Clement IV renewed the prohibition against the Talmud that had been established by Pope Gregory IX. His decree stated that any person found in possession of a copy of the Talmud would face severe penalties, including death.

Synagogues were subjected to inspections, and community leaders were pressured to surrender any copies of the Talmud for examination by church authorities. Similar actions occurred throughout Europe during this period. The Catholic Church organized public displays where representatives of the Church burned confiscated copies of the Talmud as a demonstration of power and to intimidate Jewish communities into compliance.

The Council of Basel, 1431

The Council of Basel was convened by Pope Eugene IV in 1431. He issued a papal bull prohibiting Jews from studying the Talmud, based on his belief that the teachings in the Talmud were derogatory to Jesus and Mary and that it contained other blasphemous content. Church authorities argued that the Talmud impeded Jewish conversion to Christianity, with the false assumption that the Talmud was anti-Christianity (as they had argued in the past; see the preceding section). The Church encouraged local authorities to confiscate copies of the Talmud from Jewish communities, which included raids on synagogues and homes where the Jewish community stored religious texts. The Church representatives often destroyed these confiscated books in public burnings.

Talmud Burnings in Italy, 1553

In 1553, representatives of the Church destroyed Jewish texts in several Italian cities. These burnings were part of religious and political dynamics during the Counter-Reformation. During the mid-16th century, Italy was impacted by the Counter-Revolution, which was the Catholic Church's response to the Protestant Reformation. During that time, non-Christian texts, including Jewish texts — particularly the Talmud — were viewed with hostility. In August 1553, based on the recommendations from a council of Cardinals who had examined accusations against Hebrew literature, Pope Julius III ordered that all copies of the Talmud were to be confiscated and burned.

The invention of the printing press revolutionized the production of books, including Jewish texts. In the early 16th century, Venice became a major Center for Hebrew printing (see the discussion of printing the Talmud in Chapter 2). The first complete printed edition of the Talmud in Venice prompted other editions. The printing press allowed for the dissemination of the Talmud throughout Italy — thereby making the texts more visible to non-Jewish authorities, as well, who viewed these books with suspicion.

The Roman Inquisition (started in 1542) claimed that the Talmud contained heretical teachings and teachings derogatory toward Christianity. Like in France (see the section "Debating in the Disputation of Paris," earlier in this chapter), former Jews who had converted to Christianity aided the Inquisition's actions and testified against the Talmud, eager to prove their loyalty to Christianity by denouncing Judaism.

Poland, 1757

Jacob Frank was a leader of a sect that deviated from traditional Judaism. The sect was known as the Frankists. The group was influenced by the teachings of a false Messiah whose name was Shabbetai Zevi. They gained favor with some Christian authorities, and in 1757, a Catholic bishop named Mikolaj Dembowski became involved in a dispute between the Frankists and some traditional Jewish leaders. Dembowski organized a public disputation between the Frankists and the traditional rabbis. The bishop sided with the Frankists, who argued against the Talmud. Subsequently, he ordered all copies of the Talmud in his diocese to be gathered and burned, which they did.

Jewish Persecution in Modern Times

The persecution of Jews has continued well into the modern era, with historical efforts to oppress and eliminate Jewish culture, identity, and religious practices extending beyond ancient times. In the 20th century, regimes such as the Soviet Union, Nazi Germany, Austria, Poland, and Hungary carried out targeted campaigns against Jewish communities, including systematic destruction of Jewish religious texts like the Talmud. These acts of cultural and religious suppression, including widespread book burnings, demonstrate the persistence of antisemitic violence and hostility, even in modern history.

Soviet Union, 1920s and beyond

In the Soviet Union (or the Union of Soviet Socialist Republics; USSR), government representatives confiscated and destroyed Jewish religious texts, including the Talmud, as part of antireligious campaigns aimed at suppressing religious practices and promoting atheism.

After the Bolshevik Revolution in 1917, the Soviet government, led by Vladimir Lenin and later by Joseph Stalin, attempted to establish atheism as a state doctrine. All religious institutions suffered oppression, including those of Judaism. Before the revolution, Jewish communities in Russia and Eastern Europe had many prominent centers of religious and cultural life.

Because the government saw the Talmud as a central text of Judaism, they destroyed all copies of it. The government closed Jewish schools and synagogues, and they seized religious books during the raids by state authorities, often burning them in bonfires in public squares in an effort to humiliate the Jewish community. The League of Militant Atheists was organized to promote atheism and suppress religion, confiscating books and destroying them. By the time of Stalin's death in 1953, traditional Jewish life in the USSR had significantly eroded.

Nazi Germany, 1930s–1940s

During the Nazi regime, the party organized systematic burnings of Jewish books, including the Talmud, across Germany and occupied territories. These burnings were part of the broader campaign against Jews and Jewish culture.

The Nazi party, led by Adolf Hitler, rose to power in Germany in 1933. They were known for their extreme antisemitic ideology. Their goal was to eliminate Jewish influence from all aspects of German life, including physical persecution as well as an assault on Jewish culture. The Nazis viewed Jewish books, and in particular, the Talmud, as symbols of Jewish influence, which they labeled as un-German. The Nazi regime's propaganda minister, Joseph Goebbels, orchestrated public book burnings to support Nazi ideology.

The first major book burning took place in Nazi Germany on May 10th, 1933. It was organized by the German student union and supported by Nazi officials. Twenty-five thousand books were thrown into bonfires in cities across Germany. Works by Sigmund Freud, Albert Einstein, and many other prominent Jewish personalities were included in these fires. The bonfires were public spectacles that rallied support for the Nazis and served to intimidate the opposition.

The Nazi party and its supporters made ongoing efforts during the 1930s and 1940s to confiscate and destroy Jewish texts throughout Germany. Libraries were purged of books written by Jews or containing Jewish content. These book burnings were part of a broad cultural genocide whose goal was to eliminate Jewish presence in Germany. Jewish schools and institutions were targeted for raids on their libraries. Despite these efforts, many Jews resisted by hiding books or smuggling them out of Germany and Nazi-occupied areas.

These book burnings provoked outrage in the United States. Public protests were organized to raise awareness of the dangers of Nazi ideology.

Austria, 1938

Following the Anschluss, when Nazi Germany annexed Austria, incidents of book burnings targeting Jewish literature, including the Talmud, occurred as part of the broader antisemitic policies implemented by the Nazis.

Poland, 1941

During World War II, Nazi forces in Poland burned Jewish books as part of their efforts to eradicate Jewish culture, including destruction of Talmudic texts in various ghettos and communities.

In 1941, Nazi authorities raided Jewish homes, synagogues, and community centers throughout Poland. They confiscated religious texts, including the Talmud, Torah scrolls, and other sacred Jewish writings. They also destroyed many synagogues entirely, along with their libraries. This destruction severely limited access to religious texts.

Hungary, 1944

As part of the Holocaust and anti-Jewish measures in Hungary during World War II, Nazi collaborators seized and destroyed Jewish books, including copies of the Talmud.

Nazi Germany and Occupation, 1930s–1940s

The Nazi party, led by Adolf Hitler, rose to power in Germany in 1933. They were known for their extreme antisemitic ideology. Their goal was to eliminate Jewish influence from all aspects of German life, including physical persecution as well as an assault on Jewish culture. The Nazis viewed Jewish books, and in particular, the Talmud, as symbols of Jewish influence, which they labeled as un-German. The Nazi regime's propaganda minister, Joseph Goebbels, orchestrated public book burnings to support Nazi ideology.

The first major book burning took place in Nazi Germany on May 10th, 1933. It was organized by the German student union and supported by Nazi officials. Twenty-five thousand books were thrown into bonfires in cities across Germany. Works by Sigmund Freud, Albert Einstein, and many other prominent Jewish personalities were included in these fires. The bonfires were public spectacles that rallied support for the Nazis and served to intimidate the opposition.

The Nazi party and its supporters made ongoing efforts during the 1930s and 1940s to confiscate and destroy Jewish texts throughout Germany. Libraries were purged of books written by Jews or containing Jewish content. These book burnings were part of a broad cultural genocide whose goal was to eliminate Jewish presence in Germany. Jewish schools and institutions were targeted for raids on their libraries. Despite these efforts, many Jews resisted by hiding books or smuggling them out of Germany and Nazi-occupied areas.

While the Germans expanded into other European countries during World War II, their antisemitism spread with them:

>> **Austria, 1938:** Following the Anschluss, when Nazi Germany annexed Austria, incidents of book burnings targeting Jewish literature, including the Talmud, occurred as part of the broader antisemitic policies implemented by the Nazis.

>> **Poland, 1941:** Nazi forces in Poland burned Jewish books as part of their efforts to eradicate Jewish culture, including

destruction of Talmudic texts in various ghettos and communities.

In 1941, Nazi authorities raided Jewish homes, synagogues, and community centers throughout Poland. They confiscated religious texts, including the Talmud, Torah scrolls, and other sacred Jewish writings. Though not as well publicized as the public Jewish book burnings in Germany, large gatherings were reported where Jewish books were destroyed. Also, many synagogues were destroyed entirely, along with their libraries. This destruction severely limited access to religious texts.

» **Hungary, 1944:** As part of the Holocaust and the Nazi party's anti-Jewish measures in Hungary, Jewish books, including copies of the Talmud, were seized and destroyed by Nazi collaborators.

ANTISEMITIC BOOKS ABOUT THE TALMUD FROM THE PAST

The Talmud Unmasked was published in 1892 by Justinas Bonaventure Pranaitis (1861–1917). The book is essentially a collection of quotations from the Talmud and other Jewish texts, many of which were either fictitious, taken out of context, or deliberately distorted.

Entdecktes Judenthum ("Judaism Unveiled"), written by Johann Andreas Eisenmenger in 1700, is a polemical work attacking Jewish texts, including the Talmud. It played a significant role in spreading prejudice against the Talmud.

Der Talmudjude (1871) by August Rohling follows a similar pattern of slanderous publications attacking the Talmud. Like its predecessors, it contains fictitious or distorted quotations and was heavily influenced by Eisenmenger's earlier work.

Chapter **5**

Key Terms and Concepts From the Talmud

The Talmud references hundreds of terms, but the Talmud itself often doesn't clearly identify or define these terms. The rabbis simply use them in the text, assuming the reader already knows them. Identifying and defining them not only aids in discussions and debates but also offers insight into the values underlying the Jewish way of life and thought.

In this chapter, I translate 45 terms used in the Talmud, along with definitions. Although they may appear to be just words and phrases, in fact, each has a specific legal meaning as terms utilized in Talmudic discussions and debates.

Marriage

In Judaism, marriage is not only a romantic union between two people. It's also a serious business transaction that involves many rights and responsibilities for both parties.

>> **Conjugal rights:** Called *Onah* (OH-nah); it establishes that a husband must engage in sexual relations with his wife based on the mutual agreement of the partners.

>> **Marriage contract:** Called a *ketubah* (keh-TOO -bah); a legal document that the groom gives to the bride listing his obligations both during and after marriage.

>> **Promiscuous sexual relations:** Called *zenut* (zeh-NOOT); states that no one can have sexual relations outside of a marital relationship.

>> **Wedding canopy:** Called a *chuppah* (KHOO-pah); it acts as a symbolic home entered during the wedding ceremony by the bride and groom.

Courts and the Law

In *masekhta* (mah–SEKH -tah; tractate) *Sanhedrin*, as well as elsewhere in the Talmud, the sages spell out details about Judaism's court system, discussing and debating questions such as who qualifies as a witness, how many witnesses you need to establish the facts in a case (this principle is rooted in verses such as Deuteronomy 19:15, which states, "A matter can only be established by the testimony of two or three witnesses"), and scores of other points:

>> **At times sane, at times insane:** Translation of *itim chalim, itim shoteh* (ee-TEEM khah-LEEM, ih-TEEM show-TEH); establishes that If a person has periods of sanity and insanity, all business transactions are binding while they are sane. While the person is insane, they're not responsible for their behavior. Jewish law entrusts the court with determining insanity based on various established criteria, while allowing for professional input to inform their judgment.

>> **Five types of indemnity:** called *Nezikin* (neh-zee -kin); Injury, pain, medical costs, loss of livelihood, and humiliation.

>> **Gift of a person on their deathbed:** Translation of *Matnat Shechiv Meira* (math-NAHT sheh-KHEEV meh-EAR-ah); establishes that such gifts are valid: The verbal commitment of the dying person is sufficient. An ill person may also retract their gift if they're of sound mind. Jewish law does not mandate witnesses for deathbed gifts, relying instead on the sincerity of the donor's intentions. However, practical considerations may encourage involving witnesses to avoid later disputes.

>> **Laws of Heaven:** Translation of *dinei shamayim* (DIN-ay shah-MAH-yeem); states that when a court can't enforce a law, the accused still has a moral obligation to conduct themselves in a manner that will satisfy even the laws of Heaven.

>> **The law of the land is the law:** Translation of *Dina malkhta dina* (**dee**-nah mal-**khoot**-ah dee-nah); Jews must obey the laws of the country in which they live. Jewish law encourages compliance with civil laws in most cases but prioritizes religious obligations when conflicts arise. Solutions often involve negotiation, adaptation, or reliance on rabbinic courts to mediate between the two systems.

>> **Oaths:** Translation of *shevuah* (sheh-VOO-ah); a statement invoking the name of God. The punishment for a false oath is severe. According to the Talmud, the punishment for a false oath is severe and multifaceted: The Talmud states that a person who takes a false oath "will never be forgiven by God" and will be "immediately punished," even if their life is otherwise meritorious. For intentional false oaths, the punishment is lashes administered by a human court. The Talmud emphasizes the gravity of false oaths to underscore the importance of truthfulness and the proper use of God's name in Jewish law and ethics.

>> **Pit:** called *bor* (boar); any obstruction that a person causes on public property.

>> **The requirement for an uneven number of judges:** Translation of *bet din shakul* (bet-DIN shah-**kool**); this rule avoids two equal groups who can't reach a decision.

>> **The requirement to have more than one witness:**
Translation of *Edim Shnayim* (aye-DEEM shah-NAH-yeem);
establishes that one witness can't sufficiently confirm the
facts in a court case. In fact, if the court will hear only one
witness, that witness can't even testify.

Human Behavior

The rabbis in the Talmud are highly sensitive to subtle and not-
so-subtle human behavior. Human relationships and their
dynamics are central to the Jewish legal system:

>> **Acts of kindness:** Called *gemilut chasadim* (geh-me-LOOT
khah-sah-DEEM); these are *mitzvot* (mitz-vote: commandments or obligations given by God to the Jewish people, as
outlined in the Torah, offering physical or spiritual
assistance.

>> **Behavior typical of Sodom:** Translation of *middat S'dom*
(MEE-daht suh-DOME); this term refers to selfish and cruel
behavior characterized by an unwillingness to help others
or share resources, even when it costs nothing to do so.
Enforcing unjust laws that penalize the vulnerable. Showing
cruelty to strangers and the poor.

>> **Rebuke:** Called *tochachah* (TOE-khah-khah); this act is a
mitzvah (mitz-vah, singular of *mitzvot*). The term *tochahah* is
derived from the biblical commandment in Leviticus 19:17,
which states "You shall surely rebuke your fellow, but incur
no guilt because of him." According to the Talmud, It should
be done privately and gently, to avoid embarrassing the
person being rebuked. The rebuke should be given with
the intention of helping the person improve, not out of
anger or a desire to shame them. The obligation to give
rebuke applies even to a student rebuking a teacher, if
necessary. Proper rebuke is considered an act of kindness
and love.

Personal Status

The Jewish social system is highly sensitive to various stations within the population. An individual ordained as a rabbi in Talmudic times, for example, requires certain behavior and respect. It is interesting to see, for example, that someone called a "student of the wise" occupies a highly respected position within the Jewish community. A student of Torah is a most commendable person.

Here are terms related to some of the social positions discussed in the Talmud:

>> **Disciple:** Called *talmid* or *talmidim*, plural (TAHL-mid, tahl-mee-DEEM); refers to a student who follows a rabbi (teacher) with the goal of emulating their life and teachings. This relationship was far deeper than simply acquiring knowledge; it involved a total commitment to becoming like the rabbi in all aspects of life — actions, beliefs, and behaviors. The role often goes beyond passive learning, as they are expected to challenge their teacher through questions, thereby deepening mutual understanding and sharpening intellectual engagement.

>> **Disciple-colleague:** Called *khaver* (khah-VAIR); refers to a peer who is both a student and is an intellectual equal in some respects. This term highlights the collaborative nature of Torah study, where individuals may learn from one another while maintaining mutual respect. The term is often used to describe a disciple-colleague or a companion in study. It signifies someone who is both a peer and an associate in the pursuit of Torah knowledge and observance of Jewish law.

>> **Ordination:** Translation of *semikha* (seh-MEE-khah) the term in Jewish law refers to the process of ordination, "the laying of the hands," where authority is conferred upon an individual to serve as a rabbi, teacher, or judge. Ordination could only be performed by someone who was already ordained. In Jewish law *semikha* refers to the process of ordination, where authority is conferred upon an individual to serve as a rabbi, teacher, or judge. The person granting *semikha* had to be accompanied by two other judges,

forming a court of three. However, only one of the three needed to be ordained themselves.

In the Talmud, *semikha* refers to the formal rabbinic ordination that traces its origins to Moses, who ordained Joshua through the symbolic act of laying hands on him (Numbers 27:18-23). The term *semikha* literally means "laying of hands," symbolizing the transmission of authority and responsibility from teacher to student. However, by the time of the Talmudic era, the physical act of laying hands was no longer practiced, and *semikha* was conferred through verbal or written acknowledgment.

The "laying of hands" (*semikha*) in Jewish tradition, as described in the Talmud, was a symbolic act used to confer authority or responsibility. It was performed by Moses when ordaining Joshua as his successor (Numbers 27:18–23). The act involved physically placing hands on the individual being ordained, symbolizing the transfer of leadership, wisdom, and divine authority.

>> **Rabbi:** Called *rabbi* (RAH-bye); primary teacher from whom a person learns Torah. In essence, a "Rabbi" in the Talmud is both a teacher and a leader, embodying the transmission of Jewish tradition from Moses through successive generations. Today's rabbis are not considered rabbis in the classical Talmudic sense, as they do not possess the original rabbinic ordination that was conferred through an unbroken chain of transmission beginning with Moses and ending around the 4th century CE. Instead, modern day *semicha* (seh-ME-khah, to lean on, ordination) refers to a certification or diploma granted by a rabbinical institution or a senior rabbi, signifying proficiency in Jewish law (*halacha*) and authorizing the recipient to serve as a rabbi or teacher.

While today's rabbis are not "rabbis" in the Talmudic sense, their semicha certifies them as learned authorities in Jewish law and tradition, enabling them to fulfill essential roles in Jewish communities worldwide.

>> **Sage:** Called *chacham* (KHAH-khahm); according to the Mishna, a wise man known as a sage is "one who learns from every person." This reflects humility and an openness to acquiring knowledge from diverse sources, regardless of the teacher's status or background.

Sages are often considered more honored than rabbis in terms of Torah wisdom and spiritual stature, while rabbis are highly respected for their formal roles as teachers and leaders within Jewish communities. Both reflect different aspects of reverence for Torah.

>> **Torah scholar:** Called *talmid chacham* (TAHLmeed KHAH KHAH-KHAHM); a Torah scholar studies the Holy Scriptures of Judaism, (similar but not identical to what Christians call the Old Testament) *Mishna,* and Talmud and serves Torah scholars as a disciple. He must also adopt higher standards of behavior than anyone in the community. A true *talmid chacham* integrates wisdom with piety, humility, and a deep connection to God. The term (which literally means "wise student") is used to describe an advanced scholar who excels in Torah study and embodies wisdom and moral conduct.

HISTORICAL ATTEMPTS TO REINSTATE SEMIKHA

After the Bar Kochba revolt (132–136 CE), Emperor Hadrian outlawed semikha, enforcing the death penalty for anyone who conferred or received it and even for those living in towns where it was performed. This made it exceedingly difficult to continue the practice openly. While some sources suggest semikha may have persisted in limited forms beyond this period, it ultimately fell into disuse by the end of the Talmudic era (circa 400 CE).

Throughout history, there have been several notable attempts to revive classical *semikha* (rabbinic ordination) to re-establish the Sanhedrin and restore its authority. These efforts ultimately faced significant opposition and practical challenges. Below are some of the most prominent attempts to reinstate *semikha*:

Rabbi Yaakov Beirav (1538, Safed): Rabbi Beirav sought to revive *semikha* based on Maimonides' ruling that if all or most sages in the Land of Israel agreed, *semikha* could be reinstated. He gathered 25 leading rabbis in Safed and was ordained, granting *semikha* to

(continued)

(continued)

others, including Rabbi Yosef Karo (author of the *Shulchan Aruch*). However, the Chief Rabbi of Jerusalem, Rabbi Levi ben Chaviv (Ralbach), rejected the validity of the ordination, leading to a prolonged dispute. The controversy prevented widespread acceptance, and the effort eventually faded.

Rabbi Yisroel of Shklov (1830s): A disciple of the Vilna Gaon, Rabbi Yisroel attempted to locate remnants of the Ten Lost Tribes in Yemen, believing they might have preserved *semikha*. He sent emissaries to Yemen but found no evidence of its survival.

Rabbi Aharon Mendel haCohen (1901): Rabbi haCohen sought to renew *semikha* by gathering support from 500 leading rabbis. However, his efforts were interrupted by the outbreak of World War I, and the plan was never implemented.

Rabbi Zvi Kovsker (1940s): Before the establishment of the State of Israel, Rabbi Kovsker worked toward re-establishing *semikha* as a foundation for a Sanhedrin. His efforts were disrupted by World War II and failed to gain sufficient rabbinic consensus.

Rabbi Yehuda Leib Maimon (1949): After the founding of Israel, Rabbi Maimon proposed transforming the Israeli Chief Rabbinate into a new *Sanhedrin*. However, opposition arose due to concerns about government influence on religious matters. The proposal was compared unfavorably to Napoleon's *Sanhedrin* and ultimately failed to gain traction.

Recent Efforts (2004): A group of rabbis attempted to revive *semikha* through scholarly consensus in Israel, distributing materials and organizing votes. Despite their efforts, this attempt faced significant obstacles and skepticism.

The modern form of rabbinic ordination began to develop in the Middle Ages, centuries after the cessation of classical *semikha*. This new form of ordination emerged as a practical solution to ensure the continuity of Jewish leadership and halakhic authority in the absence of the original chain of ordination. Today's *semikha* is symbolic and does not claim continuity with classical *semikha*. It is granted by rabbinical institutions or senior rabbis after rigorous study and examinations in areas such as *Shabbat*, *kashrut* (kosher laws), family purity, and other aspects of Jewish law.

>> **Descendant of Noah:** Translation of *Bnai Noakh* (Bih-**nay no**-akh); the term refers to all of humanity, as Noah and his family were the sole survivors of the Flood and thus the ancestors of all people.

>> **Two pubic hairs:** Translation of *Shtei Sa'arot* (Shu-TAY sah-ah-ROTE); when a boy is 13 and a girl is 12, or if at least two pubic hairs appear. In the Talmud, the presence of two pubic hairs is a key physical sign of sexual maturity and is used as a halachic indicator of adulthood. This concept is significant in determining when a boy or girl transitions from being a minor to an adult, which carries implications for their obligations under Jewish law and their legal status in various contexts.

>> **Righteous convert:** Called *Ger Tzedek* (gair TZEH-dekh); a righteous convert — gentile who accepts Judaism. A convert, by Jewish law, is like a newborn Jewish child, and is considered to be as Jewish as any Jew in history. The Talmud emphasizes the spiritual significance of such converts, viewing them as individuals who join the Jewish people out of genuine devotion to God and His commandments.

>> **Heretic:** Called *Apikoros* (ah-pee KORE-uhs); one who doesn't accept the fundamental principles of the Torah or the authority of the sages, or who treats them with contempt, is derived from the Greek philosopher *Apicurus*, whose ideas about denying divine providence and focusing on materialism were seen as antithetical to Jewish beliefs.

>> **Excommunication:** When the leadership of a Jewish community excommunicates someone, that person is no longer considered a member of the community, but they're still a member of the Jewish people. In the Talmud, excommunication is referred to as a form of religious censure used to enforce communal discipline and ensure adherence to Jewish law. It involves excluding an individual from the Jewish community, either temporarily or permanently, depending on the severity of their offense. The decision to excommunicate is typically made by a rabbinic court (bet din) or community leaders, depending on the severity of the offense and the local authority structure.

The Talmud outlines three levels of excommunication: *nezifah*, *niddui*, and *cherem*, each with increasing severity:

- **Rebuke:** Called *nezifah* (neh-TZIH-fah); a mild form of censure lasting one day or a short period. The individual is expected to withdraw from communal interactions, speak minimally, and reflect on their behavior.

- **Temporary exclusion:** Called *niddui* (nih-DO-ee); a more serious form of excommunication lasting 30 days, extendable if repentance does not occur. The individual is barred from social and religious interactions, including coming within six feet of others. It was often used for offenses such as disrespecting scholars, refusing to testify in court, or violating rabbinic laws.

- **Total exclusion:** Called *cherem* (KHAY-rehm); this is the most severe form of excommunication, involving total exclusion from the community. The individual is shunned entirely and barred from all communal and religious activities. This could last indefinitely until repentance or could be permanent. Rituals accompanying cherem included public announcements, curses, and symbolic acts like extinguishing candles to signify spiritual separation. Excommunication is often announced publicly in the synagogue.

Crimes

Like in the laws of today's secular society, Jewish law identifies many crimes. Some people who commit these crimes are punished by the tangible world, while others are susceptible to spiritual punishment:

>> **Burglary:** Called *maḥteret* (makh-TEH-reht); the Talmudic term for burglary, addresses the case of a thief caught breaking into a house at night. Someone who breaks into another person's home is considered a potential murderer. The victim can defend themselves and even kill the thief unless the victim knows that the thief has no intention of harming them.

>> **Destruction:** Called *Bal Tashchit* (bahl tash-KHEET); a law against destroying objects of value.

>> **Evil speech:** Translation of *Lashon Hara* (la-SHONE ha-RAH); means evil tongue and prohibits gossip. Speaking negatively about another person is prohibited, even if the gossip is true. False, disparaging remarks such as slander are even more serious

>> **Forever forewarned:** Translation of *l'olam* (lih oh-LAHM); the Talmud teaches that a person is responsible for all damages that they cause, regardless of whether the damage was caused intentionally or unintentionally. This phrase is used to emphasize that a person is perpetually considered forewarned and accountable for their actions, particularly in cases of damage or harm.

>> **Verbal mistreatment:** Translation of *Ona'at Devarim* (oh-nah-AHT deh-vah-REEM); prohibits causing distress by making statements that shame or embarrass a person. The Talmud offers a lengthy discussion of the seriousness of verbal abuse.

Mitzvot

Judaism's system of *mitzvot* (mitz-VOTE); the plural of *mitzvah*. In the Talmud and Jewish tradition, the term refers to the commandments given by God to the Jewish people, as outlined in the Torah. It includes good deeds, prescribed rituals, and forbidden actions. Judaism is particularly sensitive to peace and pleasantness between and among individuals and in society, in general:

>> **Intent:** Translation of *Kavanah* (kah-vah-NAH); *Kavanah* refers to the mindset or conscious intent to fulfill a *mitzvah* as commanded by God. It involves focusing on the act and recognizing its purpose as a Divine obligation.

>> **Repairing the world:** Translation of *Tikkun Olam* (tee-KOON oh-LUM); refers specifically to rabbinic interventions aimed at maintaining justice and social order, reflecting Judaism's commitment to ethical governance and communal well-being.

>> **Saving a life:** Translation of *Pikuach Nefesh* (pih-KOO-akh NEH-fehsh); states the effort to save a life takes precedence over all *mitzvot,* with the exceptions of idol worship, murder, and forbidden sexual relations. The Talmud explains that a Jew must not worship idols, murder, or participate in acts like incest or adultery.

>> **Ways of peace:** Translation of *Darchei Shalom* (DAHR-khay shah-LOME); *Darchei Shalom* in the Talmud represents a foundational principle aimed at creating societal harmony and ethical relationships, both within the Jewish community and with others. It highlights Judaism's emphasis on peace as a core value.

>> **Ways of pleasantness:** Translation of *darcheha darchei noam* (dahr-KHEH-khah DAHR-khay NO-ahm); the Talmudic concept of "ways of pleasantness" reflects Judaism's ethical ideal that religious practice should lead to a life of joy, kindness, and respect for others. It serves as a reminder that the Torah is not merely a set of laws but a framework for creating a just and compassionate society.

>> **Way of the world:** Translation of *Derech Eretz* (DEH-rekh EH-rehtz); refers to the integration of ethical conduct, practical living, and societal norms into a life guided by Torah values. It reflects Judaism's holistic approach to balancing spiritual aspirations with everyday responsibilities.

Human Emotions

Jewish thought is sensitive to the full range of human emotions and is surprisingly aware of subtle human feelings and their implications within life:

>> **Despair:** Translation of *ye'ush* (yeh-OOSH); the Talmudic term for despair is *ye'ush*, which refers to the emotional and legal state of giving up hope. In Jewish law, *ye'ush* is particularly significant in the context of lost objects. It denotes the point at which an owner abandons hope of recovering their lost property, thereby relinquishing their ownership rights.

>> **Fasting for a dream:** Translation of *Ta'anit Chalom* (TAH-ah-neet khah-LOHM); if a person has a troubling dream, they can fast to reverse the negative effects of that dream.

>> **Human dignity:** Translation of *Kevod HaBeriyot* (keh-VODE ha-beh-ree-OAT); this concept emphasizes the inherent respect and value owed to every human being, as all are created in the image of God. It is a central Talmudic principle that underscores the sanctity of human dignity, permitting flexibility in Jewish law to preserve respect and honor for individuals.

>> **Invasion of privacy:** *Hezek Re'iyah* (HEH-zek reh-ee-VAH); meaning "damage caused by seeing," *Hezek Re'iyah* reflects the Talmudic emphasis on respecting personal boundaries and protecting individuals from both physical and non-physical invasions of their privacy. The Talmud considers merely looking into someone else's private space as a form of harm, as it infringes on their right to privacy and dignity. It also applies to unauthorized access to personal information.

Opening the Talmud

2

Find out how the Talmud is structured and where to begin your study.

Meet the great Talmudic sages whose debates and insights shaped Jewish law and philosophy.

Explore the role of women in Talmudic discourse and historical debates about their inclusion.

Consider imaginative and philosophical ideas that stretch the boundaries of Talmudic thought.

Chapter **6**

Navigating the Talmud

W hen looking at a page of the Talmud, the first thing you notice is probably that it doesn't look like any other book you've ever seen. Where does a page begin? Where does it end? When you examine a page of the Talmud you can see a lot going on, which may feel disorienting. The Talmud isn't like a typical book in English that you buy in a bookstore. Those books begin at the top and read left to right, line by line, to the bottom of the page, after which you turn the page and begin another.

In contrast, the Talmud, often called the Sea of Talmud, has no clear beginning or end. Like diving into the sea, you can open any of its 63 volumes (called *masekhtot*, mah-sekh-tote) and start reading wherever you land. In this chapter, I describe how to navigate the Talmud, including the structure of the Talmud, in general, and then the structure of each page. And I offer advice on where to begin exploring the Talmud.

Where to Start? Anywhere!

The Talmud doesn't have an official Volume 1. Neither is there a Volume 2, nor any absolutely fixed system of reading order. Most editions of the Talmud follow the same sequence, but a student doesn't have to begin with the first *masekhta* (mah-SEKH-tah; volume). In addition, no volume of the Talmud has a page 1. All the traditional classic volumes begin with page 2. While there are various reasons that publishers begin books on page two, legend has it that just like the actual sea, the Sea of Talmud has no beginning; just jump in anywhere.

Although you can really start anywhere, if you simply open to a random page of the Talmud, you might find yourself in the middle of a highly technical discussion — surely not for a beginner. So the question remains: Where do you start? If you want a recommendation for a place among the 63 *masekhtot* (Mah-SEKH-tote; tractates) meaning detailed scholarly texts that discuss a particular topic) of the Talmud to begin, many teachers of Talmud over the centuries began teaching the Talmud with tractate Bava Metzia (BAH-vah-met-SEE-yah, The Middle Gate) because it deals with common activities like borrowing, lending, overpayment, lost items, found items and dishonest business practices. Although some teachers have a rigid idea of where to start and how to proceed, the Talmud itself recommends that you study what you want to study.

Mapping the Talmud for a beginner

Beginning on a journey into the Talmud can feel overwhelming, given its depth and scope. To ease into this world of rich discussion and diverse perspectives, consider beginning with the accessible and thought-provoking areas that I discuss in the following sections. Each part of the Talmud offers a glimpse into the Talmud's intellectual, ethical, and narrative richness, providing a strong foundation for further exploration. (For an explanation of the rather unusual page numbering, see the section "Understanding the Layout of a Talmud Page," later in this chapter.)

Begin with the sections that spark your curiosity, and take your time unpacking the layers of meaning. Approach the texts with patience, curiosity, and a willingness to ask questions. These stories and teachings can not only introduce you to the Talmud's vast landscape, but also inspire deeper engagement with its wisdom.

The Four Who Entered Pardes

Masekhta Chagigah 14b–15a: This mystical *aggadah* (ah-GAH-dah; story) describes four rabbis who journey into the spiritual realms of existence, encountering profound insights and perils along the way. It invites readers to reflect on the boundaries of human understanding and the dangers of unprepared exploration into the divine.

The Oven of Achnai

Bava Metzia 59b–60a: This famous narrative begins as a debate among sages about the ritual status of an oven, but it soon expands into broader themes, including the limits of human authority, the power of words, and the balance between tradition and innovation.

Rabbi Akiva's Transformation

Throughout the Talmud: The Talmud weaves Rabbi Akiva's extraordinary life story across multiple *masekhtot*, showcasing his journey from an uneducated shepherd to one of Judaism's greatest sages. His unwavering commitment to learning and faith provides inspiration for all who seek personal growth.

Honi HaMe'agel (Honi the Circle Maker) (1st Century BCE)

Ta'anit 23a–b: These stories recount a Talmudic personality named Honi who was known for his being able to pray for rain effectively. Honi's remarkable ability to bring rain through prayer, delves into themes of faith, community, and the relationship between human effort and divine intervention. They also highlight the power of persistence in moments of communal need.

The Creation of Adam

Sanhedrin 38a–b: In this portion, the Talmud explores the creation of humanity, pondering profound questions about human nature, equality, and the divine image. These discussions offer philosophical and ethical insights into what it means to be human.

King Solomon's Wisdom

Gittin 68b: Scattered throughout the Talmud, *aggadot* (ah-gah-DOTE; stories) the plural form of *aggadah*) about King Solomon (died 931 BCE) emphasize his unparalleled wisdom and the complexity of his judgments. The *aggadot* provide a window into the Talmud's approach to leadership and ethical decision-making.

Teachings of Hillel and Shammai

Throughout the Talmud: The contrasting views of the two great sages, Hillel and Shammai, (they lived between the first century BCE and the first century CE) frame much of the Talmudic discourse. Their debates, which often center on finding the balance between leniency and stringency, showcase the Talmud's emphasis on dialogue and respectful disagreement.

Studying your heart's desire

The Talmud discusses just about every topic under the sun. I suggest that you identify a topic of interest, and then locate where in the Talmud you can join in on the discussion. To find the portion of the Talmud of interest to you, first look up the subject in one of the topical books I recommend in the sidebar "Further reading recommendations for the beginner," in this chapter.

The topic of "studying what is your heart's desire" is found in the Talmud itself. The very first Psalm in the Book of Psalms (which contains 150 psalms) includes a verse that reads, "But his delight is in the Torah of the Lord."

The Talmud records that Rabbi Yehudah HaNasi (ca. 135 CE to 220 CE), the editor of the *Mishna* (Mish-nah; the written record of the Oral Torah) received from God at Mount Sinai along with the Written Torah, which I talk about in the following section, interpreted this verse to mean, "A person can learn Torah only from a place in the Torah that is his heart's desire." Rabbi Yehudah HaNasi explains that a person's delight is in the text that they wish to study. The Talmud presents us with an incident:

> Both Levi and the son of Rabbi Yehuda HaNasi were sitting before Yehuda HaNasi and studying a part of the Torah. When they concluded the studying of a certain book of the Torah, they had to decide which book of the Torah they should study next.

> Levi said he wanted to study the book of Proverbs, while the son of Rabbi Yehuda HaNasi said he wanted to study the book of Psalms. Rabbi Yehuda HaNasi decided to go with his son's desire and said, "Let the book of Psalms be brought in."

> When they got to the second line in Psalm 1, they read, "But his delight is in the Torah of the Lord." Rabbi Yehuda HaNasi explained the verse by saying, "A person can learn Torah only from a place that is his heart's desire." When he heard this, Levi, who wanted to study Proverbs and not Psalms, said to his teacher, Rabbi Yehuda HaNasi, "You have given me the right to rise and leave because I wish to study Proverbs, not Psalms."

FURTHER READING RECOMMENDATIONS FOR THE BEGINNER

I hope that this book can give you basic information about the Talmud while offering some experience reading the Talmud itself through the sample passages that I include throughout the book. If you want further guidance in your exploration of the Talmud, here are some other reading suggestions:

- **The Steinsaltz edition of the Talmud:** This translation and commentary of the Talmud, by Rabbi Adin Steinsaltz (first published in 1989), consists of 42 volumes (some Steinsaltz volumes contain more than one *masekhta* of the Talmud itself). Start with his Volume 1, *Berakhot* (Blessings). This *masekhta* contains an

(continued)

(continued)

explanation of the many blessings Jews say throughout the day and year, and it also contains many other subjects, including dreams and dream interpretation. In his commentary, Rabbi Steinsaltz defines important terms, offers biographical paragraphs about some of the rabbis who appear in the text, provides pictures of some of the more interesting items mentioned in the text, and more.

Due to its popularity over the centuries, Rabbi Steinsaltz published a separate volume of *Pirkei Avot* (PEER-kay AH-vote; Chapters of the Fathers). A newcomer to Talmud study can easily understand *Pirkei Avot*. You can find many editions of *Pirkei Avot,* and some translations are better than others. I always find an edition of any book translated by Rabbi Steinsaltz to be the best.

- *The Talmud: A Selection,* translated by Norman Solomon (Penguin Classic): Contains over 750 pages of translations from the Talmud. Its index and glossary can help you find Talmudic discussions about a particular topic.

- *The Talmud for Today,* by Rabbi Alexander Feinsilver (St. Martin's Press): Gives quotations from the Talmud organized by subject. The author also provides references to the page numbers in the Talmud where the quotations appear.

- *HaMafteach: Talmud Indexed Reference Guide,* by Daniel Retter (Philipp Feldheim): The very best topical index to the Talmud, this book consists of 777 pages. *HaMafteach* (ha-maf-TAY-yakh) is Hebrew for "the key."

- *Find it in the Talmud,* by Mordechai Judovits (Urim Publications): An index by subject that contains over 1,000 entries.

  Each of the topical indexes above has some overlapping but also have different approaches and choices. Both are worthwhile.

Consider taking a class at your local synagogue. Many synagogues offer Talmud classes. But I have one word of advice: If you find the class boring, then the teacher doesn't know how to teach Talmud. The Talmud is anything but boring!

Introducing the Talmud's Parts

The Talmud consists of 63 *masekhtot* (ma–SEKH–tote; tractates or books). But don't get intimidated by that number. There's a logic to the Talmud's general structure. The central text includes a

>> *Mishna* (Mish-nah): The written version of the Oral Torah that Rabbi Yehudah HaNasi gathered and edited around 200 CE, followed by its

>> *Gemara* (geh-mah-rah): Analysis of the *Mishna* can be short or go on for many pages. The word *Gemara* comes from Aramaic, meaning "completion" or "to finish." The main compiler of the *Gemara* was Rav Ashi between 375 CE to 427 CE when he died, and the final compilation was completed by Ravina around 500 CE (see Chapter 2 to meet the editors of the *Gemara*).

The following two commentaries surround the Mishna and Gemara on each page.

>> **Rashi's commentary:** The commentary by Rashi (a rabbi born in 1040) provides important explanations of the Mishna and the *Gemara*.

>> *Tosefot* (toe-sah-foat; additions): Consists of a carefully edited amalgam of commentaries. The main commentators in the *Tosefot* section of the Talmud include Rashi's grandsons and sons-in-law, who often disagree with Rashi.

Talmud study is basically the effort to understand the *Mishna* and the *Gemara*. Rashi and the Tosefot added their commentary to help the reader understand these two texts.

The order of the orders

The ritual feast held on the holiday of Passover is called a *seder* (SAY-der; arrangement). The word *seder* (order) is the singular of the word *sedarim* (say-DAHR-eem, orders). In the same way that the Passover seder has a special arrangement to it, each of the six *sedarim* of the Talmud refers to the arrangement of the *masekhtot*. In other words, each *seder* contains the *masekhtot* that most closely relate to the general contents of that *seder*. (See the section "Mishna sedarim," later in this chapter.)

Within the Talmud, each of the *sedarim* of the Mishna is divided into *masekhtot* (tractates) each of which is divided into Mishnayot (plural of mishna) which are gathered and organized into chapters called *perakim* (peh-RAH-keem); the singular is *perek* (PEH-reck).

The Talmud masekhtot

Each of the 63 tractates of the Talmud is called a *masekhta* (mah-SEKH-tah). The plural of *masekhta* is *masekhtot* (mah-SEKH-tote). Think of a *masekhta* as a book or a volume; each with its own name. (See the appendix for a complete list of all the *masekhtot* that make up the Talmud.) Each *masekhta* begins with a *Mishna*, followed by its *Gemara*.

If you look at the list of *Masekhtot* at least a couple of their names might be familiar to you. One is called *Shabbat*, which is the Hebrew name for the Sabbath. Another one is *Rosh Hashanah*, which is the Jewish New Year. The name of the tractate indicates the general topic of that particular *masekhta*.

Although each *Masekhta* of the Talmud has a name that reflects the general contents of that volume, keep in mind that the Talmud flows from topic to topic almost by free association, so you can find pages and pages that discuss a topic that seems to belong in another *masekhta* of the Talmud. For example, you can't find everything about the Sabbath in Tractate Shabbat. A lot of teachings about Shabbat are scattered throughout the Talmud. Each *masekhta* is located in one of six sedarim (seh-DAH-reem; orders).

Talmud chapters and subjects

The Talmud contains 525 perakim (chapters) spread over the 63 masekhtot. The perakim are divided into Sugyot (sug-yoat; units of study). Each of the Sugyot is called a Sugya (SUG-yah).

Outlining the Talmud's structure

In total, the entire Talmud contains 2,711 double-sided folios. So the Talmud consists of 5,422 pages! Each page of the Talmud has a lot going on. But it's not as complicated as it looks. Table 6-1 shows the general structure of the Talmud.

TABLE 6-1 Overview of the Talmud Structure

Term, Singular	Term, Plural	What It Is	Number in the Talmud
Seder	Sedarim	Order(s) or arrangement(s)	6
Masekhta	Masekhtot	Tractate(s)	63 spread across the 6 sedarim
Perek	Perakim	Chapter(s)	525 divided among the 63 Masekhtot
Mishna	Mishnayot	Individual teaching(s)	4,224
Gemara	Gemarot	Analysis of the Mishna	Not all Mishnayot have a Gemara attached to it
Sugya	Sugyot	Topic(s) or unit(s) of discussion	2,711

Mapping the Mishna and *Gemara*

The Mishna and *Gemara* are the foundation texts of Jewish learning, together forming a vast repository of wisdom, law, and ethical teachings. To navigate their depth and complexity, you first must understand their structure. The *Mishna* serves as the bedrock of the Talmud, organizing centuries of oral tradition into a systematic framework. The Talmud builds on this foundation through the *Gemara* which expands with discussions, interpretations, and debates from hundreds of rabbis and sages who have shaped Jewish thought for generations.

The Mishna contains the following *sedarim:*

- ❯❯ *Zeraim* **(Seeds):** 11 tractates, 75 chapters, 655 mishnayot

- ❯❯ *Moed* **(Festival):** 12 tractates, 88 chapters, 681 mishnayot

- ❯❯ *Nashim* **(Women):** 7 tractates, 71 chapters, 578 mishnayot

- ❯❯ *Nezikin* **(Damages):** 10 tractates, 74 chapters, 685 mishnayot

>> **Kodashim (Holy Things):** 11 tractates, 91 chapters, 590 mishnayo

>> **Tohorot (Purities):** 12 tractates, 126 chapters, 1,003 mishnayot

Table 6-2 breaks down the components in the *sedarim* of the *Mishna*.

TABLE 6-2   The Sedarim of the Mishna

Seder	Translation	Masekhtot	Mishnayot	Perakim
Zeraim	Seeds	11	655	75
Moed	Festival	12	681	88
Nashim	Women	7	578	71
Nezikin	Damages	10	685	74
Kodashim	Holy Things	11	590	91
Tohorot	Purities	12	1,003	126

Understanding the Layout of a Talmud Page

A Talmud page consists of two elements, the *Mishna* and the *Gemara* (which I talk about in the section "Outlining the Talmud's structure," earlier in this chapter).

Next to text of the Mishna and *Gemara*, you find the commentary by Rashi (a rabbi born in 1040). Rashi's commentary provides important explanations of the basic text. In the classic editions and layouts, the commentary always appears in the inside margin, next to the main text. On the other side of the basic Talmud text, the commentary called *Tosefot* (TOE-sahfoat; additions) appears. *Tosefot* consists of a carefully edited amalgam of commentaries. The main commentators in the *Tosefot* section of the Talmud include Rashi's grandsons and sons-in-law, who often disagree with Rashi. The layout of a page of Talmud has been standard since the 16th century.

If you want to study Talmud, you must get to know Rashi and *Tosefot* — their commentaries have appeared on every page since the 16th century. For more background and detail on Rashi, his life, and his legacy, as well as *Tosefot*.

A page of the Talmud contains more than these elements; but for now, just focus on the central text, the commentary by Rashi, and the commentary by the *Tosefot*.

TECHNICAL STUFF

In medieval times, scribes wrote manuscripts on both sides of parchment or vellum. The front side was called the *recto* and the back of that was called the *verso*. Writers also used A and B to distinguish the two sides. One side of a page is referred to as an *amud* (AH-mood), so to single out one side, you might say "*Amud Aleph*" or "*Amud Beit.*" *Aleph* and *Beit* are the Hebrew equivalent of A and B, or 1 and 2. When bound books began to appear, each side of a page had a number, with those numbers going up in order through the pages. Odd numbers were on the right and even numbers were on the left. Books published today use the same format. The Talmud is one of the only books still printed that has A sides and B sides. Every edition has the same pagination. So, for example, if you go to page 22b in the *masekhta* of the Talmud called *Shabbat*, every edition of the Talmud has the same text on that page.

A PHOTOGRAPH OF A FOUNTAIN

Rabbi Adin Steinsaltz, the renowned Jewish scholar (see Chapter 2 for more about Rabbi Steinsaltz), suggested that a good way of thinking about the Talmud is to picture it as a photograph of a fountain. The Talmud, like a fountain, keeps moving. Over the centuries, various publishers added commentaries based on popular demand. The text always changes. So don't imagine the entire Talmud is a fixed text. Great rabbis throughout the centuries have earned the right to have their work become a part of the text and placed on the margin of a page — at times, even at the top of the page. Some commentaries also get printed in the back of the *masekhtot* of the Talmud.

(continued)

(continued)

This is a very important point: Although books generally have fixed content, the Talmud can add commentaries on a page to help explain the original *Mishna* or *Gemara*.

Another reason why comparing the Talmud to a photograph of a fountain is apt involves the fact that the Talmud basically records debates and discussions. The Talmud doesn't offer a record of a whole debate, but rather a general idea of the positions taken in the debate by the various sides. The text on a page of Talmud gives only that one moment in the discussion (that photo of the fountain). The reader has to imagine, with the help of commentators, the active debate represented by the clues in the still photograph.

Other voices in the margins

Rashi's commentary and the commentary of the *Tosefot* are the two main commentaries on just about every page of the Talmud. In addition, you can find other commentators in various editions of the Talmud, who add depth and guidance in the outer margins of Talmudic pages. These scholars provide insights, context, cross-references, and summaries that aid in understanding the discussions at the center of each page:

>> **Rabbenu Hananel:** (b. 1050 CE) His commentary appears on the outside margin of many Talmudic *masekhtot*. Rabbenu Hananel provides a synopsis of the Talmudic discussion, rather than a detailed explanation.

>> **Rabbi Yehoshua Boaz:** (b. 1530 CE) Located on the outside margin of the page, he provides source references so that the reader can find relevant citations to the scriptural sources for verses cited in the Talmud.

>> **Rabbi Yoel Sirkes:** (b. 1561 CE) Offers suggestions for textual *emendations* (improvements) in both the Talmud generally and Rashi's commentary specifically.

>> **The Gaon of Vilna:** (b. 1720 CE) These notes suggest emendations to the text. You can find them within the text as a square Hebrew letter within square brackets.

>> **Rabbi Akiva Eiger:** (b.1761 CE) Often provides references to similar or contradictory sources within the Talmud.

Still more commentators

There are other commentators appearing in various editions of the Talmud, as well. They include

>> The Meiri (Menachem ha Meiri), (b. 1249. CE) who wrote a commentary on the entire Talmud.

>> Rashba (Solomon ben Adret), (b. 1235 CE) a Spanish commentator.

>> Ritva (Rabbi Yom Tov Asevilli), (b. 1250 CE) also a Spanish commentator.

>> Maharsha (Samuel Edels), (b. 1555 CE) who analyzes Rashi and Tosefot.

>> Maharam (Meir Tublin) (b. late 16th century) who also analyzed Rashi and Tosefot.

The Stories and Laws of the Talmud

Generally, you can find two types of material in the text of the Talmud, stories and legal discussions: stories, called *aggadah* (ah GAHD-ah from "to tell"), that usually have a moral or teaching imbedded within it, and legal material, called *halakhah* (ha-LAH-chah from "to walk"), discussions that usually include points of view that become matters of law.

REMEMBER

The Talmud isn't a law book. Don't go to the Talmud to find out what the Jewish law is. Instead, look to codes of law (such as the *Shulchan Arukh* (SHOOL-khan Ah-RUKH) and *Mishneh* Torah (MISH-neh TOE-Rah) like how to light Chanukah candles properly, or questions about kosher food) that can answer those kinds of questions. The Talmud records the discussions and debates about Jewish law.

Both *aggadah* and *halakhah* are essential components of the Talmud, but a running debate throughout the centuries deals with determining which is more important, the stories in the Talmud or the laws that tell us specifically what to do and what not to do:

>> **Story people:** The people who think the *aggadah* are more important might say that the moral of a story has a greater impact on the reader because the abstract idea of the moral imbedded within the story addresses questions of ethical behavior, while the *halakhah* may or may not have an impact outside of the possible observance of that particular law. A story has a human-interest aspect whereas a law is more of a technical question.

>> **Law people:** The people who think the *halakhah* are more important than the *aggadah* represent the view that the laws are concrete and are specific, whereas the moral of the story can sometimes be vague and not always agreed upon.

Aggadah: Hillel on the roof

Before I share the text of this *aggadah* with you, I want to point something out before we even get started. This story appears in *Masekhta Yoma* (Mah-SEH-khet YOM-ah), which is basically about the Jewish holy day of Yom Kippur. But Yom Kippur has little if anything to do with this *aggadah*. However, if you look at the Talmud text that comes right before this story, the *Gemara* is discussing poverty and wealth. In fact, it was a perfect place for the editors of the Talmud to place this well-known *aggadah*.

The aggadah

Every day, Hillel the Elder earned half a *dinar* (a very small coin). Hillel worked as a wood chopper, and he paid half of his income to the guard of the study hall and half for his family's needs.

On one particular day, Hillel couldn't earn any money, so he couldn't pay the fee required to enter the study hall. He had an idea: Climb on the roof of the study hall and sit on the roof near the skylight to listen to Shemaya and Avtalyon, the spiritual leaders of that generation, give their Torah lessons.

On this eve of the Sabbath, it was wintertime. Snow fell on Hillel while he listened to the lessons. He was so focused on the lessons that he didn't even realize that the snow was slowly burying him.

The next morning, Shemaya said to Avtalyon, "Why is it dark in the room today? Usually, the light comes through the skylight. Is it a cloudy day?"

They looked up, and through the skylight, they saw what looked like a man's shape. They went to the roof and saw a man covered with 3 cubits of snow (a *cubit* is the ancient yardstick, from the elbow to the tip of the middle finger). They dug him out, brought him downstairs, washed him, sat him before the fireplace, and lit a fire. Hillel was revived. Even though it was the Sabbath, when observant Jews aren't permitted to light a fire, Shemaya and Avtalyon were exempt from this law because God always allows saving a life, even on the Sabbath.

The Steinsaltz Talmud includes Rabbi Steinsaltz's comment: "Poverty is not an excuse for failure to attempt to study Torah. Hillel's thirst for learning motivated him to do what he had to do to learn from his teachers."

Even though the story reminds us that observant Jews can't light a fire on the Sabbath except to save a life, and even though the story reminds us that saving a life takes precedence over the laws of the Sabbath, this isn't a text of *halakhah*. The story contains no discussion of law, no source for the law, nor any arguments to justify this law. Clearly, this is an *Aggadic* (ah=GAD-ick) passage: a story that includes lessons for the reader.

Did this really happen? Does it matter?

Before discussing the lesson or lessons in the story of Hillel on the roof, I want to note that this *aggadah* doesn't seem terribly plausible. Was Hillel actually buried beneath 3 cubits of snow for the night? And if he was and did survive, would a fireplace thaw him out?

The *aggadah* may contain a germ of actual reality. Perhaps Hillel did listen to the lessons through the skylight, and perhaps it did snow that night. But to be buried under several feet of snow all night, and then to survive, seems a bit implausible.

The purpose of this *aggadah* is to illustrate Hillel's dedication to Torah study. Jewish children learn this story from the Talmud early in their religious studies. Not only does the story show Hillel's dedication to study; because Hillel ultimately became a great teacher and leader for the Jewish people, it tells the reader that devotion to one's Torah study pays off.

I know from my own studies that Rabbi Elazar ben Azarya, when he was in a leadership position in Judea in the first century CE, changed the rule and thereby permitted anyone to enter the study hall for free.

Aggadah: The sins of the city of Sodom

This *aggadic* passage in the Talmud is one of my favorites! It talks about the wicked city of Sodom. In the story as I present it here, **the bold** words are close to the actual words in the Talmud, and the words in regular type are my effort to help tell the story.

When you think of the city of Sodom in the Bible, sexual sins may come to mind (the word *sodomy* is derived from the name of the city). The Talmudic version of Sodom is much different. The *aggadah* does mention sins of the body, but it goes much further.

Describing Sodom

REMEMBER

The bold typeface is the story from the Talmud, and the regular type is my interpretation.

In the Mishnah, we read that **the people of Sodom will have no place in Heaven. The book of Genesis says, The Men of Sodom were wicked and sinners before the Lord exceedingly (Gen. 13:13).** "Wicked" in this world and "sinners," disqualifying them from entering heaven.

Rabbi Yehuda offers a different explanation. He says, **"Wicked"** refers to sins **with their bodies. And "sinners"** refers to sins committed **with their money. "Before the Lord"** refers to **cursing God,** and **"exceedingly"** refers to **sinning intentionally.**

Note: The approach of the Talmudic rabbis is to believe that every word in the Torah and the Talmud has meaning.

The Sages taught that the people of Sodom were haughty, and they sinned **as a result of God bestowing a lot of success and wealth on them.** In Sodom, **bread grew from the earth, and the stones were all sapphires,** and **the dust** of Sodom **was made of gold.** In addition, **no birds of prey flew within Sodom, no wild beasts came to Sodom, and no lion came in the vicinity.** Sodom was a wealthy and safe city.

Immigrants: Keep out

The people of Sodom thought they had everything they needed. **So, they passed laws forbidding outsiders from coming to the city.**

Also, they were hostile **to landowners,** so **they often put them seated next to a flimsy wall and pushed the wall on them, killing them, and thereby taking their property.**

Rava taught: What is the meaning of the words in the book of Job (24:16), **"In the dark they dig through houses, by day they shut themselves up, they know not the light." They would give rich people some balsam to put near their money, and at night they would sniff like a dog, locate the balsam and steal the money.**

Rabbi Yose taught in Tzippori how thieves steal. The people who attended the lecture learned how thieves steal, **and they took their knowledge and stole.**

The people of Sodom would say, "Anyone who has an ox shall herd all the oxen in the city for one day. But if you didn't have any oxen you had to do it for two days."

In Sodom, **anyone who had a row of bricks saw that people just stole one brick until there were none. And anyone who put out onions or garlic to dry would have them stolen by people just taking one — until there were none.**

There were four judges in Sodom. Their names were Liar, Habitual Liar, Forger, and Perverter of Justice. Someone hit a pregnant woman, and she miscarried. The judges said, give the woman to the one who hit her so he can impregnate her.

Crazy logic

Another case in Sodom involved **a man who cut the ear off another person's donkey. The judges said, give the donkey to the one who cut the ear off until the ear grows back.**

There was also a case where **someone wounded another person, and the one who did the wounding can charge the victim for bloodletting.** (*Bloodletting* was an ancient healing technique.)

In Sodom, they passed a law saying **that if you cross the river on the ferry, you must pay four dinars. But if you cross the river in the water without the ferry, you must pay eight dinars.**

They had beds that guests would lay on. When the guest was longer than the bed, they would cut their legs to fit. If the person was shorter, they would stretch their legs.

There was a law in Sodom that it was forbidden to give charity to the poor. **There was a woman who gave bread to the poor in a pitcher so that people would not see it.** People found out about her charity, and **they smeared her with honey and put her on a wall. Hornets came and ate her. And that is the meaning of the verse, "And the Lord said: The cry of Sodom and Gomorrah is great."** And whose cry was it? It was the woman who was killed for giving bread to the poor.

Considering the aggadah's issues

This piece of *aggadah* from the Talmud discussing Sodom contains many teachings. You can draw conclusions about

>> The tendency of some rich people to be insensitive to the poor

>> The frequent results of greed

>> Conformity (by wanting everyone to be the same size!)

>> Perverted justice

The issues discussed in this *aggadah* go beyond Jewish law; they really offer life lessons.

If you want to read the whole story, get a copy of the Steinsaltz Talmud, pages Sanh. 109a-b. I left out some crazy details regarding the sick society in Sodom. (But I think you get the idea.)

Halakhah about lost objects

One of the *masekhtot* of the Talmud, *Bava Metzia*, has a large section about lost objects. The rabbis go into a lot of detail, trying to figure out just what a lost object is and a person's responsibility when they find a lost object.

The first half of this *Mishna* spells out how a person should handle items that they find:

> "If one found lost scrolls, he reads them once in 30 days.
>
> And if does not know how to read, he rolls them.
>
> But he shall not study in them for the first time.
>
> And another shall not read with him.
>
> If one found a garment, he shakes it once in 30 days, and he spreads it out for its sake, to ventilate it, but he may not use it as a decoration for his own prestige."

This *Mishna* (like almost all *Mishnayot,* in fact) is written in an abbreviated style. It raises some questions, including

>> What is a scroll?

>> How do you roll it?

>> Why can't a person study the text if it's their first time?

>> How can a person read it with another?

>> How do you shake a garment?

>> What does it mean to "spread it . . . not for prestige"?

Getting answers to your Mishna questions

As you can read about in the section "Outlining the Talmud's structure," earlier in this chapter, most *Mishnayot* are followed by a *Gemara*, which is a lengthy expansion or explanation responding to questions that come up when examining the *Mishna*. The *Gemara* for this *Mishna* explains

» *Scrolls* refer to Torah scrolls or scrolls that contain educational text. In Talmudic times, books came in the form of scrolls.

» If you borrow a Torah scroll from someone, you may not lend it to a third party.

» If you borrow a Torah scroll, you may not rent it out to someone else.

» Even if you think that the owner of the scroll would like you to lend it, you can't do it.

» You can open and read from a borrowed Torah scroll, but not if you're reading that text for the first time.

» You need to unroll a scroll to air it out.

» While you air a scroll out, you can read it.

» You take care of an old Torah scroll differently than you do a new Torah scroll.

» If two people are reading the scroll at the same time, be careful to read the same passage at that time. If you read different passages at the same time, you could rip the scroll by pulling the scroll in different directions at the same time.

» The Talmud uses this example to explain that when you find a lost object, you must take care of it properly.

I'll stop at nine points made in the *Gemara* about the care of a found scroll. This particular *Gemara* contains many more.

Laying down the law

This Talmud passage contains several *halakhot* (ha-lah-KHOAT), including

>> If you rent something from someone, you can't rent the item to a third party.

>> If you find *tefillin* (Tlh-FIL-in; leather boxes containing scrolls), you need not take care of it. You can sell it and hold the money if someone looks for it. (As opposed to today, when *tefillin* are very expensive, in Talmudic times, factories made *tefillin* in bulk, and you could buy them very inexpensively.)

>> If you deposit a Torah scroll with someone for safe keeping, they must care for it properly until you return to claim it.

Questions for the lost and found

Here's a sample of some further issues brought up in the various *Mishnayot* regarding lost objects:

>> For how long must a person try to find the owner of a lost object?

>> What if the lost object is an animal?

>> How do you determine whether an object is really lost?

>> What if you find an animal in a stable?

>> What if you find two lost objects, and you know that one belongs to your father and the other belongs to your teacher? Who should you attend to first?

You can find in-depth and compelling discussions about these issues in the *Gemara*.

Navigating debates and the promise of Elijah

Sometimes in a Talmud discussion, no one reaches a clear conclusion. The rabbis participating in the discussion simply can't come to an agreement about the law or don't have enough information. Sometimes, they argue for many pages without coming to a consensus. When a debate or a discussion remains unresolved, at the end of the discussion, the editors of the gemara place the word *Teyku* (TAY-koo). The word itself is connected to an Aramaic word, *teikum* (TAY-koom; it will stand). But the majority of scholars throughout history say that the source of the word *Teyku* is an acronym for "Elijah will answer questions and problems."

For example, the Talmud records that the schools of Hillel and Shammai had over 300 debates, with many debates remaining unresolved. By putting the word *Teyku* at the end of a discussion or debate, the Rabbis were saying that they couldn't figure out the conclusion — but that when Elijah comes, he'll resolve all the conflicts.

Halakhah versus aggadah — a parable

Rav Ami and Rav Asi sat before Rabbi Yitzḥak Nappaḥa. One sage said to Rabbi Yitzḥak Nappaḥa: "Let the Master say words of *halakhah*." And the other sage said to Rabbi Yitzḥak Nappaḥa: "Let the Master say words of *aggadah*." Rabbi Yitzḥak Nappaḥa began to say words of *aggadah*, but one sage did not let him. So he began to say words of *halakhah*, but the other sage did not let him.

Rabbi Yitzḥak Nappaḥa said to them: "I will relate a parable. To what can this be compared? It can be compared to a man who has two wives, one young and one old. The young wife pulls out his white hairs, so that her husband will appear younger. The old wife pulls out his black hairs so that he will appear older. And it turns out that he is completely bald due to the actions of both his wives."

Chapter **7**

Greeting the Great Talmudic Masters

The Talmud is largely a collection of wisdom as taught by hundreds of rabbis and sages. Generally, the rabbis of the Talmud are referred to as sages. Sages are profoundly wise people, praised for their knowledge and experience.

When you study the Talmud, you probably notice that some names repeat themselves over and over again. Some sages made only one statement in the entire 63 volumes of the Talmud, while others take part in discussions hundreds of times.

Students of the Talmud become familiar with the sages who appear very often. Although you can find quotes from at least several hundred sages in the Talmud, a relative few become leaders and sources of a huge number of teachings and wisdom.

In this chapter, I take pleasure in introducing you to some of the greatest rabbinical personalities in all of Jewish history.

Praising the Rabbi Currently Known as Prince

It stands to reason that when the Talmud refers to an individual sage throughout as simply *Rebbe (REH-bee)* or *Rabbi,* he must be an important personality. Although the text often identifies him by his name, it also often just identifies him by the honorific of Rebbe.

His name was Judah, also known as Rabbi Yehudah; but his complete identifying name is Rabbi Yehudah HaNasi, translated as "Rabbi Judah the Prince." The term *Nasi* refers to a great leader, which definitely applies in Rabbi Yehudah's case. However, the term *Nasi* is also the title of the highest-ranking member of the *Sanhedrin,* the Supreme Court of the Jewish people.

During his life, Rebbe was also known as *Rabbenu haKodesh* (ra-BAY-new Ha-KOH-desh; Our Holy Rabbi). In addition to his scholarship, he was the great-grandson of Hillel. (I talk about Hillel in the section "Pairing Two by Two (Rabbis, Not Animals)," later in this chapter.)

Rebbe was also the teacher to some of the next generation's leading rabbis.

Rabbi Yehudah HaNasi had two rare qualities: He was both a superb scholar and the foremost political figure of his generation. His father, Rabban Shimon Ben Gamaliel, was the *Nasi* before him. (Ironically, he was, in reality and at his core, an ascetic, but he appeared in great splendor.) The Talmud says, "From Moses to Rebbe, we do not find another who was supreme both in Torah and in worldly affairs." His life included much sickness, and he abstained personally from any luxuries, yet he lived in a palace. The Talmud says that Antoninus, the Roman Emperor who was a close friend of Rabbi Yehudah HaNasi placed Roman guards at his residence to protect him from anyone who wanted to do him harm.

It's peaceful — so let's get busy

According to the Talmud, Rabbi Yehudah HaNasi's close ties to Roman rulers, and in particular to Emperor Antoninus, contributed to the peaceful time that allowed for Rabbi Yehudah HaNasi to compile the *Mishna*. He had the wisdom to realize that the peace would give him and his colleagues an opportunity to do something unthinkable: to write down the oral tradition.

Moses received two Torahs at Mount Sinai (which you can read about in Chapter 1):

>> **The Written Torah:** The Five Books of Moses

>> **The Oral Torah:** An essential part of the Divine communication between God and the Children of Israel. However, Jewish tradition deliberately kept this communication between God and Moses oral to allow the tradition to remain fluid and flexible.

It says in the Talmud itself, "matters that were written, you may not express them orally, and matters that were taught orally, you may not express them in writing." In other words, don't paraphrase what appears in the written Torah. Every letter has meaning. And don't write down the oral law because the oral law must remain fluid. In a few places in the Talmud we find the warning not to write down the oral tradition, and that the oral tradition must remain fluid to encourage creativity and innovation, and to allow the tradition to adapt to new situations, but the leadership at the time of Yehuda HaNasi, and Yehuda HaNasi himself saw that if the oral tradition wasn't written down it very well might be lost.

Rebbe and his colleagues had the vision to see that they could take advantage of the relative peace at the time and commit the oral tradition to writing. The result of that effort is known as the *Mishna*, the foundation of the Talmud itself. In a sense, the writing down of the oral tradition was a transgression. But the compromise, at the time, appeared to be absolutely necessary. The Jewish leadership came to see the wisdom in their decision.

Although Rabbi Akiva (see the section "Rabbi Akiva: Announcing the Talmud's Superstar," later in this chapter) and Rabbi Meir organized all of the oral teachings into general topics (and other rabbis made similar efforts), Rabbi Yehudah HaNasi completed the job.

Writing down the oral law

The *Mishna* (the word means "repetition") began as an effort to sort all of the oral laws and legends into general categories. They became known as the six *sedarim* (sh-DAR-eem; orders) of the *Mishna*. The *sedarim* were split into smaller groupings by topic. Each of these smaller books was referred to as a *masekhta* (mah-SEKH-tah; tractate). The *masekhtot* (mah SEKH-tote; plural of *maskheta*) were then divided into *perakim* (pe-RAH-keem; chapters), and they in turn were divided into still smaller units called *Mishnayot* (mish-NAH-yote; individual teachings).

Rebbe's contribution was not so much to design the system as it was to write the oral laws in a somewhat precise format. He also had as his students the cream of the crop. They ultimately preserved centuries of wisdom into a well-organized work. Of course, the greatest result of Rabbi Yehudah HaNasi's work on the *Mishna* was that it became the basis of the Talmud itself. If there wasn't a *Mishna*, there simply wouldn't be a Talmud.

The *Mishna*'s language required precision and brevity. Each sentence had to encapsulate a collection of oral teachings. It was crucial for Rebbe to document widely accepted issues, although numerous matters still demanded resolution.

At times in the *Mishna*, Rebbe provides the reader with several conclusions. A close examination of the *Mishna* can lead to the resolution of many controversies, but many disagreements among the sages remained unsettled. Ultimately, the *Mishna* was considered a holy book, second to the Torah itself.

In one of his most well-known statements, Rebbe said, "I have learned a lot from my teachers, and even more from my colleagues, and the most from my students."

And on his deathbed, he lifted his ten fingers toward Heaven and said, "Master of the world, it is revealed and known before you that I toiled with my ten fingers in the study of Torah, and I did not derive any personal pleasure from even my little finger. May it be Your will that there will be peace in my resting place."

Rabbi Akiva: Announcing the Talmud's Superstar

Rabbi Akiva is undoubtedly the superstar of the Talmud. His personal story alone — forgetting about his wisdom for a moment — is downright cinematic.

Akiva was an ignorant shepherd. He didn't even know the alphabet. But Rachel, the daughter of ben Kalba Savua, one of the richest men in all of Jerusalem (whom Akiva worked for), fell in love with him. She undoubtedly saw something in him that was special. She recognized his potential.

One day, she said to him, "If you study Torah, I will marry you." And that's just what Akiva did. But when his father-in-law found out about just who his daughter married — an ignorant shepherd — he disowned her. She lived in dire poverty while her husband was away teaching students. He managed to accumulate 24,000 students. When his father-in-law saw what Akiva had become, they reconciled.

The love story of Rabbi Akiva and Rachel

This is how the Talmud tells the story of Rabbi Akiva and Rachel:

> The daughter of ben Kalba Savua saw that Akiva was humble and refined. She said to him: "If I marry you, will you go learn Torah?"
>
> He said yes to her.
>
> She married him in secret and encouraged him to pursue his studies. When he found out about this secret marriage, her father grew furious. He banished her from his home and declared that she would inherit none of his wealth. (In Judaism, a vow carries significant weight and is binding unless a court intervenes.)
>
> In the winter, Rabbi Akiva and Rachel would sleep in a straw storage shed, where Rabbi Akiva would often remove strands of

straw from her hair. He would tell her, "If I had the means, I would adorn you with a Jerusalem of gold, a golden crown."

Rabbi Akiva spent 12 years studying at a study hall in the town of Lod with Rabbi Eliezer and Rabbi Yehoshua.

When he returned home in Jerusalem, he brought back 12,000 students with him. When he neared home, he overheard an old man asking Akiva's wife, "How long will you live like a widow of a living man, all alone while your husband is away?" She replied, "If he would heed my advice, he would study for another 12 years."

When Rabbi Akiva heard her words, he felt empowered to return to the study hall for another 12 years. When he eventually returned, he had brought with him 24,000 students. His wife rushed out to greet him, and while she approached, she bent down and kissed his feet. His students tried to push her away, not recognizing her.

Akiva told them, "Leave her be; my Torah knowledge and yours truly belong to her."

Meanwhile, her father heard that a great rabbi came to the town. He decided to find him with the hope that the rabbi could nullify his vow against his daughter so that he could support her.

When ben Kalba Savua came to Rabbi Akiva to ask about nullifying his vow, Rabbi Akiva said to him: "Did you vow thinking that this Akiva would become a great man?"

Ben Kalba Savua said to Rabbi Akiva: "If I had believed he would know even one *perek* (chapter) or even one *halakhah* (law), I would not have been so harsh."

Rabbi Akiva said to ben Kalba Savua: "I am he." Then ben Kalba Savua got on his knees and kissed his feet, and he gave Akiva half of his money.

Everything that God does, He does for the best

One of Rabbi Akiva's most significant and challenging teachings revolves around an obligation outlined in the *Mishna:* Even when receiving negative news, one must recite a special blessing: "Blessed is the true judge. . . ." You must recite a blessing for the bad, just like one for the good.

However, in the Gemara (geh-MAH-rah; completion; The Gemara is a commentary on the Mishna. The Mishna and the Gemara together make up the core of the Talmud. The Gemara includes debates, discussions, legends, and much more.) Rava clarified that the Mishna's instruction emphasizes accepting bad news with the same joy that we embrace good news, rather than dictating which blessing to recite.

Rav Aḥa then asks what verse supports this idea: "I will sing of loving-kindness and justice; unto You, O Lord, will I sing praises" (Psalms 101:1). Rav Aḥa interprets this verse as: "Whether it is loving-kindness or justice, I will sing. I will thank God for misfortune just as I do for joy."

Rabbi Shmuel bar Naḥmani offers further proof: "In God, I will praise His word; in the Lord, I will praise His word" (Psalms 56:11). The Gemara explains that this verse reflects God's goodness with "In God, I will praise His word," while "In the Lord, I will praise His word" shows acceptance of suffering; meaning, "Even when faced with hardship, I will continue to praise Him." Rabbi Shmuel bar Nahmani interprets the repetitious lines of Psalm 56 as implying two different things. He speculates that one refers to goodness and the other refers to hardship.

Rabbi Tanḥum presents additional evidence: "I will lift up the cup of salvation and call upon the name of the Lord" (Psalms 116:13) and "I found trouble and sorrow, but I called upon the name of the Lord" (Psalm 116:3–4).

The Rabbis in the same passage of the Gemara also cite: "The Lord has given, and the Lord has taken away; blessed be the name of the Lord" (Job 1:21). Often when the Gemara quotes "the Rabbis" they are stating a consensus among the rabbis of the Gemara.

Rav Huna recounts that Rav, (Rahv, teacher; the leading rabbi of his generation; while he has a first name, he was so illustrious that he only needed to be referred to as Rav and everyone knew who he was.) said that Rabbi Meir taught in the name of Rabbi

Akiva: One should always be inclined to say: "Everything that God does is for the best." It is interesting to note that generally rabbis from Babylonia were referred to as "Rav" while rabbis of Israel were referred to as "Rabbi."

Rabbi Akiva sleeps in a field

The *Gemara* recounts an incident involving Rabbi Akiva:

> While traveling, Rabbi Akiva reached a certain city and asked for lodging, but no one offered him a place to stay. He then declared, "Everything that God does, He does for the best."
>
> Rabbi Akiva spent the night in a field, accompanied by a rooster, a donkey, and a candle. A strong wind blew out his candle, a cat ate the rooster, and a lion devoured the donkey. Yet, Rabbi Akiva continued to affirm, "Everything that God does, He does for the best."
>
> That night, an army invaded the city and took its residents captive. Because Rabbi Akiva was outside the city, with no lighted candle, noisy rooster, or braying donkey to reveal his position, he was spared. He then remarked, "Didn't I tell you? Everything that God does, He does for the best."

The extraordinary death of Rabbi Akiva

The sages in the *Gemara* taught:

> After the Bar Kochba rebellion from 132 to 136 CE in Judea (Israel today), the oppressive Roman Empire declared that Israel could not study or practice Torah. Pappos ben Yehuda approached Rabbi Akiva, who was publicly gathering people to study Torah.
>
> Pappos asked him, "Akiva, aren't you afraid of the government?"
>
> Rabbi Akiva replied, "Let me share a parable. This situation is like a fox walking by a riverbank, who notices fish darting around in a panic. The fox asked, 'What are you fleeing from?' The fish responded, 'We're escaping from the nets thrown at us.'

The fox suggested, 'Would you like to come onto dry land and live with me, just as my ancestors lived with yours?'

The fish retorted, 'Are you the one they call the cleverest of animals? You are mistaken; you are foolish. If we are afraid in the water — our natural habitat that sustains us — then we'd be even more afraid in an environment that leads to our demise.'

The moral is clear: Thus, as Jews engage in Torah study, which is referred to as, 'For that is your life, and the length of your days' (Deuteronomy 30:20), we feel fear from the government; if we stop studying, abandoning it like a place of death, our fear of the empire would increase."

Not long passed before the Romans imprisoned Rabbi Akiva, and they also arrested Pappos ben Yehuda alongside him. Rabbi Akiva asked, "Pappos, what brought you here?" Pappos responded, "Blessed are you, Rabbi Akiva, for your charge is that of studying Torah. Woe to me, for I was taken for engaging in trivial pursuits."

The execution

When they took Rabbi Akiva out to be executed, it was time for the recitation of Shema. "Hear O Israel, the Lord our God, the Lord is One." And while the Romans raked his flesh with iron combs, he was reciting Shema, accepting upon himself the yoke of Heaven.

His students said to him: "Our teacher, even now, while you suffer, you recite Shema?"

He said to them: "All my days, I have been troubled by the verse 'With all your soul,' meaning 'Even if God takes your soul.' I said to myself: 'When will the opportunity be afforded me to fulfill this verse?' Now that it has been afforded me, shall I not fulfill it?"

His last word was "One"

To the last moment of his life, Rabbi Akiva focused his mind on the notion that everything is "One" meaning the Oneness of God.

Rabbi Akiva prolonged his uttering of the word "One" until his soul left his body, so his final word was "One."

A voice descended from Heaven and said: "Happy are you, Rabbi Akiva, that your soul left your body while you said 'One.'"

And then the Divine Voice emerged and said: "Happy are you, Rabbi Akiva, because you are destined for life in the World-to-Come; your portion is already in eternal life."

Rabbi Akiva the great

Students of the Talmud consider Rabbi Akiva great for several reasons:

>> He developed a method of Torah study that significantly influenced Jewish tradition.

>> He gathered 24,000 disciples.

>> His personal transformation, from an ignorant shepherd to a revered Talmudic sage, can provide an inspiration to all students of the Torah.

>> His martyrdom represented extraordinary faith and dedication.

>> Among his thousands of students were some of the greatest Talmudic sages, including Rabbi Meir, Rabbi Shimon ben Yohai, Rabbi Yose ben Halafta, Rabbi Eleazar ben Shammus, and Rabbi Nehemia.

Pairing Two by Two (Rabbis, Not Animals)

Before the many rabbis who contributed most of the teachings in the Talmud, the Jewish people lived in an era called *zugot* (zoo-goat; pairs). Essentially, they considered two Talmudic personalities the Jewish leaders at the time.

The *Sanhedrin*, which was the Supreme Court of the Jewish people — in other words, the judicial body that defined the Jewish community at the time — had two leaders. One was essentially the president or Nasi (nah-SEE; *literally "prince"*) of the

Sanhedrin, and the other was known as the *Av Beit Din* (ahv bet din; Father of the Court), who functioned like a vice president.

These pairs began a time-honored tradition of two people with different views who want to find the truth. Imagine a pair of people today, one being liberal and one being conservative, who balance each other and come up with a third position that tries to synthesize two extremes.

The *Sanhedrin* had five pairs of leaders between 170 BCE and 30 CE:

- ➤ Yose ben Yoezer and Yose ben Yochanan (170 BCE to 140 BCE)

- ➤ Joshua ben Perachiah and Nittai of Arbela (140 BCE to 110 BCE)

- ➤ Judah ben Tabbai and Simeon ben Shetach (110 BCE to 70 BCE)

- ➤ Shemaya and Abtalion (70 BCE to 40 BCE)

- ➤ Hillel and Shammai (40 BCE to 30 CE)

Hillel and Shammai go at it

Each of the five pairs of the *Sanhedrin* leaders had disputes, the most well-known and significant being the disputes between Hillel and Shammai. Hillel was the *Nasi* (essentially, the president), and Shammai was the *Av Beit Din* (the vice president). They helped create a phenomenon in Jewish life, that of two different schools of thought that often clashed. They came to be known as *Bet Hillel* (the House of Hillel) and *Bet Shammai* (the House of Shammai).

The two schools had many disputes, sometimes vehement, but both schools' ideas and philosophy fell well within the boundaries of Jewish thought and life.

The disputes that the schools had sometimes extended to several generations. And generally, Bet Hillel's positions on questions of how to interpret Jewish law and some general approaches to life (see the stories below) won most of these disputes by consensus of the rabbis.

The two schools, Bet Hillel and Bet Shammai, often reflected the personalities of their founders. Hillel's approach to life was humble and simple, while Shammai's was rather strict with himself and others.

The best way to understand their difference is to review some of the most well-known stories about them and clashes between them, which you can read about in the following sections.

Hillel always maintained equanimity

In the Talmud, we read about Hillel:

> Two friends once made a bet with each other; one claimed he could provoke Hillel's anger. The other said he could not.
>
> On a Friday afternoon, Hillel was busily preparing for Shabbat.
>
> The friend who thought he could anger Hillel walked by his house while Hillel was washing his hair. He yelled, "Is Hillel here? Is Hillel here?" Hillel quickly dressed and went to the door to greet him. He asked, "My son, how can I assist you?" The man said, "I have a question." Hillel said, "Ask my son. Ask!"
>
> The man inquired, "Why are Babylonians' heads so round?" Hillel replied, "My son, that's a profound question. It's due to the lack of qualified midwives."
>
> After a while, the man returned and called out, "Is there a Hillel here? Is there a Hillel here?" Hillel went to the door and asked, "My son, what do you seek?"
>
> The man responded, "I have a question for you." Hillel encouraged him, saying, "Ask, my son. Ask." The man then questioned, "Why do Tarmodians [people from a Syrian oasis] have such bleary eyes?"
>
> Hillel answered, "My son, you've asked another profound question. It's because they live in a sandy region, and their smaller eyes protect them from the blowing sand."
>
> The man left again but returned, shouting, "Is there a Hillel here? Is there a Hillel here?" Hillel came to the door once more,

saying, "My son, how can I assist you?" The man replied, "I have a question." Hillel urged him, "Ask, my son. Ask!" He asked, "Why are the feet of Africans so wide?"

Hillel replied, "My son, you have asked an important question. It is because they live in swamplands."

The man then said to Hillel, "I have a lot of questions to ask you, but I am afraid you will become angry with me."

Hillel sat in front of him and replied, "Feel free to ask any questions you have."

The man said, "Are you the man named Hillel who is the *Nasi* of the Jews?"

Hillel said, "Yes."

So, the man said, "If it is really you, I hope there are not too many like you."

Hillel said, "Why would you say that?"

The man said, "Because of you, I lost 400 *zuz* [an ancient Jewish coin]!" and told Hillel about his bet.

Hillel remarked, "My son, it's important to remain calm with others. Losing an extra 400 *zuz* is worth it. I won't take offense."

A potential convert

Here is another story showing the kind of flexible personality Hillel had.

One day, a non-Jew approached Shammai and asked, "How many Torahs do you possess?" Shammai replied, "We have two Torahs: one that is written and one that is oral."

The non-Jew responded, "I believe the Written Torah is from God, but not the Oral Torah. I wish to convert, but I only want to learn the Written Torah." Shammai yelled at him and sent him away.

The non-Jew then went to Hillel with the same request, and Hillel agreed to convert him. Hillel was sure that the man would ultimately comprehend the importance of the Oral Torah.

The Golden Rule

This is probably the most well-known story about Hillel and Shammai. It contains the concise statement of the essence of Judaism.

> A non-Jew approached Shammai, requesting, "Convert me to Judaism if you can teach me the entire Torah while standing on one foot." Shammai, who was doing work as an architect and holding a ruler, pushed him away with it.

> The non-Jew then turned to Hillel with the same request. Hillel accepted him, stating, "What is hateful to you, do not do to anyone else. This is the whole Torah. Everything else is commentary. Now go and study."

"These and those are the words of the living God"

Though not technically considered pairs, there are several rabbis in the Talmud who often seem to be at odds with one another.

Now, don't get me wrong: they didn't hate each other or even dislike each other. They often simply had different points of view on many questions and, most importantly, they understood that debating each other was a fine way to get to the truth.

The Talmud contains an expression associated with the disputes between Hillel and Shammai, but really it forms the background to almost all the disputes in the Talmud — and you can find plenty of them. The phrase is, *Eilu v'eilu dirvrei Elohim Chayim.* (Ay-loo veh ay-loo, div-ray el-oh-heem chay-eem; These and those are the words of the living God). This phrase is profound. It teaches that two opposing views can both be acceptable to God. Life is not always black or white.

For example, sometimes the dispute between Hillel and Shammai concludes with the victory of Hillel's point of view as judged by the consensus of the rabbis, but the Talmud adds, "These and those are the words of the living God." This statement inspired respect for different opinions and supported an atmosphere of constructive dialogue.

Some famous sparring partners in the Talmud are

>> Rabbi Yohanan and Resh Lakish

>> Rav and Shmuel

>> Abaye and Rava

>> Rabban Gamliel and Rabbi Yehoshua

Grasping the Unforgettable Nachum Ish Gamzu

Nachum ish Gamzu (Nachum, the man of "this too." He was known to cultivate the attitude that everything is for the best. He'd say "this too" is for the good.) is one of the most colorful personalities in the entire Talmud.

And although we know that he was the great Rabbi Akiva's teacher for 22 years, he is mentioned on only a handful of pages. I personally find him to be the most compelling individual in the Talmud's 63 volumes.

The Talmud introduces Nachum ish Gamzu with a question:

Why did they call him Nachum of Gam Zu? The reason is that, regarding any matter that occurred to him, he would say: "This too (*gam zu*) is for the good [*gam zu l'tova*]."

In the section "Rabbi Akiva: Announcing the Talmud's Superstar," earlier in this chapter, I talk about the fact that Rabbi Akiva, Nachum's student for 22 years, believed that everything that God allows to happen is for the best. Rabbi Akiva often said, "All that the Merciful One does, He does for good."

Where did Rabbi Akiva first hear this point of theology? Undoubtedly from Nachum ish Gamzu.

Praying to suffer

A particularly powerful story is related about Nachum. In the Talmud, you can read:

It was generally known about Nachum of Gam Zu that he was blind in both eyes, both his arms were amputated, both his legs were amputated, and his entire body was covered in boils.

He was lying on a bed in a dilapidated house, and the legs of his bed were placed in buckets of water so that ants should not climb onto him.

Once, his students sought to remove his bed from the house and afterward remove his other vessels. He said to them:

"My sons, remove the vessels first, and afterward remove my bed, as I can guarantee you that as long as I am in the house, the house will not fall."

They removed the vessels and afterward they removed his bed, and immediately the house collapsed.

His students said to him: "Rabbi, you are obviously a wholly righteous man. We have just seen that as long as you were in your house it did not fall. Why has this suffering happened to you?"

He said to them: "My sons, I brought it upon myself."

Nachum ish Gam Zu related to them the following: "Once, I was traveling along the road to my father-in-law's house, and I had with me a load distributed among three donkeys, one of food, one of drink, and one of delicacies. A poor person came and stood before me in the road, saying: 'My rabbi, sustain me.'

"I said to him: 'Wait until I unload the donkey, after which I will give you something to eat.' So, I delayed helping him for a while. And I had not managed to unload the donkey before his soul left his body [he died].

"I went and fell upon his face and said: 'May my eyes which had no pity on your eyes be blinded; may my hands which had no pity on your hands be amputated; may my legs which had no pity on your legs be amputated.' And my mind did not rest until I said: 'May my whole body be covered in boils.'"

Nachum of Gam Zu prayed that his suffering might atone for his failure. His students said to him: "Even so, woe to us that we have seen you in this state."

He said to them: "Woe is me if you had not seen me in this state, as this suffering atones for me."

Rabbi Nachum's miracles

Another story from the Talmud about Nachum further illustrates his personality and his theology:

Once, the Jews wished to send a gift to the house of the emperor.

They asked: "Who should go and present this gift? Let Nachum ish Gamzu go. He is accustomed to miracles."

They sent with him a chest full of jewels and pearls, and he went and spent the night in a certain inn. During the night, the residents of the inn took all of the precious jewels and pearls from the chest and filled it with earth.

The next day, when he saw what had happened, Nachum ish Gam Zu said: "This, too, is for the good."

When he arrived at the ruler's palace, they opened the chest and saw that it was filled with earth. The king wished to put all the Jewish emissaries to death. He said: "The Jews are mocking me."

Nachum of Gam Zu said: "This too is for the good."

Elijah the Prophet came and appeared before the ruler as one of his ministers. He said to the ruler: "Perhaps this earth is from the earth of their father Abraham. When he threw earth, it turned into swords, and when he threw grain stubble, it turned into arrows. It is written in a prophecy that the sages interpreted this verse as a reference to Abraham: 'His sword makes them as the dust, his bow as the driven stubble.'"

The Romans had yet to conquer a particular province. They took some of this earth, tested it by throwing it at their enemies, and conquered that province. When the ruler saw that this earth indeed had miraculous powers, his servants entered his treasury and filled Nachum of Gam Zu's chest with precious jewels and pearls, and sent him off with great honor.

When Nachum of Gam Zu came to spend the night at that same inn, the residents said to him: "What did you bring with you to the emperor that he bestowed upon you such great honor?"

He said to them: "That which I took from here, I brought there."

When they heard this, the residents of the inn thought that the soil upon which their house stood had miraculous powers. They tore down their inn and brought the soil underneath to the king's palace. They said to him: "That earth that was brought here was from our property."

But the miracle had been performed only in the merit of Nachum of Gam Zu. The emperor tested the inn's soil in battle, and it was not found to have miraculous powers. He had these residents of the inn put to death.

Excommunicating Rabbi Eliezer the Great

The excommunication of Rabbi Eliezer the Great is one of the most important stories in the entire Talmud. It starts off quite simply, but by the end, it grows to express a profoundly important point of Jewish theology.

I offer you an abridged version. And I reveal the importance of the story in the section "Interpreting the story of excommunication," later in this chapter. *Note:* Excommunication does not mean throwing a person out of the religion. Once a Jew, always a Jew. It means a kind of shunning and public pressure.

But first, let me introduce Rabbi Eliezer. His actual name was Eliezer ben Hyrcanus, but even in his own lifetime, he became known as Rabbi Eliezer the Great. Born into great wealth, he became one of the leading sages after the destruction of the Second Temple (circa 70 CE).

Rabbi Yochanan ben Zakkai, (see Chapter 2 for more about this great sage) said of Rabbi Eliezer that if all the sages of Israel were on one side of a scale and Eliezer ben Hyrcanus on the other, he would outweigh them all. Rabbi Eliezer had a remarkable memory. And, in fact, he claimed to never say anything that he failed to hear from his teachers. All of the sages of the next generation were students of his, the most prominent being Rabbi Akiva (see the section "Rabbi Akiva: Announcing the Talmud's Superstar," earlier in this chapter).

From verbal abuse to ritual purity

The story of Rabbi Eliezer the Great begins during a discussion that the leading rabbis of the time were having about verbal mistreatment. According to Jewish law, embarrassing a person in public is like killing them.

Then the story shifts to a discussion about an oven. You don't need to understand the details of this very difficult subject area — ritual purity and impurity. But Rabbi Eliezer had one opinion, and the other rabbis disagreed with him. A *Mishna* (Kelim 5:1), describes how if you cut an earthenware oven widthwise into segments and place sand between each segment, Rabbi Eliezer deemed it ritually pure, but the other rabbis deemed it ritually impure.

Note: Just remember that almost all of the sages involved with the subject were of one point of view, and Rabbi Eliezer took the opposite view.

Rabbi Eliezer tried to convince the other rabbis

The sages taught:

> On that day, when the rabbis discussed this matter, Rabbi
> Eliezer answered all possible responses in the world to support
> his opinion, but the rabbis did not accept his explanations.

After failing to convince the rabbis with arguments, he began to try to convince them with amazing wonders:

> Rabbi Eliezer told them: "If the law aligns with my view, let this carob tree be a proof." The carob was uprooted from its location, with some claiming it was 100 cubits away, while others claimed it was 400 cubits.
>
> The Rabbis responded: "One cannot use the carob tree as evidence."
>
> Rabbi Eliezer then stated: "If the law follows my opinion, let the stream serve as proof." The water in the stream reversed course and began flowing backward.
>
> They replied: "One does not use a stream as evidence."
>
> Rabbi Eliezer then said: "If the law aligns with my opinion, let the walls of the study hall provide proof." The walls of the study hall tilted inward and appeared to fall.
>
> Rabbi Yehoshua shouted at the walls: "If Torah scholars dispute among themselves regarding the law, what is your role in this matter?"

The *Gemara* explains that the walls didn't collapse out of respect for Rabbi Yehoshua, but they didn't straighten out of respect for Rabbi Eliezer.

After all the miraculous demonstrations by Rabbi Eliezer failed to convince the rabbis that he, Rabbi Eliezer, was right and they were wrong, Rabbi Eliezer resorted to the best evidence possible — he asked Heaven to back him up:

> Rabbi Eliezer then said: "If the law is in accordance with my opinion, Heaven will provide proof." A Divine Voice issued from Heaven, stating: "Why are you arguing with Rabbi Eliezer, when the law consistently follows his opinion in every issue he addresses?"

Ignoring a Divine Voice

The rabbis were unimpressed by the Divine Voice Rabbi Eliezer elicited (see the preceding section):

> Rabbi Yehoshua stood on his feet and said: "It is written: 'It is not in Heaven.'"

The *Gemara* asks:

> What is the relevance of the phrase "It is not in Heaven"?

Rabbi Yirmeya says:

> Because God already gave the Torah at Mount Sinai, we don't regard a Divine Voice, as You, God, already wrote at Mount Sinai, in the Torah: "After a majority to incline." (Exodus 23:2) In other words, if there is a dispute among the rabbis as to what a certain verse in the Torah means, a vote is taken and the majority view "wins" the argument. The majority of rabbis disagreed with Rabbi Eliezer's opinion, so the law is not ruled in accordance with his opinion.

The *Gemara* relates:

> Years later, Rabbi Natan encountered Elijah the prophet and said to him: "What did the Holy One, Blessed be He, do at that time when Rabbi Yehoshua issued his declaration?"

> Elijah said to him: "The Holy One, Blessed be He, smiled and said: 'My children have defeated Me; My children have defeated Me.'"

Excommunicating Rabbi Eliezer

The sages reached a consensus concerning Rabbi Eliezer and excommunicated him:

> And the sages said: "Who will go and inform him of his excommunication?"

> Rabbi Akiva, his beloved disciple, said to them: "I will go."

What did Rabbi Akiva do? He wrapped himself in black, as an expression of mourning, and sat before Rabbi Eliezer at a distance of 4 cubits, which is the distance that one must maintain from an excommunicated individual.

Rabbi Eliezer said to him: "Akiva, what is different about today from other days that you comport yourself in this manner?"

Rabbi Akiva addressed him, saying: "My teacher, I sense that your colleagues are drifting away from you."

Rabbi Eliezer then tore his garments and took off his shoes, as per the tradition of an excommunicated individual, and he descended from his seat to sit on the ground.

Interpreting the story of excommunication

The key point in this story happens when Rabbi Yehoshua says, "It is written: 'It is not in Heaven.'"

Rabbi Yirmeya then clarifies that Rabbi Yehoshua meant that because God gave the Torah at Mount Sinai, the rabbis don't take into consideration a Divine Voice. As stated in the Torah at Mount Sinai: "After a majority to incline," Given that most rabbis opposed Rabbi Eliezer's viewpoint, the prevailing law doesn't follow Rabbi Eliezer's interpretation.

Essentially, God bestowed the Torah upon humanity; so the word of God "is no longer in Heaven." When questions arise about the Torah's meaning, we disregard heavenly voices and miracles. Instead, the sages of the generation deliberate and vote. As the Torah itself emphasizes, the majority's decision determines the outcome.

After all is said and done, this story communicates one major idea: God gave the Torah to the people. God no longer has a role in interpreting the Torah for people; the sages of the Jewish people have the responsibility of this interpretation. This is what the phrase "The Torah is not in Heaven" means.

Meeting the Talmud's Heretic

Elisha ben Abuyah was a student of Rabbi Akiva. It's difficult to imagine that a man with such a powerful teacher could sink as low as Elisha did. He became the heretic of the Talmud, and to this day, students of the Talmud refer to him as *Acher* (AH-khair; the other one) so that they don't have to say his name.

Elisha came from a prestigious Jerusalem family and earned a reputation as an extraordinary scholar; but he had a crisis of faith that caused him to not only leave Judaism, but encourage others to leave.

The Talmud records that he witnessed the death of a child while the child was in the act of doing a *mitzvah* (a commandment from the Torah) — a *mitzvah*, it is taught, whose reward was supposed to be a long life. A boy, at the request of his father, climbed a tree to chase away the mother bird while the boy confiscated the eggs from her nest.

The boy fell out of the tree and died. Elisha ben Abuyah witnessed the tragedy.

And if that wasn't enough, Elisha saw a pig running in the street with the tongue of a man named Rabbi Yehudah, the baker, in its mouth. The pig has ripped the tongue from Rabbi Yehuda, the baker. According to the Talmud, upon seeing this desecration, Elisha said, "From this tongue, pearls of pure light used to come. Is this the reward for observing the Torah?"

A crisis of faith

The Talmud contains many informative passages about Elisha ben Abuyah, yet none fully explain why he abandoned his faith and instead studied Greek philosophy:

> Throughout the day, Greek songs lingered on his lips. Once a respected sage, he transformed into a man who discouraged children from studying the Torah. When he rose from his pretense of engaging in Jewish studies, books of heresy would tumble from his lap.

Visions of Metatron

The Talmud recounts that when Elisha ben Abuya experienced mystical visions in the *Pardes,* he observed Metatron sitting, instead of standing. Typically, anyone in the heavenly realm stands before God. Unbeknownst to Elisha, God had granted Metatron a special privilege to sit. Elisha mistakenly believed this indicated the presence of two supreme powers.

Elisha himself admitted to his colleague, Rabbi Meir, that he desecrated Yom Kippur by riding a horse in front of the Holy of Holies. Some narratives suggest that after being branded a heretic, he adopted a mindset of enjoying worldly pleasures as his main priority in life.

Additionally, he allegedly visited prostitutes. Upon recognizing him, one prostitute expressed her disbelief that he would seek her services, especially on Shabbat. In response, Elisha uprooted a radish, an act forbidden on Shabbat, to signify that he no longer observed its laws.

Elisha shared a distinct bond with Rabbi Meir. Despite Elisha abandoning the observance of *mitzvot* and renouncing Judaism, Rabbi Meir continued to learn from him. So devoted was Rabbi Meir that he declared, "When I die, I will plead for *Acher*'s sentence to Hell, believing it preferable for him to be judged and bear the consequences of his actions, cleansing his soul." After Rabbi Meir passed away, smoke was reported to rise from his grave, suggesting his success in advocating for his teacher, Rabbi Elisha ben Abuya, to enter Heaven.

To this day, Elisha is referred to as *Acher* in most of the Talmud, yet he is named in *Pirke Avot* (peer-KAY ah-VOYE; The Chapters of the Fathers, a section of the *Mishna.*) This duality reflects Judaism's complex feelings towards Elisha. On one side, the sages deemed him a heretic; on the other, they recognize him as an outstanding scholar. This ambivalence is evident in his inclusion in the Talmud, appearing sometimes as *Acher* and at other times by his full name, Elisha ben Abuya.

Recognizing the Five Sages in the Passover Hagaddah

In the Passover *Haggadah* (ha-GAD-ah) the book that families read during the Passover dinner (called a seder; say-dehr), five rabbis remain awake all night to discuss the Exodus from Egypt. The *Haggadah* emphasizes that, despite their expertise as rabbis, they still have to remember the details of the Exodus each year during Passover as commanded by the Talmud. If anyone at a Passover seder claims that they already remembered the Exodus or that they know the details without going over them, they still have to recount them annually. The *Haggadah* provides a prime example of this requirement because these five distinguished rabbis recount the Passover story to one another.

All the rabbis mentioned in the *Haggadah* are well-known among Talmud students. By the next Passover, if you join a seder, you'll recognize them too:

>> **Rabbi Eliezer:** A student of Rabbi Yohanan ben Zakkai and played a significant role in revitalizing Jewish scholarship after the Second Temple's destruction (circa 70 CE). He was crucial in establishing the academy at Yavne, an important Jewish institution.

>> **Rabbi Yehoshua ben Perachia:** Distinguished himself through scholarship and leadership, emphasizing the value of friendship. He taught, "Acquire for yourself a friend." The term *acquire* (kah-NEH in Hebrew) suggests that nurturing friendships requires intentional time and effort.

>> **Rabbi Elazar ben Azariah:** Among the youngest Talmudic rabbis, he was revered for his wisdom, despite his age. He was appointed *Nasi* at around 18 years old, and legend has it that his beard turned white overnight, giving him an elderly appearance. When his wife expressed concern about the burden of his new role, he famously replied, "Should one not drink out of a crystal glass for fear of it breaking?"

>> **Rabbi Akiva:** The greatest Jewish scholars regard him as one of the greatest rabbis, if not the greatest, in the Talmud. (You can read all about Rabbi Akiva in the section "Rabbi Akiva: Announcing the Talmud's Superstar," earlier in this chapter).

>> **Rabbi Tarfon:** One of Rabbi Akiva's mentors who was both wealthy and generous. He earned the title The Father of All Israel and is recognized for his poignant observation: "The day is short, and the labor is plentiful; the laborers are lazy, and the reward is immense, while the master of the house is urgent. You are not obliged to complete the work, but neither are you free to refrain from it."

Following the Four Rabbis into the Mystical Garden

One of the most fascinating episodes recorded in the Talmud concerns four famous rabbis who traveled to the depths of mystical Judaism. When the sages tell us in the pages of the Talmud that these four rabbis entered the "garden," you can't take the word at face value. The word in Hebrew is *pardes*, which does mean garden or orchard. But the word *pardes* has a far deeper meaning. In Hebrew, the word *pardes* is also an acronym, spelled as the Hebrew equivalent of PRDS:

>> *P'shat* (puh-**shot**; literal): Interpret the words literally.

>> *Remez* (**reh**-mehz; hint): Explore the hints within the words.

>> *D'rash* (dud-rahsh; a story that has a message): Discern the moral lessons of the stories.

>> *Sod* (sowd; secret): Uncover the secret, mystical meanings of the Torah.

In essence, when the four rabbis entered the *pardes*, they engaged with all four levels of meaning, including the most abstract and esoteric interpretation of the Torah, known as the *Sod*. Here are the rabbis who entered the *pardes*, their fates, and their philosophies:

>> **Ben Azzai:** Ben Azzai caught a glimpse of the Divine Presence and died. The verse says about him: "Precious in the eyes of the Lord is the death of His pious ones" (Psalms 116:15).

Recognized for his piety, he was a disciple of Rabbi Akiva. He stated, "Do not disdain any person and do not belittle anything. For there is no individual who does not have his moment, and no object that lacks its significance."

>> **Ben Zoma:** Ben Zoma saw a glimpse of the Divine Presence and was harmed. The verse states regarding him: "Have you found honey? Eat as much as is sufficient for you, lest you become full from it and vomit" (Proverbs 25:16). Some claim he lost his sanity due to being unprepared for the complex teachings, which led to confusion.

Renowned for his insight: "Who is Wise? The one who learns from everyone." The rabbis taught that if someone sees ben Zoma in a dream, they may aspire to gain wisdom.

>> *Acher* **(The Other),** referring to Elisha ben Abuyah: He "uprooted the shoots," or severed the branches of a sapling, representing his self-imposed disconnection from a genuine grasp of Judaism. (I talk about Acher in the section "Meeting the Talmud's Heretic," earlier in this chapter.)

He earned the title The Other because of his philosophical pursuits and traumatic experiences that led him away from the path of Judaism.

>> **Akiva:** Rabbi Akiva entered the *pardes* safely and exited safely. He warned the others: "When you come across pure marble stones, avoid saying, 'Water. Water.' Because it is written: 'He who speaks falsehood shall not be established before My eyes' (Psalms 101:7)." Have you seen polished marble that looks wet? It's an illusion. Rabbi Akiva was warning his colleagues that, while exploring the depths of mysticism, don't get fooled by surfaces and illusions.

Many consider Rabbi Akiva the foremost leader among all Talmudic rabbis (see the section "Rabbi Akiva: Announcing the Talmud's Superstar," earlier in this chapter). He remarked, "A man whose wife engages in good deeds is truly a wealthy man."

Seeing What Others Say

The 63 volumes of the Talmud contain the teachings of over 1,000 rabbis. Some appear only once. Others appear twice. Still others appear hundreds of times. The Talmud covers the teachings from several generations.

The frequency with which certain rabbis appear has little to do with their importance. As I talk about in the section "Grasping the Unforgettable Nachum Ish Gamzu," earlier in this chapter, Nachum ish Gamzu appears only a handful of times in the pages of the text, but his influence has been enormous. After all, he was Rabbi Akiva's teacher for 22 years!

One teacher in the Talmud had the unusual name of ben Bag Bag (ben bahg bahg). He was probably a convert to Judaism. We don't even know his first name. Only the name of his father is identified (*ben* means "son of"). And he only appears a few times in the Talmud. And yet one of his sayings has become among the most famous lines in the entire Talmud: "Turn it over and turn it over, for everything is in it. Reflect on it and grow old and gray with it. Do not turn from it, for nothing is better than it." This saying emphasizes the richness of the Torah. It's meant to encourage study and meditation on the Torah every day and for life because all wisdom can be found in the Torah.

The phrase "And others say" is used throughout the Talmud when some rabbis in the Talmud give alternative opinions. The phrase reflects the fact that many diverse opinions appear in the Talmud, which offers multiple perspectives.

Throughout *The Talmud for Dummies*, I emphasize that the Talmud frequently doesn't give a single authoritative point of view. In fact, when people who have decided, after a lifetime of ignorance about Judaism, to return to Jewish faith and observance, they often don't really like the Talmud very much: They're busy looking for answers, not questions.

The Talmud is based on questions, and often you can find several possible answers to each question. In the Talmud, the text explores ideas from many points of view. Countless rabbis participate in those discussions.

Chapter **8**

Apologies and Reflections on Women in the Talmud

O n behalf of all the Jewish members of my gender (whether they agree with me or not), *I'm sorry.*

I'm sorry that the 63 volumes of the Talmud record, with a few exceptions, the views of men but not women. Of course, the Talmud reflects the patriarchal norms of its time. But I'm sorry that it has taken so long for qualified women to receive rabbinic ordination and that many people in some corners of the Jewish world still have great resistance to the ordination of women.

Even a quick glance at the list of the six *sedarim* (she-DAH-reem; orders) of the *Mishna* (MISH-nah; to repeat) and you can see trouble up ahead. The *Mishna* contains a whole *seder* (SAY-der; order) titled "Women," but none titled "Men." I have to face it — the Talmud is more or less a men's club. But women today can and do teach Talmud and learn Talmud in numbers unprecedented in the history of the Jewish people.

In this chapter we will explore the status of women in Judaism, and why some Jews have a problem with women as rabbis. We'll also explore why some people even have objections to women studying the Talmud. Then I will discuss how, in our generation, there is change afoot. And finally we will learn about some remarkable women in Jewish history and in the Jewish world today who have become agents of significant change in the entire situation of woman and their relationship to the Talmud.

As Rabbi Adin Steinsaltz points out in his book, The *Essential Talmud*, the Talmud was never completed. We must add to it from one generation to the next. It's therefore about time — no, indeed it's overdue — that we invite, not just allow, women to pull up their chairs and participate fully in all Talmudic discussions. One can only imagine how different (and I suspect more humane) the Talmud and Jewish law could be. It's not too late! In fact, the time is now!

Looking at How Women Are Represented in Judaism

Up until recently — as in, within my lifetime — there was no such thing as a woman rabbi. (Some would say there still isn't because they reject the very idea of a woman as a rabbi). Although hundreds of women have graduated from rabbinical programs over the last half century, there remain conflicting ideas on the attitude toward women in the role of rabbi. Here are the five movements or organizations in Judaism today, each of which have different official positions on the subject of the role of women in Jewish life. These movements have synagogue networks, some of which ordain rabbis (see below), and have different standards and positions on a host of contemporary issues.

>> **Reform:** (The Union of Reform Judaism). Reform Jews view women as equal participants in their movement. It ordains women as rabbis and expects them to perform all the rabbinic responsibilities required of male rabbis. They began ordaining rabbis in 1972, when American Sally Priesand was ordained by the Hebrew Union College-Jewish Institute of Religion in Cincinnati, Ohio.

>> **Reconstructionist:** (The Reconstructionist Rabbinical College and the Reconstructionist Movement) Reconstructionist Jews ordained their first woman in 1974 when Sandy Eisenberg Sasso became a rabbi after attending the Reconstructionist Rabbinical College in Philadelphia, Pennsylvania.

>> **Jewish Renewal:** While not a formal movement, there is an umbrella organization, established in 1993, called the Aleph Alliance for Jewish Renewal that ordains Jewish Renewal rabbis and oversees other activities. The loosely defined (at the time) Jewish Renewal Movement ordained Lynn Gottlieb as their first woman rabbi in 1981. Lynn Gottlieb was ordained by rabbis Zalman Schachter-Shalomi, Everett Gendler, and Shlomo Carlebach before the Rabbinic Ordination program of the Aleph Alliance for Jewish Renewal was even formed. This ordination program, largely developed and led by Reb Marcia Prager several years after the official organization was formed, has ordained several dozen woman rabbis over the past 20 years.

>> **Conservative:** (United Synagogue of Conservative Judaism) Conservative Jews were slower than the Reform Movement in deciding to ordain women as rabbis, but now it has established complete equality for men and women. The decision was made in 1983, and the Jewish Theological Seminary of America in New York City ordained their first woman rabbi, Amy Eilberg, in 1985. They have a rabbinic organization, including men and women, called the Rabbinical Assembly.

>> **Orthodox:** There are several independent movements within Orthodox Judaism. Orthodox Judaism maintains what it considers traditional Jewish values and is faithful to

time honored traditions. The two major organizations are the Orthodox Union. and the Rabbinical Council of America. They are, in principle, against women as rabbis. But in 1999 Orthodox Rabbis Avi Weiss and Saul Berman established a new movement known as Open Orthodoxy. They also established a school known as Yeshivat Chovevei Torah (KhOWE-vah-vey TOE-rah; "lovers of Torah") that supports an expanded role for women in leadership positions. It later transitioned into a full rabbinical school. Rabbi Weiss and Rabbi Berman also founded Yeshivat Maharat which trains women as clergy, although they do not use the title "Rabbi" but rather confers titles like Maharat (an acronym of a Hebrew phrase which translates as "female leaders of Jewish law, spirituality and Torah") and Rabba (the female form, in Hebrew, of the word "rabbi.") Yeshivat Maharat ordained their first three rabbis, Ruth Balinsky Friedman, Rachel Kohl Finegold and Abby Brown Scheier in 2013. But they did not receive the formal title of Rabbi but were given the title Maharat instead. In the Orthodox world, the issue of women and their authority as rabbis is still in flux due to its controversial nature within Orthodoxy.

Women as Orthodox Rabbis? Why Not?

The traditional Orthodox ordaining institutions don't accept woman as rabbinical candidates, even though anyone can see that many Orthodox woman would prove to be as knowledgeable and skilled in rabbinic responsibilities as their male counterparts. These responsibilities include teaching Torah (including Talmud), officiating at funerals and weddings, leading prayer services and being counted in a minyan (MIN-yan; a quorum of ten people required for certain prayer services).

Orthodox Jews who do advocate the ordination of women as rabbis feel that women rabbis can encourage more women to study Torah. They recognize that many women have the same intellectual accomplishments and spiritual gifts as men. They also feel that equality is simply the correct way to live.

Case in point: Rabba Sara Hurwitz was the first woman to be ordained as an Orthodox rabbi, back in 2009, by two modern Orthodox rabbis, Rabbi Avi Weiss and Rabbi Daniel Sperber. Yet the traditional Orthodox Jewish community doesn't generally recognize her ordination.

Some Orthodox movements and ordaining institutions voice objection to women candidates for the rabbinate because of the general hesitation to innovate in any way, as well as the expressed fear that if women become rabbis, the traditional gender structure of Judaism will fall apart.

HISTORIC RABBAS: EXTRAORDINARY EXCEPTIONS

Born in 1902, Regina Jonas wanted to be a rabbi for most of her life. Born in Berlin, Germany, Jonas grew up in a religious home in that city. While on the path to becoming a teacher, she decided to enroll in the Higher Institute for Jewish Studies of the Academy for the Science of Judaism. She took courses designed for future rabbis, and at a certain point, she announced that she wished to become a rabbi herself. Regina Jonas wrote a thesis titled "Can a woman become a rabbi according to *halakhic* (Jewish law) sources." She concluded that it was permissible.

Although her teachers praised her thesis, she was given only a teachers' certificate. She continued to lobby to become a rabbi, and despite protests from some of the membership of the Liberal Rabbis' Association in the German city of Offenbach am Main, she was ordained on December 27, 1935. She worked as a pastoral counselor at the Jewish Hospital in Berlin. In June of 1944, she was arrested by the Nazis and murdered in Auschwitz at the age of 42. A book written by Rabbi Elisa Klapheck titled *Fraulein Rabbiner Jonas: The Story of the First Woman Rabbi* (Jossey-Bass), which includes a translation of her thesis, was published in 2004.

Further back in history, there was a woman in the late 14th or early 15th centuries whose name was Miriam Spira-Luria. Her father was

(continued)

(continued)

Rabbi Solomon Shapira, who was a descendant of Rashi (the greatest Biblical and Talmudic commentator — who lived in the 11th century. His Talmudic commentary appears on every page of the Talmud. See Chapter 2 for more about Rashi). Her brother was Rabbi Peretz of Konstanz. Her husband was Rabbi Aharon Luria. So now you know the names of her father, brother and husband. Ordinarily, that would be the extent of a Jewish woman's biography in the Middle Ages. But Miriam Spira-Luria was an exception because Miriam was a Talmud scholar! In fact, she ran a *yeshiva* (Yeh-SHEE-vah; a traditional Jewish school) in Padua, Italy. She was also known to give public lectures. They called her Rabbanit Miriam. She was known for her scholarship and — for better or worse — actually known for her beauty, as well. What we know about her life comes mainly from a brief report by one of her descendants, Yochanan Luria, in the late 15th century. He writes that when she taught in her *yeshiva*, she did so from behind a curtain so that none of the students could gaze at her. (Oy!)

(Baseless) Arguments Against Women Studying and Teaching the Talmud

The main arguments against women learning Talmud are rooted in traditional interpretations of Jewish law and cultural beliefs:

>> **The word from authorities:** Some Jewish authorities, such as Maimonides (born in 1135), argue that teaching Talmud to women is akin to teaching them *tiflut* (tif-LOOT; silliness/immorality), suggesting that women lack the capacity for such study.

>> **A focus on expected roles:** Traditional views emphasize women's roles in family and community over intensive Torah study, suggesting that learning Talmud might detract from these responsibilities.

>> **A question of capacity:** Some rabbis believed women weren't intellectually suited for the complexities of Talmud study, leading to concerns about trivializing the text.

Teaching the Talmud as a Woman

Women are certainly qualified to teach the Talmud. *Yeshivat Maharat,* located in New York City, was founded in 2009 to ordain women as clergy and educators. This school has ordained many women who occupy roles as teachers, chaplains, and synagogue leaders, and was the first Orthodox *yeshiva* to ordain women as clergy. *Yeshivat Maharat* has faced major criticism from other establishments in the Orthodox Jewish world, yet it continues its important work. Both the Rabbinical Council of America and the Orthodox Union have condemned the ordination of women. The Rabbinical Council of America forbids their membership from hiring women who represent themselves as rabbis.

The Susi Bradfield Women's Institute of Halakhic Leadership of Ohr Torah Stone is a five-year, elite institute in Israel that trains women scholars in Talmud and *halakhah* (Ha-lah-KHAH; Jewish law), giving women the equal opportunity to learn and gain recognition and respect for their studies. The studies provide the necessary tools for leadership in Jewish communities, educational institutions, and diverse organizations. Graduates are certified as spiritual leaders authorized to provide direction in matters of *halakhah.*

Many Orthodox and non-Orthodox women *are* qualified and actively teach Talmud. One interesting case is that of Judith Hauptman. Rabbi Judith Hauptman was ordained as a rabbi in May 2003 by the Academy for Jewish Religion (founded in 1956 as a pluralistic rabbinic and cantorial training program, located in Yonkers, New York). Judith Hauptman has taught Talmud since 1973 at the Conservative Movement's Jewish Theological Seminary, which, among other functions, is the ordination wing of the Conservative movement. Hauptman now teaches Talmud in an institution that for many years didn't ordain woman as rabbis.

Prominent women teaching Talmud at the time I write this book include

>> **Rabba Sara Hurwitz:** Dean of *Yeshivat Maharat*

>> **Rabba Melanie Landau:** A graduate of *Yeshivat Maharat* and founder of *Yeshivat Kol Isha,* a post-denominational women's *yeshiva* in Jerusalem

Educating Jewish Women

After many centuries of excluding women from serious Jewish study, a revolution slowly began to take shape regarding the Jewish education of women.

Before World War I, it became clear that a trend of assimilation was spreading throughout the Jewish world among Jewish girls because they didn't receive a Jewish education. For centuries, the Jewish community felt that by simply living in a Jewish home, girls learned what they needed to know by watching their mothers. But the influence of the outside world began to make inroads into Jewish society, and young Jewish women began to leave their sheltered lives, attracted by the world around them.

Beginning with a seamstress's school

In 1917, a woman named Sarah Schenirer founded the first school dedicated to serious Jewish education for girls, located in Krakow, Poland. She named her school Beis Yaakov (Base yah-ah-kove; The House of Jacob) based on the phrase in the book of Exodus, "So shall you say to the House of Jacob." The phrase "*Beis Yaakov*" is traditionally interpreted as meaning "the women of Israel."

Schenirer was a seamstress with a vision. In her dressmaking studio in Krakow, she began to offer classes of Jewish education for Orthodox girls. By 1921, 4 *Beis Yaakov* schools existed in Poland, and by 1924, 54 such schools offered women a Jewish education.

The curriculum consisted of secular, as well as Jewish, studies, including Jewish history, ethics, and Torah.

And Sarah's creation of her schools had an impact on the rest of the Jewish world:

>> **1921:** Rabbi Yosef Leib Bloch established an Orthodox high school for girls in Telz, Lithuania inspired by *Beis Yaakov* schools. The curriculum consisted of the study of the Five Books of Moses and the books of the Prophets which are part of the Hebrew Scriptures.

>> **1922:** The *Agudat ha-Rabbanim*, (ah-goo-DAHT He-rah bah-neem; the Union of Orthodox Rabbis of Poland) advocated education for Jewish girls and young women, and established schools for this purpose.

>> **1923:** *Agudath Israel* (ah goo-DAT Yis-row-ale; Union of Israel), the political organization of Orthodox Jewry, helped to run the *Beis Yaakov* movement.

>> **1924:** Sarah Schenirer founded a teachers' seminary in Krakow to train teachers for the *Beis Yaakov* schools. Also in 1924, the first *Beis Yaakov* conference was held in Warsaw, Poland.

>> **The 1930s:** The *Beis Yaakov* schools had spread to parts of Europe, Palestine, and even to North America.

>> **1935:** Sarah Schenirer died; but by then, over 250 *Beis Yaakov* schools existed, with more than 30,000 students.

Published after World War I, Rabbi Israel Meir Kagan (known by the title of his book, *Chofetz Chaim* (khowe-fitz khah-yeem; Pursuer of Life), published the following statement: "It seems that all of this [prohibition against women learning Torah] applies only to times past when all daughters lived in their fathers' home and tradition was very strong, assuring that children would pursue their parents' path. As it says, 'Ask your father, and he shall tell you.' On that basis, we could claim that a daughter needn't learn Torah, but merely rely on proper parental guidance. But nowadays, in our iniquity, as parental tradition has been seriously weakened, and women, moreover, regularly study secular subjects, it is certainly a great *mitzvah* (*mitz-vah*; commandment from the Torah), to teach them Chumash (*Choo-Mahsh; The Five Books of Moses*), *Menorat Hamaor* (*men-ohr-aht ha-mah-ohr*) and the like, so as to validate our sacred belief; otherwise they may stray totally from G-d's path and transgress the basic tenets of religion, G-d forbid."

Although Rabbi Kagan's statement offered great support to the expanding movement for Jewish education for girls, no one offered the study of the Talmud — the most important religious work after the Torah itself — in the curriculum of women's education.

Dealing with fear of change

Fear of assimilation provided an impetus to correct the lack of educational opportunities for Jewish girls and women. But fear has also often caused cultural resistance to change.

During the 20th century, Jewish continuity was threatened by an escalator-like type of assimilation. Generations moved from Orthodox to Conservative to Reform, and then to no affiliation. So, whatever the liberal denominations did threatened the Orthodox group, who felt they were accelerating the escalator. Because Orthodox rabbinical boards, such as the Rabbinical Council of America, usually have older rabbis in charge, they may feel especially influenced by this fear of change, although younger rabbis point out that the escalator phenomenon no longer occurs (and hasn't for a while).

Yet, the Modern Orthodox Movement has a good foundation for taking a better path. Its most prominent figure, Rabbi Joseph Soloveitchik — popularly referred to as The Rav — inaugurated the advanced Talmud program at Stern College for Women in 1977, with a speech in which he stated emphatically, "It's important that not only boys should be acquainted, but girls as well," with the Talmud. His son, Dr. Haym Soloveitchik, who founded the program, said that as a child he had studied with his father, The Rav, together with his older sisters, Atarah and Tovah.

Despite the opposition of some, but not all, *Haredi* leaders (the ultra-orthodox branch of Judaism), the program continues to this day. The Modern Orthodox movement is relatively small, but today has proven the escalator theory long gone because of the movement's vibrant growth. Hopefully, that can create the confidence to overcome past prejudices and continue the progress toward inclusion of women in all of Jewish life.

Getting help and hindrance from the Talmud itself

A source that delayed progress in the inclusion of women in Talmudic study came from the Talmud itself, in which Rabbi Eliezer the Great (see Chapter 7 for more about Rabbi Eliezer the Great) stated in the Mishna, "Anyone who teaches his daughter Torah, it is as if he taught her licentiousness."

All arguments supporting this incredible statement are sexist, pure and simple. Maimonides, for example, wrote that most women lack the intellectual capacity for in-depth study!

Fortunately, Ben Azzai, another Talmudic sage, responds to Rabbi Eliezer by saying, "A person is obligated to teach his daughter Torah."

And so the debate has raged for centuries.

Meeting the Women in the Talmud

There are several women who stand out as you go through the Talmud. Unfortunately they are not known by their names. For example, there is the wife of Mar Ukva, whose life was devoted to helping the poor; the wife of Rabbi Chanina ben Dosa, who was known for her great piety and faith; the wife of Abba Chilkayah, known as a completely righteous woman; and Yalta, known for the breath of her knowledge. It is wonderful that the editors of the Talmud recognized these exceptional women, but sadly they were not identified by name.

But there is, in fact, a small list of women whose names are known and who stand out as exceptional individuals. Let me introduce you to them.

Berurya

Berurya was undoubtedly the most illustrious woman in the pages of the Talmud. Her reputation was that of a brilliant scholar. She also has the honor of being the only woman in rabbinic literature who made *halakhic* (legal) decisions that the male sages of the time accepted and respected.

Her father, Rabbi Hananiah ben Teradyon, a great sage, likely acted as her teacher. And Berurya was the wife of the great Rabbi Meir, well-known for sharpness in his Torah study. (His reputation was that of one of the greatest scholars of his generation.)

The following sections offer eight passages about Berurya from the pages of the Talmud.

She learned 300 laws

Berurya, wife of Rabbi Meir and daughter of Rabbi Hananiah ben Teradyon, was so smart and had such a good memory that she learned 300 *halakhot* in one day from 300 sages.

Hate the sin, not the sinner

Hooligans in Rabbi Meir's neighborhood caused him a lot of anxiety. Rabbi Meir prayed to God that they should die.

Rabbi Meir's wife, Berurya, said to him: "What are you saying? Why would you pray for the death of these hooligans? Are you saying this based on the verse 'Let sins cease from the land' (Psalms 104:35), which you might interpret to mean that the world would be better if the wicked were destroyed?

"But the passage doesn't read 'Let sinners cease'; it says, 'Let sins cease.' You should pray for an end to their sins, not for the death of the sinners. At the end of the verse, it says: 'And the wicked will be no more.' Instead, pray for God to have mercy on them, that they should repent. If they repent, then the wicked will be no more, as they will have repented."

Rabbi Meir saw that Berurya was correct. He prayed for God to have compassion for them, and they repented.

Berurya and the heretic

A heretic said to Berurya: "It is written: 'Sing, barren woman who hasn't given birth.' Because you haven't given birth, should you sing and rejoice?"

Berurya responded to the heretic and said: "Fool! Go to the end of the verse where it is written: 'For the children of the desolate shall be more numerous than the children of the married wife, said the Lord.'"

Berurya makes a point

Rabbi Yosei HaGelili was walking along a road and met Berurya. He said to her: "On which path shall we walk in order to get to Lod?"

Sarcastically, she said to him: "Foolish Galilean, didn't the sages say: 'Do not talk much with women?' You should have shortened your question to: 'Which way to Lod?'"

Study loudly

Berurya encountered a certain student who was whispering his studies, rather than raising his voice.

She kicked him and said to him: "Isn't it written: 'Ordered in all things and secure,' which is interpreted to mean if you exert your entire body in studying, it will be secure, and if not, it won't be secure."

The *Gemara* also relates that Rabbi Eliezer had a student who would study quietly, and after three years, he forgot his studies.

The death of Berurya's father

When Rabbi Yosei ben Kisma was ill, Rabbi Hananiah ben Teradyon went to visit him.

Rabbi Yosei ben Kisma said to him: "Hananiah, my brother, don't you know that Rome forbids us to teach Torah? But I heard about you that you sit and engage in Torah study, and you bring people together in public and have a Torah scroll placed in your lap, completely disregarding the decrees issued by the Romans."

Rabbi Hananiah ben Teradyon said to him: "Heaven will have mercy and protect me."

Rabbi Yosei ben Kisma said to him, "I am being reasonable, and you say to me: 'Heaven will have mercy'? I wonder if the Romans will not burn both you and your Torah scroll by fire."

Rabbi Hananiah ben Teradyon said to him, "My teacher, what will become of me? Am I destined for life in the World to Come?"

Rabbi Yosei ben Kisma said to him, "Did any incident happen to you which might be an indication of whether you will have a life in the World to Come?"

Rabbi Hananiah ben Teradyon said to him, "I confused my own coins that I needed for Purim with coins of charity, and I distributed them all to the poor at my own expense."

Rabbi Yosei ben Kisma said to him, "If that is so, may my portion be of your portion, and may my lot be of your lot."

Not even a few days passed before Rabbi Yosei ben Kisma died of his illness. All the Roman notables went to bury him, and they praised him with a great eulogy. When they returned, they found Rabbi Hananiah ben Teradyon engaging in Torah study.

They brought him to be sentenced, wrapped him in the Torah scroll, and also wrapped him with bundles of branches, and they set fire to this bundle. They brought tufts of wool and soaked them in water, and placed them on his heart so that his soul couldn't leave his body quickly, but rather that he would die slowly.

His daughter Berurya said to him, "Father, must I see you like this?"

Rabbi Hananiah ben Teradyon said to her: "If I alone were being burned, it would be difficult for me, but now that I am burning along with a Torah scroll, God will seek retribution for the insult to the Torah scroll and will also seek retribution for insulting me."

His students said to him: "Our teacher, what do you see?"

Rabbi Hananiah ben Teradyon said to them, "I see the parchment burning, but its letters are flying up to the heavens."

They said to him, "You should also open your mouth, and the fire will enter you, and you will die quickly."

Rabbi Hananiah ben Teradyon said to them, "He who gave me my soul should take it away, and one should not harm oneself to speed his own death."

The executioner said to him, "My teacher, if I increase the flame and take off the tufts of wool from your heart, so that you will die sooner and suffer less, will you bring me to the life of the World to Come?"

Rabbi Hananiah ben Teradyon said to the executioner, "Yes."

The executioner said, "State an oath that what you say is true."

Rabbi Hananiah ben Teradyon took the oath, and the executioner immediately increased the flame and took off the tufts of wool from the Rabbi's heart, causing his soul to leave his body quickly. The executioner then leaped into the fire and died.

A Divine Voice said, "Rabbi Hanaiah ben Teradyon and the executioner are destined for the life of the World to Come."

Upon hearing this, Rabbi Yehuda HaNasi wept and said, "There are some who acquire their share in the World to Come in one moment, such as the executioner, and there are some who acquire their share in the World to Come only after many years of work, such as Rabbi Hananiah ben Teradyon."

Berurya's sister

Berurya said to her husband Rabbi Meir, "It is a disrespectful that my sister is sitting in a brothel [she was arrested by the Romans and forced to work there]; you must do something to save her."

Rabbi Meir took some money and went. He said to himself, "If no transgression was committed by her, a miracle will be performed for her; if she committed a transgression, no miracle will be performed for her."

Rabbi Meir went and dressed as a Roman knight, and said to her "Bow to my wishes and engage in intercourse with me."

She said to him, "I am menstruating and cannot."

He said to her, "I will wait."

She said to him, "There are many women in the brothel, and there are many women here who are more beautiful."

He said to himself, "I can conclude from what she said that she did not commit a sin, as she presumably says this to all who come."

Rabbi Meir went over to her guard and said to him, "Give her to me."

The guard said to him, "I fear that if I do so I will be punished by the government."

Rabbi Meir said to him, "Take this money; give half to the government as a bribe, and half will be for you."

The guard said to him, "But when the money is finished, what shall I do?"

Rabbi Meir said to him, "Say: 'God of Meir, answer me!' And you will be saved."

The guard said to him "Who can say that this is the case, that I will be saved by these words?"

Rabbi Meir said to him, "You will now see."

There were wild dogs that would eat people; Rabbi Meir took some earth, threw it at them, and when they came to eat him, he said, "God of Meir, answer me!" The dogs then left him alone. After seeing this, the guard gave the daughter of Rabbi Hananiah ben Teradyon to Rabbi Meir.

Ultimately, the matter was heard in the king's court, and the guard, who was taken to be hanged, said: "God of Meir, answer me!"

They then lowered him down because they couldn't hang him.

They said to him, "What is this?"

He said to them, "This was the incident that occurred," and he proceeded to relate the entire story to them.

They then engraved the image of Rabbi Meir at the entrance of Rome where it would be seen by everyone, and they said, "Anyone who sees a man with this face should bring him here."

One day, Romans saw Rabbi Meir and ran after him, and he ran away from them and entered a brothel to hide. Some say he then escaped capture because he saw food cooked by gentiles and dipped one finger in the food and tasted it with that other finger, thereby fooling them into thinking that he was eating their non-kosher food, which they knew Rabbi Meir would not do.

A TALMUDIC MAGIC TRICK

The text of the Talmud says, "Some say he [Rabbi Meir] escaped capture because he saw food cooked by gentiles and dipped one finger in the food and tasted another finger, thereby fooling them into thinking that he was eating their non-kosher food, which they knew Rabbi Meir wouldn't do." Well, an area in the literature of magic tricks has to do with thimbles. One of the sleight-of-hand techniques for "thimble magic" uses the same move that Rabbi Meir used to fool the Romans who were looking for him. (See Figure 8-1.) There are many tricks magicians perform by manipulating thimbles. In some of them, the magician confuses the spectator by leading the spectator to think that the thimble is on one finger when it is really on another finger. It can actually look like the thimble is jumping from one finger to another magically. Rabbi Meir did the same thing. It's what magicians refer to as "misdirection."

I can't explain the "move" in detail. Nor can this still photo illustrate it. Magicians don't reveal their secrets. As a member of the Society of American Magicians (SAM) and the International Brotherhood of Magicians (IBM) I am sworn to secrecy. In this photo I am suggesting to Rabbi Steinsaltz, in a vague way, how the trick can work.

FIGURE 8-1: The author, Arthur Kurzweil (left), with Rabbi Adin Steinsaltz, discussing the sleight-of-hand move that Rabbi Meir used to disguise himself as a non-Jew.

Some say that he escaped detection because Elijah came, appeared to the Romans as a prostitute and embraced Rabbi Meir. The Romans who were chasing him said, "Heaven forbid, if this were Rabbi Meir, he would not act in that manner."

The death of Berurya's children

While Rabbi Meir was teaching on a Sabbath afternoon, both of his sons died from the plague that was affecting their city.

When Rabbi Meir returned home, he asked Berurya, his wife, "Where are our sons?"

She handed him the cup for *havdalah* [the ritual at the conclusion of the Sabbath], and he said the blessing.

Again, he asked, "Where are our sons?"

She brought food for him, and he ate. When he had finished eating, Berurya said to her husband, "My teacher, I have a question. A while ago, a man came and deposited something precious for me to hold for him. Now he has come back to claim what he left. Shall I return it to him or not?"

Meir responded, "Isn't one who holds a deposit required to return it to its owner?"

So, she took his hand and led him to where their two children lay.

He began to weep, crying "My sons, my sons."

She comforted him by quoting the *midrash* on the book of Psalms (*MID-rahsh;* the word *midrash* comes from the Hebrew root *"darash"* which means to seek or inquire. A *"midrash"* usually expands on a text from the Torah. In this case the verse being expanded is from the book Psalms.) "The Lord gave, the Lord took. May the Name of the Lord be blessed."

Imma Shalom

Imma Shalom was a descendent of King David (the second King of Israel, he is perhaps best known from the story of David and Goliath. He is also the author of most of the Book of Psalms). Her husband, Rabbi Eliezer, was one of the great sages of his time. Imma Shalom had beautiful children, and she attributed this beauty to her husband's extreme modesty.

You can find an interesting story about her in the Talmud that I relate in this section. As you read this story, keep in mind that the reader can't always easily understand stories in the Talmud. Sometimes, you have to read them a few times. Sometimes, you need to have words defined. When reading anything from the Talmud, please take your time. You can do it! Here's the Talmud story about Imma Shalom:

Imma Shalom, the wife of Rabbi Eliezer, was Rabban Gamliel's sister. A heretical philosopher in their neighborhood was trying to promote a reputation that he (the philosopher) doesn't take bribes.

Imma Shalom and Rabban Gamliel wanted to mock him and reveal his true nature.

Imma Shalom privately gave him a golden lamp as a bribe, and then she and her brother came before him, acting like they wanted a judgment about a certain question.

She said to the philosopher: "I want to share in the inheritance of my father's estate." He said to them: "Divide it."

Rabban Gamliel said to him: "It's written in our Torah: 'In a situation where there is a son, the daughter does not inherit.'"

The philosopher said to him: "Since the day you were exiled from your land, the Torah of Moses was taken away and the *avon gilyon* [a heretical text] was given in its place. The *avon gilyon* says: 'A son and a daughter shall inherit equally.'"

The next day, Rabban Gamliel brought the philosopher a Libyan donkey as a bribe.

Afterward, Rabban Gamliel and his sister came before the philosopher for a judgment. He said to them: "I proceeded to the end of the *avon gilyon*, and it says, 'I did not come to subtract from the Torah of Moses, and I did not come to add to the Torah of Moses.'"

He offered the opposite judgment from the day before — as a result of Rabban Gamliel's bribe. He said: "In a situation where there is a son, the daughter does not inherit."

She said to him, hinting at the bribe he took: "May your light shine like a lamp," alluding to the lamp she had given him.

Rabban Gamliel said to him: "The donkey came and kicked the lamp," thereby revealing the entire episode.

What happened in this story? First, we hear of a man who wants to convince people that he doesn't take bribes. That gives us a clue that he probably *does* take bribes. Imma Shalom wanted to bust him, so she bribes him with a gold lamp, and then asks him a question. She assumes that he will take the bribe and rule in her favor. She says that she wants to share in an inheritance, even though the law says that when it comes to an inheritance, if the deceased has a son, that son gets the inheritance. (You may not like this — I don't. But it was the law as explained elsewhere in the Talmud.) But the man rules that the inheritance is split, despite the law. In other words, the bribe worked!

Then Rabban Gamliel approaches the man and offers his own bribe: a donkey (which was a valuable animal because donkeys help farmers in many ways including carrying heavy loads, pulling small carts, and plowing small fields). The man claims that he can't change the Torah law, and when asked the same question about an inheritance, he rules in favor of Rabban Gamliel, who had just offered a bribe. The man ruled the opposite of what he ruled previously, proving that he can in fact be bribed.

Rachel, the wife of Rabbi Akiva

Rachel, the wife of Rabbi Akiva (considered to be the greatest rabbi in the Talmud. See Chapter 7 for a lot more on this illustrious scholar and leader.), appears as a major female figure in the Talmud.

Rachel was the daughter of one of the richest men in Jerusalem. She met one of the shepherds on her father's property, Akiva ben Joseph, and must have detected something special about him. Despite his being unable to even recite the alphabet, Rachel said to him that if he would study Torah, she would marry him. Akiva took the challenge. Ultimately Akiva became Rabbi Akiva and rose to become the superstar of the entire Talmud (the additional appendix, found at www.dummies.com/go/talmudfd, gives you the full story of Rabbi Akiva).

The Times They Are A-Changin'

From Talmudic times until the present, a lot of changes have taken place regarding the status of women in Judaism. Just one example is the fact that only relatively recently have girls had a *bat mitzvah* ceremony, which is a coming-of-age ceremony, in the synagogue. Boys have had public ceremonies (called a *bar mitzvah*) since the Middle Ages, but girls didn't have a public ceremony until the 20th century. The first *bat mitzvah* ceremony took place on March 18, 1922, in the United States. Today, it's a common occurrence.

Just to be clear, the idea of a boy becoming a man at age 13 and a girl becoming a woman at age 12 has existed since Talmudic times: "Twelve years and one day for a girl and thirteen years and one day for a boy." So the concept of a Jewish child's transition into adulthood existed as early as in ancient times, but the Jewish community didn't have public ceremonies until much later.

Seeing What the Torah Has to Say

What does the Torah — the Five Books of Moses — teach us about the role of women? Here are some of the stories that inform the role of women in Jewish life:

>> **In the beginning:** The Torah begins with a world where men have a dominant role, with God creating Eve from Adam's rib.

>> **Sarah's advice:** But the text provides us with hope for gender equality in the form of a new family. The first marital advice ever given is from God to Abraham: "Listen to your wife." God didn't mean hear Sarah out, but rather follow her lead.

>> **Rebecca's wisdom:** Sarah and Abraham's son Issac eventually learns that only his wife Rebecca gets it right about which son should inherit their legacy (Jacob).

>> **Miriam's faith:** Only Miriam, Moses's sister, has the faith and foresight to look after his welfare after his mother casts him in the Nile.

>> **Deborah's courage:** The Bible has several prominent female warriors, such as Deborah, who's the only hero capable of defeating Sisera, the Canaanite commander who oppressed the Israelites for 20 years. And she did so in spite of his 900 chariots (versus Deborah's none).

But most important and encouraging, the Torah offers a unique approach to overcoming evils in the laws of the Torah. The Torah tackles many kinds of societal oppression, such as slavery, poverty, and treatment of captives of war. Every case proceeds from the same perspective: The sages lay out a path to eliminate wrongs in steps that bring justice incrementally. The Torah acknowledges that human nature is stubborn, and you can't break and then immediately repair a societal wrong. But the Torah does say that you can correct and rechannel wrongs. This philosophy is the tradition that the writers of the Talmud believed.

Chapter **9**

Thinking Like a Talmudic Rabbi

The Talmudic sages dedicated themselves to pursuing the truth. They didn't just accept ideas blindly. If a certain rabbi offered a theory, the other rabbis needed to test the theory to see whether it was logical, sensible, and correct. One of the ways that they did these tests involved taking something to its logical extreme. The Talmud includes absurdities as a method of clarifying Jewish law and ideas, a sort of thought experiment. People unfamiliar with the Talmud are often critical of it because they don't understand that strange scenarios in the Talmud are really tools for exploring legal principles. The Talmud often discusses implausible situations, but it does so in the pursuit of truth.

People often fail to see that these absurd scenarios provide ways to test or explore ideas and laws, with the goal of shedding light on legal principles and keeping the text engaging at the same time. In this chapter, you can see just how the rabbis crafted these scenarios, and I offer some rather amusing examples of this kind of analysis.

Absurdities as a Tool for Exploring Truth

Strange Talmudic scenarios often highlight the complexity of an issue or topic. The use of these absurdities actually reflects the Talmud's literary sophistication. They explore ideas and enhance our understanding of them through what I might call creative legal imagination. The sages could also use the absurd scenarios to sharpen their debating skills.

REMEMBER

Some people erroneously view these scenarios as outdated or irrelevant because they seem absurd or inaccurate. But the sages posing these scenarios never meant them to reflect reality. The sages are far more sophisticated than that! The Talmudic approach is similar to the principle of *reductio ad absurdum* (reduction to absurdity) used in philosophy. You try to prove that a premise is false by illustrating that its logical consequence is absurd or contradictory.

Jewish intellectual tradition has always used absurdities in this way. Debate and discussion are an essential part of a Jewish scholar's education. This method sheds light on a tradition central to critical thinking. In a way, the bizarre situations also act as brain teasers, helping to sharpen one's analytical skills. They also provide a teaching method that can help make complex legal principles more interesting.

The following sections give you some examples of these debates.

A fish and a goat

A law in the Torah says, "You should not plow with an ox and a donkey together." The reason for this law, according to the sages in the Talmud, is that because the animals don't have equal strength, the combination would actually increase the workload of both and would cause them unnecessary suffering.

On page 55a of *Masekhta Bava Kamma* (Mah-sekh-tah bah-vah Kah-mah; Tractate The First Gate), the rabbis have a discussion about this law, and they wonder whether the prohibition would include the combination of a goat and a fish. The Talmud says,

"Rahava raises a problem: Regarding someone who drives a wagon with a goat and a *shibuta* [She-boo-tah; a freshwater carp] together, if it was pulled by the goat on the land and by the fish in the sea, what is the law?"

Because a goat lives on dry land and a fish lives in the water, if a wagon or a plow was pulled by the fish in the water and the goat on the land, would the law's prohibition apply? The Talmud points out that a fish cannot live on dry land and a goat cannot live in the water. The whole situation is impossible, but the rabbis wanted to test the ideas, so they imagined a fish and a goat hooked up to a wagon.

Teaching the whole Torah while standing on one foot

In Chapter 7, I introduce you to two famous sages, Hillel and Shammai, who often disagreed with one another. One of the most well-known incidents recorded in the Talmud is when a pagan asked a question of Shammai and then asked the same question of Hillel. The question — it was really a request — was "Convert me on the condition that you teach me the entire Torah while I'm standing on one foot."

Shammai impatiently chased the pagan away for asking such a ridiculous request. After all, how is it possible to teach the entire Torah while someone is standing on one foot?

However, Hillel took the request as an opportunity to actually summarize the whole Torah in one sentence, thereby teaching the pagan, and teaching all of us, what the foundation principle of Judaism is.

Hillel said, "That which is hateful to you, do not do to another; that is the entire Torah, and the rest is commentary. Go and study."

Hillel's teaching is the negative form of the Golden Rule ("Do unto others as you would have them do unto you"). (Confucianism also teaches the Golden Rule in the negative — "What you do not wish for yourself, do not do to others.")

The day a carob tree jumped across a garden

Rabbi Eliezer (whom you can read about in Chapter 7) used every logical argument to try to convince the other rabbis that he was right and they were wrong about a certain issue. But there was no convincing them. They rejected all his arguments.

The Talmud actually says that he used every argument in the world. It was no use. Over and over again, they rejected his position. So he said, "If I'm right, let this carob tree prove it." And the carob tree jumped across the field.

The story doesn't mention the miracle of the tree actually moving, but that the rabbis disagreed about whether the tree jumped 100 cubits or 400 cubits. Seemingly, the carob tree actually uprooted itself and dug itself in the soil across the garden, but the rabbis weren't phased by that.

The rabbis insisted that you can't win arguments because of miracles, and so they rejected Rabbi Eliezer's argument.

Rabbi Eliezer also said, "If I am right, let the stream of water prove it." And the flowing stream of water reversed itself! The rabbis once again insisted that legal disputes are not solved by streams going in the opposite direction.

And finally, the Rabbi Eliezer asked that Heaven weigh in — and a voice from Heaven said, "Rabbi Eliezer is always right." The rabbis point out that questions of Jewish law are not solved by voices from Heaven.

With this story, the Talmud is trying to make the point that miracles don't decide the resolution of disputes, nor do impressive magic tricks. A majority vote among the rabbis resolves legal disputes, as the Torah itself says. The Talmudic rabbis didn't hesitate to invent a story that includes wild so-called miracles to make this important point.

By the way, I'm a magician (a card-carrying member of the Society of American Magicians and the International Brotherhood of Magicians). So, I know that magicians can do tricks that inspire audiences to say, "That's impossible!" Therefore, I'm pleased when the Talmud rejects miracles in an argument — because I know how easy it is to fool an audience.

A nest on a person's head

This story provides a great example of how the rabbis would sometimes invent strange scenarios to test a principle. The Torah has a law called *shiluach haken* (shih loo-akh Ha-Kehn; sending away the nest).

The Torah says, "If, along the road, you chance upon a bird's nest in any tree or on the ground that holds fledglings or eggs, and the mother's sitting over the fledglings or on the eggs, don't take the mother together with her young. Let the mother go, and take only the young, in order that you may fare well and have a long life."

The Talmud includes a discussion about the phrase in the Torah "in any tree or on the ground." What, for example, does the verse mean when it says that a Jewish person has an obligation to chase away the mother to get the eggs or fledglings from a nest that is "on the ground"?

Masekhta Chullin (Mah-sekh tah khoo-leen; Tractate "profane items") contains the following discussion:

> The residents of Pappunya asked *Rav* Mattana: "If you find a nest on the head of a person, what's the law with regard to the *mitzvah* [mitz-vah; a commandment whose purpose is to connect with God] of sending away the mother? Is the nest considered to be on the ground, so therefore one is obligated in the *mitzvah*?" And *Rav* Mattana answered: "Yes."

The Talmud uses this scenario to clarify the boundaries of halakhic principles. Though physically improbable, it emphasizes that the law applies regardless of the nest's location, provided it meets the Torah's criteria.

Using the Torah verse "And earth upon his head," the Talmud concludes that if a nest is on someone's head, the top of the head is considered earth, and therefore the law in the Torah includes something on top of someone's head as "on the ground." The mitzvah is rooted in compassion, discouraging cruelty to animals. Even in bizarre cases, the Talmud reinforces ethical conduct

While no real-world instances are recorded, this discussion informs debates about applying ancient laws to novel situations, such as nests in urban environments.

A rabbi hides under his teacher's bed

A well-known story in the Talmud (which I share in more detail in Chapter 12) talks about a man named *Rav* Kahane who once hid under an illustrious rabbi's bed and listened while the rabbi and his wife made love. Now, between you and me, I don't think it happened. And, by the way, the illustrious rabbi in the story wasn't just some rabbi; he was the leader of his generation and was simply known as Rav (Rahv; teacher). The story says that *Rav* Kahane heard the couple "chatting and joking" — which is a reminder that a couple making love should use words, if necessary, to get his or her partner "in the mood" (a teaching found in the Talmud). But the conclusion of the story is the story's climax (no pun intended):

> When Rav discovered *Rav* Kahane under his bed, Rav protested and said it was inappropriate. And *Rav* Kahane replied, "It is a matter of Torah, and I'm required to learn."

 A story like this one can make the point strongly that sex education is an important part of an individual or couple's life.

Clarifying the Law Through Absurdities

Here are some examples of the sometimes absurd scenarios that the sages use in the Talmud to help clarify an idea or a point of law:

> » *A weasel enters the womb of another animal and swallows the fetus.*

The weasel hypothetical underscores the Talmud's method of using extreme or imaginative scenarios to test legal boundaries. The Talmud raises the question of a weasel inserting its head into the womb of a pregnant cow, swallowing the fetus, and then reinserting its head into another animal's womb. This scenario is part of a series of theoretical dilemmas posed by Rava to clarify the legal concept of peter rechem (peh-tehr reh-khem; opening the womb), which determines whether a firstborn animal attains sanctity. Modern commentators note its unexpected relevance to debates about surrogate motherhood and medical ethics.

>> *During the first three hours every day, God spends the time studying the Torah.*

The Talmud details the Divine Schedule:

First three hours — God engages in Torah study.

Second three hours — God judges the world.

Third three hours — God provides sustenance for creation.

Fourth three hours — God "sports with the leviathan" (a symbolic act of cosmic order)

This framework emphasizes Torah study as the foundational divine activity, reflecting its supreme value in Jewish thought. The structure also serves as a model for human prioritization of Torah learning, urging Jews to emulate this dedication. Some sources suggest that Torah study sustains the world's existence.

>> *A demon who looks like a serpent with seven heads appears in the study hall; Rabbi Aha begins to pray, and each time he bows, one of the serpent's heads falls off.*

The seven-headed serpent (tanina) evokes Mesopotamian and Ugaritic chaos-dragon myths (for example, Leviathan), repurposed here to illustrate Torah's triumph over destructive forces. While rare, such vivid demonic accounts often serve allegorical purposes, addressing internalized fears, for example, distractions or arrogance or external threats to Torah study.

>> *The sage Peleimu asks, "If a person has two heads, on which head does he put on his tefillin [teh-fill-in; a set of small black leather boxes with straps, containing scrolls of parchment with Torah verses]?"*

Some argue the individual is a single entity, requiring tefillin on one head only (likely the dominant one.) While the text provides no definitive answer on tefillin placement, it underscores the Talmud's method of using extreme cases to clarify foundational principles. Some suggests tefillin must be placed on both heads if each possesses independent consciousness. Later authorities continue to debate the implications, reflecting Judaism's dynamic engagement with extraordinary circumstances.

>> *A righteous man named Honi falls asleep and wakes up 70 years later.*

Honi was troubled by the verse in the Book of Psalms, "When the Lord restored the fortunes of Zion, we were like those who dream." He wondered how 70 years of exile could feel like a fleeting dream. While traveling, Honi encountered a man planting a carob tree, which takes 70 years to bear fruit. When asked why he planted it, the man replied, "Just as my ancestors planted for me, I plant for my descendants." After eating, Honi fell asleep, and a rocky enclosure hid him for 70 years. Upon waking, he found the carob tree fully grown and met the planter's grandson. Returning home, he discovered his grandson was alive, but no one recognized Honi. Honi went to the study hall, where scholars revered his legacy but dismissed his identity. Grieving this loss of connection, he prayed for death and died. The story critiques reliance on miracles and emphasizes intergenerational responsibility.

>> *A tower flies through the air.*

This passage underscores the Talmud's method of using imaginative scenarios to probe legal principles. Today, it sparks discussions about technology (such as airplanes, space travel) and their Jewish legal implications. The Talmud discusses a hypothetical scenario of a tower flying through the air within a broader legal discussion about ritual impurity, *tum'ah* (too-mah), and priestly conduct. This passage uses the concept of a "floating tower" as a thought experiment to explore Jewish legal boundaries. If a tower or vessel flies over a cemetery, does it transmit ritual impurity to its occupants? The Talmud debates whether airborne objects are subject to the same impurity laws as ground contact.

›› Two rabbis deliver the exact same sermon, word for word, at the exact same time in two different cities.

The Talmud attributes this synchronicity to the Holy Spirit guiding Torah scholars, emphasizing that profound insights can transcend physical separation when rooted in shared spiritual truth. The story reflects the Talmudic belief that Torah scholars operating at the highest spiritual levels may receive identical revelations. This account remains a touchstone for discussions about communal unity, divine providence, and the transcendent nature of Torah wisdom.

›› A snake swallowed a frog the size of 60 houses. A raven swallowed the snake and sat in a tree.

This story appears within a series of fantastical accounts shared by Rabbah bar Bar Ḥana, a sage known for recounting extraordinary tales to convey moral or allegorical lessons. The story is interpreted as a symbolic vision of world empires:

The frog represents ancient Greece, known for its intellectual pursuits. The snake symbolizes Rome, destructive and cunning like the serpent in Eden. The raven signifies Islamic caliphates, which conquered Rome's territories. The tree represents Abraham, the "tree of life" whose spiritual legacy sustains Israel through exile.

The tale critiques reliance on transient power structures and emphasizes faith in divine providence. The raven's ascent to the tree hints at eventual redemption through ancestral merit.

›› King Solomon had 1,000 wives. Each wife would prepare dinner for the King at her home in case he decided to eat with her that day.

This practice underscored the extravagance of Solomon's court and his deviation from Torah ideals for kings. The Talmud uses this anecdote to critique his accumulation of wives and reliance on luxury rather than divine wisdom.

This narrative serves as a cautionary tale about the dangers of excess and the importance of adhering to Torah principles.

>> *When God created Adam from dust, the dust for his torso was taken from Babylonia. His head was made from the dust of Israel. His limbs were made from the dust of all the other lands. And his buttocks were made from the dust of Akra De'agma (a Babylonian town).*

The Talmud explains that Adam's composite origin emphasizes humanity's shared ancestry and the interconnectedness of all nations. By gathering dust from diverse regions, God ensured "no nation could claim superiority by saying, 'Our soil produced Adam!'" Rashi notes that Adam's head being from Israel highlights the land's spiritual centrality. The Talmud explains that Adam's composite origin emphasizes humanity's shared ancestry and the interconnectedness of all nations. The Talmud uses this narrative to reject ethnic exceptionalism, asserting that all people derive from a single, divinely crafted source.

3
Living the Talmud Way

IN THIS PART . . .

Understand how the Talmud shapes Jewish holiday observance and religious traditions.

Discover the Talmudic perspectives on food and prayer, and their deeper meanings.

Explore how the Talmud approaches marriage, divorce, and family life.

See what the Talmud teaches about relationships and intimacy.

Examine how Talmudic principles influence Jewish legal proceedings and ethical decision-making.

IN THIS CHAPTER

» **Experiencing the Sabbath on Shabbat**

» **Expressing gratitude through holy days**

» **Finding joy on holy days**

» **Using holidays for self-reflection**

Chapter **10**

Observing the Holidays as Holy Days

"Thou shall not labor on the Sabbath." Sounds simple enough, doesn't it? But if it were so simple, the Talmud wouldn't have one large tractate devoted to the subject. Although the subject is rather complicated, I hope that this chapter can give you a good sense of what the Sabbath is about. I also take a look at the Jewish holy days of Chanukah, *Sukkot*, Purim, Passover, Rosh Hashanah, and Yom Kippur.

The Jewish calendar has a lot of holy days, and the Talmud deals with just about all of them. But please remember that the Talmud isn't a how-to guide for observing these holy days; it's where the sages discuss and debate certain issues regarding the holy days.

Shabbat: The Day of Rest

Shabbat begins on Friday at sundown and ends on Saturday night, one hour after sundown. And during that period of time, the goal is to rest. This doesn't mean that you should sleep all day. You can find plenty to do on the day of rest, but what you do and how you do it makes Shabbat what it is. Preparation for the next Shabbat begins as soon as Shabbat is over. It's six days of climbing back to a spiritual peak.

The book of the Talmud that directly deals with the Sabbath consists of 157 double-sided pages. That's 314 pages total. In the following sections, I go over just a few of the topics and issues that the Talmudic sages discussed in *Masekhta Shabbat (mah-sekh-tahv Shah-baht*; Tractate Shabbat).

Other than Shabbat, all of the Jewish holy days happen once a year. In part because Shabbat happens weekly, it's arguably the most important holy day on the Jewish calendar. After all, it's the only holy day included in the Ten Commandments (and the longest of the Ten Commandments, at that):

> This is one of the texts from the Torah concerning itself with the Sabbath. It is in one of the two versions of the Ten Commandments that appear in the Torah:
>
> "Remember the Sabbath and keep it holy. Six days you shall labor and do all your work, but the seventh day is a Sabbath of your God. You shall not do any work — you, your son or daughter, your male or female slave, or your cattle, or the stranger who is within your settlements. Because, in six days, God made Heaven, and earth, and sea — and all that is in them — and then rested on the seventh day; therefore, God blessed the Sabbath day and hallowed it."

The Ten Commandments appear twice in the Torah, with slightly different wordings. For example, the first version of the Sabbath commandment says "Remember the Sabbath" and the second version says "Observe the Sabbath day." The Talmud says that anyone who is obligated to observe is obligated to remember.

Perhaps the most important aspect of Shabbat is your inner attitude. In the Talmud, Rabbi Hanina said,

"A joyous spirit should be a rule on the Sabbath day."

Why is Shabbat different from the other days of the week?

A story in the Talmud tries to explain why Shabbat is different than the other days of the week. It concerns Turnus Rufus and Rabbi Akiva. Turnus Rufus was the governor of Judea and a treasury officer for Rome. He was cruel to the Jews, enacting several cruel measures against the Jewish population, including sentencing Rabbi Akiva to death.

Often in the Talmud there are conversations recorded between a sage and a Roman official or between the sages and other members of the community:

Rabbi Akiva comes up with a clever way to teach Turnus Rufus, the governor of Judea, why the Sabbath is so special:

> Turnus Rufus, the wicked Roman governor of Judea, asked this question of Rabbi Akiva: "And what makes this day, Shabbat, different from other days?"
>
> Rabbi Akiva said to him, "What makes you more distinguished than other men?"
>
> Turnus Rufus said to him, "I am more distinguished because my master the emperor wants it that way."
>
> Rabbi Akiva said to him, "Shabbat too is unique because my Master wants it that way; He has sanctified that day."

And this is one of the most famous passages from the Talmud about Shabbat:

> Rabbi Yosei bar Yehudah says, "Two ministering angels accompany a person on every Shabbat evening from the synagogue to their home, one good angel and one evil angel.
>
> "And if they reach their home and find a lamp burning, and a table set, and their bed made ready for Shabbat, the good angel says, 'May it be Your will that it shall be like this for another Shabbat.'

"And the evil angel answers against their will, 'Amen.'

"And if a person doesn't prepare the person's home for Shabbat in that manner, the evil angel says, 'May it be Your will that it shall be so for another Shabbat.' And the good angel answers against their will, 'Amen.'"

What exactly is "labor"?

The Talmudic sages taught that labor consists of 39 categories of work corresponding to 39 types of labor involved in building the Tabernacle in the desert. This is the passage found in Tractate Shabbat. The Talmudic discourse often jumps between different categories, elaborating on some more than others, and introducing related concepts and rulings.

It's worth noting that while Tractate Shabbat is the primary source for these laws, other parts of the Talmud and later rabbinic literature also discuss and interpret these prohibitions in various contexts. This passage is from an important Mishna in Tractate Shabbat that defines the 39 categories of forbidden "labor" on Shabbat. They identified 39 different activities used in the building of the Temple, and used this to determine the activities identified as "work" on the Sabbath.

> One who sows, and one who plows, and one who reaps, and one who gathers sheaves into a pile, and one who threshes, removing the kernel from the husk, and one who winnows threshed grain in the wind, and one who selects the inedible waste from the edible, and one who grinds, and one who sifts the flour in a sieve, and one who kneads dough, and one who bakes.

> Additional primary categories of prohibited labor are the following:

> One who shears wool, and one who whitens it, and one who combs the fleece and straightens it, and one who dyes it, and one who spins the wool, and one who stretches the threads of the warp in the loom, and one who constructs two meshes, tying the threads of the warp to the base of the loom, and one who weaves two threads, and one who severs two threads for constructive purposes, and one who ties a knot, and one who unties a knot, and one who sews two stitches with a needle, as well as one who tears a fabric in order to sew two stitches.

One who traps a deer, or any living creature, and one who slaughters it, and one who flays it, and one who salts its hide, a step in the tanning process, and one who tans its hide, and one who smooths it, removing hairs and veins, and one who cuts it into measured parts.

One who writes two letters and one who erases in order to write two letters. One who builds a structure, and one who dismantles it, one who extinguishes a fire, and one who kindles a fire.

One who strikes a blow with a hammer to complete the production process of a vessel and one who carries out an object from domain to domain.

All these are primary categories of labor, and they number forty-less-one.

Behave yourself

The Talmud discusses how you should behave differently on Shabbat. The Jewish Scriptures contains the following passage in the book of the prophet Isaiah. The passage emphasizes the importance of honoring the Sabbath by refraining from one's usual activities and pursuits. It suggests that by properly observing the Sabbath, one will find joy in the Lord and receive blessings:

> "If you keep your feet from breaking, from pursuing your affairs on My holy day, and you call Shabbat a delight, the Lord's holy day honorable, and you honor it by not going your own way, from attending to your affairs and speaking idle words, then you will find your joy in the Lord, and I will cause you to ride in triumph on the heights of the land and to feast on the inheritance of your father Jacob. For the mouth of the Lord has spoken."

Watch how the Talmud comments on the words spoken by the prophet Isaiah, a few words at a time, phrase by phrase:

> The rabbis derived from the words "and you honor it" that your dress on Shabbat shouldn't be like your dress during the week because Rabbi Yohanan would refer to his clothing as "my honor," indicating that appropriate clothing is a form of respect for God.

The words "going your own way" mean that how you walk on Shabbat should not be like your walking during the week. These are the ways the sages describe the way to walk on Shabbat. The difference in walking on Shabbat is meant to embody several key aspects of Shabbat observance. The practical implications are:

>> Slowing Down: On Shabbat, one is encouraged to walk at a more leisurely, relaxed pace. This contrasts with the hurried, purposeful stride often adopted during the workweek. Walking on Shabbat should be done at a normal or leisurely pace, avoiding brisk or hurried movement.

>> Mindfulness: The change in walking pace promotes a greater awareness of one's surroundings and inner state, aligning with the contemplative nature of Shabbat. Walks on Shabbat are often taken for pleasure, health, or to reach the synagogue, rather than for utilitarian purposes.

>> Rest and Rejuvenation: By walking differently, one physically enacts the concept of rest that is central to Shabbat, distinguishing it from the other days of the week. There are traditional limits on how far one may walk on Shabbat, known as "techum (TEY-khum; boundary.) It is typically set at 2,000 cubits (approximately 0.596 miles) outside one's city limits on Shabbat." The altered walking style serves as a reminder that Shabbat is a time for spiritual pursuits rather than mundane activities.

"From attending to your affairs" means that you can't deal with your weekday affairs and speak about them on Shabbat. However, you can talk about affairs of Heaven (meaning those pertaining to *mitzvot* [mitz-VOTE; specific actions commanded by God]).

"And speaking idle words" means that you should speak differently on Shabbat than you do during the week. You shouldn't discuss your weekday affairs on Shabbat. The prohibition against speaking "idle words" on Shabbat is derived from the Book of Isaiah, which instructs people to honor the Sabbath by "not doing your own ways, nor finding your own pleasure, nor speaking your own words." This concept has been interpreted in various ways within Jewish tradition:

Many commentators understand this to primarily prohibit discussing business matters or weekday affairs on Shabbat. This includes planning work-related activities, discussing financial transactions, and making deals, and refraining from phrases like "I will do such-and-such thing tomorrow" or discussing future business plans.

Some interpret it as discouraging excessive casual or frivolous talk that doesn't contribute to the spiritual nature of the day. Discussions that cause worry or distress are also considered inappropriate for Shabbat, as they detract from the day's restful and joyous character. The goal is to elevate one's speech to focus on more meaningful topics. The general principle is that one's speech on Shabbat should be noticeably different from everyday conversation. This aligns with the broader concept of making Shabbat a distinct and holy time.

Preparing for Shabbat: Make an Effort!

Shabbat is more than just a day of rest; it's an opportunity to connect with tradition, family, and faith. The preparation for Shabbat is not merely about physical tasks, but also about setting the intention for the spiritual and communal experience it brings. To properly observe this day, you must invest time, effort, and even resources. This investment signifies the importance of Shabbat because it demands that we honor it in a way that reflects its significance.

Spending money on the necessary preparations — whether for food, clothing, or other essentials — offers a way of demonstrating the value of this sacred day. In fact, Jewish tradition teaches us to believe that a person's entire livelihood for the year is allocated during the period from Rosh Hashanah (the Jewish New Year) to Yom Kippur, and the preparation for Shabbat provides an expression of that divine provision. It acknowledges that by making a sincere effort to prepare for Shabbat, you're engaging in a cycle of blessing and renewal that spans far beyond the week ahead.

Spend money to prepare for Shabbat

It is a special expression of devotion to the Sabbath when a person spends as much as he or she can to make the Sabbath extra-special. How much to spend Is determined in this way:

A person's entire livelihood is allocated to them during the period from Rosh Hashanah to Yom Kippur. (More about Rosh Hashanah and Yom Kippur later in this chapter.)

During this period of time, God judges everyone, God decrees exactly how much money a person will earn for all their expenditures of the coming year, except for expenditures for Sabbaths, festivals, and the school fees of their sons' Torah study.

In these areas, God determines no exact amount at the beginning of the year; rather, if a person reduces the amount that they spend for these purposes, their income reduces, and they earn that much less money in that year. And if they increase their expenditures in these areas, their income increases to ensure that they can cover the expense.

Therefore, one can borrow money for these purposes because God guarantees that a person will have enough income to cover whatever they spend.

Eat the finest food

Food is another way to express devotion to the Sabbath:

The Talmud teaches: "They said about Shammai the Elder that throughout his life he would eat in honor of Shabbat."

"How so?"

"If he found a choice animal, he would say: 'This is for Shabbat.'

"If he subsequently found a better one, he would set aside the second for Shabbat and eat the first.

"He would eat the first to leave the better-quality animal for Shabbat, which continually rendered his eating an act of honoring Shabbat."

Dress in your finest clothes

How one dressed is also a reflection of one's attitude toward Shabbat and is another way to express one's feeling about the special nature of Shabbat. The Talmud records:

Rabbi Ḥanina would dress in his finest garments on Shabbat eve and say: "Come and we will go out to greet Shabbat, the queen."

Rabbi Yannai put on his garment on Shabbat eve and said: "Enter, O bride. Enter, O bride."

10 QUOTATIONS ABOUT SHABBAT FROM THE TALMUD

Shabbat occupies a central place in Jewish life, and the Talmud offers rich insights into its significance. The following are a selection of ten key quotes from the Talmud about Shabbat scattered throughout the text:

- "The Sabbath was given to you, not you to the Sabbath."

- "Shabbat is equal to all the other commandments."

- "One who observes Shabbat according to its laws, even if he worships idols, is forgiven."

- "If Israel were to keep two Sabbaths according to the laws thereof, they would be redeemed immediately."

- "Shabbat is one-sixtieth of the World to Come."

- "On Shabbat, a person receives an additional soul."

- "Whoever delights in the Sabbath is granted his heart's desires."

- "The Sabbath is a gift from God's treasure house."

- "He who blesses the Sabbath is blessed, and he who calls it a delight shall inherit an unbounded heritage."

- "The Sabbath is the source of blessing."

Lighting Up the World on Chanukah

First things first: Let me clear something up just in case you're misinformed about Chanukah (KHAH-new-cah). Chanukah is *not* the Jewish Christmas. The two religious observances are generally around the same time on the calendar (December), but that's where the similarity ends. And the custom of giving gifts to children on Chanukah is a relatively new activity — undoubtedly, to let Jewish children enjoy some presents while their Christian friends and neighbors are doing just that.

The custom of gift-giving during Hanukkah has evolved over time, with different practices emerging at various points in history. Some scholars suggest that the practice of giving coins during Hanukkah may date back to the time of the Maccabees (during the 2nd century BCE), as a way of distributing war booty. In Europe, there was a tradition of giving small amounts of money to Torah teachers during Hanukkah, possibly dating back to the 18th century. The shift towards more extensive gift-giving began in the late 19th century, coinciding with the commercialization of Christmas in America. The practice of giving presents during Hanukkah significantly increased in the 1950s in the United States. The growth of Christmas as a national holiday in America also influenced the Jewish custom of gift-giving.

REMEMBER

It's important to note that while gift-giving has become common, it is not a traditional part of Hanukkah observance. The practice of giving money or chocolate coins is older and more deeply rooted in Jewish tradition than the exchange of wrapped presents.

The battle of the Maccabees is an important part of Jewish history, typically associated with the story of Hanukkah. It involved a Jewish revolt against the Seleucid Empire in the 2nd century BCE fight against melting into the main culture, and provides a reminder to Jews not to abandon their unique Jewish identities. Hanukkah represents the importance of maintaining Jewish identity and commemorating the military victory of the Maccabees, a small group of Jewish rebels who fought against the Greeks. The fighting during the Maccabean Revolt primarily took place in several locations in the region of Judea, which was part of the Seleucid Empire at the time.

The military victory gave the Jews the opportunity to rededicate the Holy Temple in Jerusalem, which the Greeks had desecrated. Lighting flames or candles and increasing them each day during the holy days is a symbol of the desire to increase God's light in the world.

Chanukah receives just a few pages in the entire Talmud. But this basic controversy related to Chanukah was discussed in the those pages:

Chanukah has eight days, and the Chanukah menorah (men-oh-rah; a nine-branched candelabra) has space for eight candles, one for each day (plus the ninth space, where you place the candle used to light the others).

The question arises: Do you light one candle the first day, and two the second day, and so on, until the eighth day, when eight candles are lit? Or do you start with eight candles and diminish them day by day, with the second day lighting seven candles, and then six, and so on?

Beit Shammai and Beit Hillel disagreed (see Chapter 7 for more on this quarreling pair of rabbis). Here's what the Talmud has to say:

> The sages taught: The basic commandment of Chanukah is to have a light kindled by a person, the head of the household, for himself and his household each day.
>
> And those who are meticulous in the performance of *mitzvot* [mitz-VOTE; Divine commandments] kindle a light for each one in the household.
>
> And those who are even more meticulous, adjust the number of candles daily.

Here's how the controversy is expressed in the Talmud:

> Beit Shammai says, "On the first day, one kindles eight lights and, from there on, gradually decreases the number of lights until, on the last day of Chanukah, they kindle one light."

And Beit Hillel says, "On the first day, one kindles one light, and from there on, gradually increases the number of lights until, on the last day, they kindle eight lights."

One person said "The reason for Beit Shammai's opinion is that the number of lights corresponds to the incoming days, meaning the future. On the first day, eight days remain in Chanukah, so one kindles eight lights; and on the second day, seven days remain, so one kindles seven lights, and so on.

"The reason for Beit Hillel's opinion is that the number of lights corresponds to the outgoing days. Each day, the number of lights corresponds to the number of the days of Chanukah that were already observed."

Ultimately, the rabbis in the Talmud decided in favor of Beit Hillel's position:

The reason for Beit Hillel's opinion is that the number of lights is based on the principle that one elevates to a higher level in matters of sanctity, and one does not downgrade.

7 QUOTATIONS FROM THE TALMUD ABOUT CHANUKAH

Throughout the pages of the Talmud, you can find many brief teachings about Chanukah. Here are some:

- "These days are for praise and thanksgiving."

- "These lights we kindle for the miracles, and the wonders, and the salvations; and for the battles which You performed for our forefathers in those days at this season through Your holy priests."

- "The zealous kindle a light for each person in the household."

- "One who sees a Chanukah light must recite a blessing."

- "Place the Chanukah light outside the doorway of your house."

- "In times of danger, you can place the light on the table."

Dwelling in a Sukkah on Sukkot

Sukkot, also known as the Feast of Booths or the Feast of Tabernacles, is a joyous seven-day Jewish holiday that typically falls in autumn. It commemorates the Israelites' 40-year journey through the desert after the Exodus from Egypt and celebrates the fall harvest.

The central symbol of Sukkot (sue-COAT) is the sukkah (sue-KAH), a temporary outdoor shelter with at least three walls and a roof made of natural materials that allows starlight to peek through. During the holiday, Jews are encouraged to eat meals, socialize, and even sleep in the sukkah.

Sukkot is marked by festive meals, prayer services, and community gatherings, emphasizing themes of divine protection, gratitude for the harvest, and the importance of hospitality.

In the Torah, when describing the holy days (seven days) of *Sukkot*, also known as the Feast of Booths, the Torah text doesn't give us much information about just what it means by *sukkot* (booths). Here are the two Torah verses that mention booths:

> You shall live in booths seven days; all citizens in Israel shall live in booths.
>
> After the ingathering from your threshing floor and your vat, you shall hold the Feast of Booths for seven days.

The question is, of course, "What's a booth?"

Here's where the Talmud comes in. When God dictated the Written Torah to Moses, He made no mention of just what a booth looks like. But the Talmud (the oral transmission of the teachings of God) goes into great detail about what a booth is, what it looks like, how you build it, and what requirements it has to fulfill.

In fact, in the Talmud, you can find a description of how to make a *sukkah* (sue-KAH; booth) in *Masekhta Sukkah* (Tractate Booth). The instructions on how to make a *sukkah*, in modern book terms, cover more than 50 pages!

You must ask five fundamental questions when approaching the task of building a *sukkah*:

>> What are the minimum and maximum dimensions of a *sukkah*?

>> What structure must the *sukkah* have? Is it square, rectangular, some other shape?

>> What materials can you use to build a *sukkah*?

>> How and when does one build a *sukkah*? Do you have to build it at special times?

>> Where do you locate a *sukkah*? Where can you build a *sukkah*?

The Written Torah answers none of these questions, but the Oral Torah (the Talmud) deals with all of them, in great detail.

What does the Mishna say?

As I explain in Chapter 1, the *Mishna* (MISH-nah) is a part of the Talmud. (And just about every *Mishna* has an analysis, called the *Gemara* [Geh-MAR-ah]). The *Mishna* is written in Hebrew, and it records the detail of the law as the sages remember it. But as you can see from the following several *Mishnayot*; (portions of the *Mishna*) from *Masekhta Sukkah*, the sages had a lot disagreement about what exactly the law says.

WARNING

The *Mishnayot* (plural of *Mishna*) in the following sections get very technical, which helps illustrate why Talmud study can reach to very advanced levels. But if you read each *Mishna* carefully, and consult the commentary of Rabbi Steinsaltz, you can understand the *halakhot* (hah-lah-KHOT; laws) discussed in each *Mishna*.

In each of the following sections, the first portion of text comes from the *Mishna*, and the following text is part of Rabbi Adin Steinsaltz's commentary on the Talmud, (see my discussion of this publication in Chapter 16), helping the reader to better understand the festival of sukkot). The major topic is the building of a sukkah.

The Talmud offers a detailed analysis of each *Mishna* and usually resolves disagreements and adds other details. Each *Mishna* is relatively short — only a few lines.

The height of the sukkah

The roofing of a *sukkah* is the main and most crucial element of the *mitzvah*, and if it's more than 20 cubits high, it's unfit.

Rabbi Yehudah says it is acceptable.

Blocking a sukkah

If you establish a *sukkah* beneath a tree, it's the same as if you established it inside the house, which makes it unfit (because the tree would block the sky).

If one established a *sukkah* atop another *sukkah*, the upper *sukkah* is fit and the lower *sukkah* is unfit (because the sky would not be blocked.)

Rabbi Yehudah says: If there are no residents in the upper *sukkah*, the lower *sukkah* is fit (again, the sky would not be blocked).

Using sheets in a sukkah

If one spread a sheet over the roofing as protection for those sitting in the *sukkah* due to the sun, or if one spread a sheet beneath the roofing as protection due to the falling leaves, or if one spread a sheet as a canopy over the frame of a four-post bed, the area in the *sukkah* beneath the sheets is unfit. The roof must be made of raw, unfinished vegetable matter that is no longer attached to the ground.

In the first two cases, because the sheet is susceptible to ritual impurity, it renders the otherwise fit roofing unfit. In the case of the canopy, you're not sitting under the roofing of the *sukkah*; rather, you're sitting inside a tent.

However, you may spread the sheet over the frame of a two-post bed, which has one post in the middle of each end of the bed. When spreading the sheet over the posts, it forms an inclined, rather than a flat, roof. And it doesn't consider a tent that has an inclined roof a significant structure.

Using climbing plants

If you attach climbing plants, such as grapevines, gourd plants, or ivy, to trellises as part of a *sukkah* while those plants are still attached to the ground, and you then add roofing atop the trellises, the *sukkah* is unfit.

If the amount of fit roofing was greater than the plants attached to the ground, or if you cut the climbing plants so that they no longer attach to the ground, it's fit.

No bundles on the roof

You may not make a roof for the *sukkah* by using bundles of straw tied with rope, or bundles of wood, or bundles of twigs.

And with regard to all of the bundles, if you untie them, they're fit for use in roofing the *sukkah*. The reason that the bundles are unfit is because the bundles are tied (and would block the sky).

And even when tied, all of the bundles are fit for use in constructing the walls of the *sukkah*.

No wide boards on the roof

You may make a roof for the *sukkah* by using boards such as those used in the ceiling of a house; this is the statement of Rabbi Yehudah.

Rabbi Meir prohibits their use.

If you place a board that's four handbreadths wide atop the *sukkah*, the *sukkah* is fit. They fulfill their obligation, provided they don't sleep beneath the board.

How boards can serve as roofing

In the case of a roof made of boards that are four handbreadths wide which have no plaster coating, Rabbi Yehudah says that Beit Shammai and Beit Hillel disagree with regard to the manner in which to render it fit.

Beit Shammai says, "You can move each board, and then it's as though you placed the board there for the sake of the *mitzvah* of *sukkah*; and you then remove one board from among the boards and replace it with fit roofing.

Beit Hillel says, "You need not perform both actions; rather, you must either move the boards or remove one from among them."

Rabbi Meir says, "You remove only one board from among them and don't move the others."

Using an elephant as a wall

The walls of the *sukkah* are discussed in the building details of an acceptable *sukkah* (see the section "Dwelling in a Sukkah on Sukkot," earlier in this chapter). *Masekhta Sukkot* focuses on four areas of concern:

>> **Materials:** You can make walls of any sturdy material that withstands normal wind.

>> **Height and structure:** Walls must be a minimum of 32 inches (1.7 cubits) high but no more than 20 cubits. And a *sukkah* requires at least two walls and part of a third wall. (A cubit is the ancient yardstick. It is from the tip of your middle finger tip your elbow.)

>> **Placement:** Walls need to be no more than 9 inches (one half of a cubit) above the ground.

>> **Stability:** Walls must be stable and not sway in the wind.

I have my doubts that someone would build a *sukkah* by using an elephant as one of the walls, but the rabbis of the Talmud were big fans of testing out ideas. They asked, "What if someone wanted to use an elephant as a wall? Would it pass the test of the Talmudic requirement for building a *sukkah*?"

Rabbi Meir and Rabbi Yehudah disagreed on the question.

>> **Stability:** Rabbi Meir asked just how stable an elephant, a living creature, could be as a wall. Rabbi Yehudah felt that if you tie up the elephant in an effective way, it could serve as a *sukkah* wall.

>> **Mortality:** Both rabbis had concerns about what would happen if the elephant died. But the sages determined its body would probably meet the requirements of the height of the wall.

Here's a small piece of how the discussion goes in the Talmud:

The *Gemara* asks: What is the reason for the opinion of Rabbi Meir, who rules that an animal is unfit for use as a partition in areas of *halakhah* [ha-la-KHAH; law] that require a partition?

Abaye says: Because of the concern that the animal might die, leaving the *sukkah* without a wall.

Rabbi Zeira says: Because of the concern that it will flee.

The *Gemara* explains the practical *halakhic* (ha-LA-khik; legal) differences between the two opinions:

In the case where one established a wall with a tied elephant, everyone agrees that the *sukkah* is fit because, even if it dies and falls, its carcass still has a height of 10 handbreadths and is fit for the wall of a *sukkah*.

They disagree in the case of an elephant that's not tied. According to the one who said: "Because of the concern lest the animal die," we aren't concerned in this case because the carcass would remain a fit wall.

10 QUOTATIONS ABOUT SUKKOT FROM THE TALMUD

Here are 10 quotations culled from various parts of the Talmud about the holy days of Sukkot:

- "All of Israel is worthy to dwell in one *sukkah* [booth]."

- "The *mitzvah* [Divine commandment as stated in the Torah (Five Books of Moses)] of *sukkah* is to make the *sukkah* a permanent dwelling and one's house a temporary dwelling."

- "A *sukkah* higher than 20 cubits is unfit."

- "A *sukkah* which does not have three walls, and which doesn't have more shade than sunlight, is unfit."

- "The minimum size for a *sukkah* is 7 handbreadths by 7 handbreadths."

- "One who's uncomfortable [because of rain, illness, and so on] is exempt from dwelling in the *sukkah*."

- "One who has not seen the joy of the water-drawing ceremony [a beautiful ritual in the Temple] has never seen joy in their life."

- "The flute is played for five or six days [during *Sukkot*]."

- "The world is judged for water on *Sukkot*."

- "The *sukkah* commemorates the Clouds of Glory [Divine protection in the desert]."

Masquerading on Purim

Purim is a fascinating holy day. It celebrates the victory of the Jews against antisemitism, and is the only day of the year when everyone — not only children — dress up in costumes. It's also the only day of the year when it's recommended (by the Talmud) that you drink enough alcohol to get at least a little tipsy. What's going on?

The Book of Esther, in the Torah, tells the story of a Jewish woman named Esther who becomes the queen of Persia. Her cousin Mordechai uncovers a plot by Haman, an advisor to the king, to murder all the Jews. Esther reveals her Jewish identity to the king and pleads for her people, leading to Haman's downfall.

The Talmud references this story when talking about Purim:

> Rava said: "A person is obligated to become intoxicated with wine on Purim until he's so intoxicated that he doesn't know how to distinguish between 'cursed is Haman' and 'blessed is Mordechai.'"

The word "megillah" comes from Hebrew, meaning "scroll" or "roll," derived from the root "g-l-l" which means "to roll." In Jewish tradition, the most well-known megillah is the Scroll of Esther, which is read publicly during Purim celebrations. This scroll tells the story of how Queen Esther saved the Jewish people from destruction in ancient Persia.

In the Talmud, *Masekhta Megillah* (meh-GILL-ah; Tractate Megillah) discusses these things:

>> Laws related to reading the entire *megillah*

>> Rules about writing a *megillah*

>> Other Purim customs, such as gift giving and charity

>> The public reading of the whole book of Esther from the Holy Scriptures.

Many commentators and authors over the centuries have pointed out that The Book of Esther has no mention of God; many of those commentators take the position that God is so present in every detail of the story, that the story has no need to mention God's name.

Wearing costumes

Although the custom of wearing costumes on Purim developed after Talmudic times, the story in the Book of Esther certainly has a theme of hiddenness, which is at the root of the custom to wear costumes.

A major theme of the holy day of Purim involves concealing and revealing.

In the story:

>> Esther conceals her identity.

>> God seems absent from the story.

>> Divine intervention doesn't obviously occur.

Giving gifts and giving charity

Unlike Halloween, when children go door to door asking for things, on Purim, Jews go from door to door giving gifts to their friends. Jews also customarily give charity to at least two recipients on Purim.

SIX QUOTATIONS FROM THE TALMUD ABOUT PURIM

Here are 6 quotations from various parts of the Talmud about Purim:

- "To fulfill the Purim requirement of giving presents to the poor, you must give at least two gifts to two people."

- "These days are for praise and thanksgiving."

- "Mordechai recorded these events, and he sent letters to all the Jews throughout the provinces of King Xerxes, near and far, to have them celebrate annually the 14th and 15th days of the month of Adar."

- "He wrote them to observe the days as days of feasting and joy, and giving presents of food to one another and gifts to the poor."

- "A person should be more liberal with his presents to the poor than to be lavish in his preparation of the Purim feast or in sending portions to his friends."

Preparing for Passover

Passover, which lasts eight days, commemorates the exodus of the Children of Israel from Egypt. The highlight of Passover is a family feast known as a seder (SAY-der). During the feast, the participants sitting around the table read from the *Haggadah* (Hah-GAH-dah; the story), a book that describes the ritual performed during the evening of the seder as well as the story of the Exodus. The text of the *Haggadah* is actually based on passages from the Talmud, (Tractate Pesachim; Peh-SAKH-eem, plural of Pesach) but the text has evolved over the centuries.

Here's a Haggadah timeline:

>> **2nd century CE:** The basic elements of the seder were developed and recorded in the Talmud. *Rabban* Gamliel was instrumental in the development of the *Haggadah* at that time.

>> **7th to 8th centuries:** The rabbis in Babylonia compiled various versions of the *Haggadah*, including some additions, rewordings, and re-orderings of the text.

>> **10th century:** The oldest manuscript containing a *Haggadah* was found in the Cairo *Genizah* (geh-NEE-zah; a storage place for worn out books, sacred parchment, and other items that have God's name on them).

>> **13th to 14th centuries:** During this time, various Jewish and non-Jewish artists created manuscripts of the *Haggadah* that contained beautiful illustrations.

>> **1482:** Unknown artists created the first printed *Haggadah* in Spain.

>> **16th century:** Several haggadahs became quite popular, and the text of the *Haggadah* became more or less fixed.

>> **Today:** Over 3,000 versions of the Passover *Haggadah* exist, many containing additions to make the *Haggadah* and the Holy Days of Passover more relevant to the times.

The following sections offer six examples of pieces from the Haggadah. You will read the passages from the Talmud and then from a contemporary *Haggadah*, so that you can see how the text of the *Haggadah* has evolved over the centuries and is based on the text of the Talmud.

Observing a night of Passover

One of the most cherished Passover traditions is the recital of "The Four Questions." Often it is the youngest family member who is able to read who asks these four questions:

>> **From the Talmud:** The *Talmud* lists each of the questions. Why is this night different from all other nights?

On all other nights, we eat leavened bread and matzah as preferred; on this night, all our bread is matzah.

On all other nights, we eat other vegetables; on this night, we eat bitter herbs.

On all nights, we eat sitting upright or reclining. And on this night, we all recline!

The *Mishna* continues its list of the questions.

When the Temple was standing, one would ask: On all other nights, we eat either roasted, stewed, or cooked meat, but on this night, all the meat is the roasted meat of the Paschal lamb.

The final question was asked, even after the destruction of the Temple: On all other nights, we dip the vegetables in a liquid during the meal only once; however, on this night, we dip twice.

>> **From the *Haggadah*:** The child asks *Ma Nishtana* [mah nish-TAH-nah; "What is different"].

What makes this night different from all [other] nights?

On all nights, we need not dip even once. On this night, we do so twice!

On all nights, we eat *chametz* [CHAH-maytz; certain grains that rise in contact with water] or matzah. And on this night, only matzah.

On all nights, we eat any kind of vegetables. And on this night, *maror* [maw-roar; bitter herbs].

On all nights, we eat sitting upright or reclining. And on this night, we all recline!

>> **From the Talmud:** The sages taught: If his son is wise and knows how to ask, his son asks him. And if the son is not wise, his wife asks him. And if even his wife is not capable of asking or if he has no wife, he asks himself. And even if two Torah scholars who know the *halakhot* of Passover are sitting together with no one else present to pose the questions, they ask each other.

Telling the Passover story

The central activity on Passover night is the retelling of the exodus from Egypt. The Haggadah gives some of the detail and those participating in the celebration are encouraged to add details:

>> **From the *Haggadah*:** Even if all of us were wise, all of us understanding, all of us knowing the Torah, we would still be obligated to discuss the exodus from Egypt; and everyone who discusses the exodus from Egypt at length is praiseworthy.

>> **From the Talmud:** The concept likely predates these written sources, as it reflects a longstanding rabbinic tradition. The Mishnah, compiled around 200 CE, contains the earliest known reference to this idea, though not in these exact words.

Explaining the Passover foods

A major part of the Passover holy days are the foods both eaten and avoided. The foods eaten at the Passover seder are symbolic and help to tell the story:

>> **From the Talmud:** *Rabban* Gamliel would say: "Anyone who did not say these three matters on Passover has not fulfilled his obligation: The Paschal lamb, matzah, and bitter herbs. When one mentions these matters, he must elaborate and explain them: The Paschal lamb is brought because the Omnipresent *pesach* [PAY-sakh; passed over] the houses of our forefathers in Egypt, as it is stated: 'That you shall say: It is the sacrifice of the Lord's Paschal

offering, for He passed over the houses of the children of Israel in Egypt when he smote the Egyptians and delivered our houses.'"

>> **From the *Hagaddah*:** *Rabban* Gamliel used to say: "Whoever doesn't discuss the following three things on Passover has not fulfilled his duty, namely the Passover sacrifice, the matzah, and the *maror* (bitter herbs)." The Talmudic discussions and later interpretations emphasize that eating maror and matza is not merely a ritual act, but a deeply meaningful experience designed to evoke reflection on the Exodus story and its ongoing relevance to Jewish life.

Recognizing your part in the story

A significant part of the holy days of Passover is reviewed every Passover. Participants are reminded to identifying with the Passover seder and personally connect with it. This Talmudic passage, now in every Haggadah, reminds us of this:

>> **From the Talmud:** The rabbis of the *Mishna* further state: "In each and every generation, a person must view themselves as though they personally left Egypt because the Talmud states: "And you shall tell your son on that day, saying: 'It is because of this which the Lord did for me when I came forth out of Egypt.'" In every generation, each person must say: 'This, which the Lord did for me,' and not: 'This, which the Lord did for my forefathers.'"

>> **From the *Haggadah*:** In every generation, a person is obligated to regard themselves as if they had come out of Egypt, as the Haggadah says: "You shall tell your child on that day, 'It is because of this that the Lord did for me when I left Egypt.'"

Praising God's miracles

Passover is filled with opportunities to express gratitude to God:

>> **From the Talmud:** Therefore, we are obligated to thank, praise, glorify, extol, exalt, honor, bless, revere, and laud

the One who performed for our forefathers and for us all these miracles: He took us out from slavery to freedom, from sorrow to joy, from mourning to a Festival, from darkness to a great light, and from enslavement to redemption. And we will say before Him: "Halleluiah." At this point, the *Hallel* is recited [HAH-layl; a joyous praise of God] that you say on all joyous days.

>> **From the *Haggadah*:** Thus it's our duty to thank, to laud, to praise, to glorify, to exalt, to adore, to bless, to elevate, and to honor the One who did all these miracles for our parents and for us. He took us from slavery to freedom, from sorrow to joy, from mourning to festivity, from deep darkness to great light, and from bondage to redemption. Let us therefore recite before Him Halleluiah.

Explaining the use of matzah

When most people think of Passover, they think of matzah, the unleavened bread eaten throughout the eight days of the observance of the holiday:

>> **From the Talmud:** *Rabban* Gamliel explains: "The reason for matzah is because our forefathers were redeemed from Egypt, as it is stated: 'And they baked the dough that they took out of Egypt as *matzot* [maht-ZOAT; plural of matzah] because it wasn't leavened. Because they were thrust out of Egypt and could not tarry.'"

>> **From the *Haggadah*:** "This matzah that we eat, for what reason? Because the dough of our parents didn't have time to become leavened before the King of the kings of kings, the Holy One, Blessed be He, revealed Himself to them and redeemed them."

Thus it is said: "They baked matzah from the dough that they had brought out of Egypt because it wasn't leavened; they had been driven out of Egypt and could not delay, and they had also not prepared any provisions."

SEVEN THINGS THE TALMUD SAYS ABOUT MATZAH

Here are seven topics concerning matzah that appear in the Talmud:

- In the Talmud, *Rabban* Gamliel said one must explain the significance of matzah during the seder. Rabban Gamliel states:

  "This matzah that we eat, for what reason? Because the dough of our fathers did not have time to become leavened before the King of Kings, the Holy One, Blessed be He, revealed Himself to them and redeemed them."

- Symbolizes the unleavened bread that the Israelites took when fleeing Egypt.

  The Talmud discusses the haste with which the Israelites left Egypt, as they didn't have time for their bread to rise.

- The types of grain that can be used to make matzah.

  The Talmud discusses five specific grains that can be used to make matzah for Passover: wheat, barley, spelt, oats, and rye

- Can matzah be made from anything other than flour and water, such as wine, oil, honey, or eggs for use on the first seder night?

  According to the Talmud and Jewish law, the answer is no. The core principle behind the discussions in the Talmud is that Passover matzah should be simple, reflecting the haste and affliction of the Exodus. Traditional matzah for fulfilling the Passover obligation is made only with flour and water.

- Guard matzah to prevent leavening.

  The Talmud introduces the concept of "shemurah matzah" (shmor-ah matz-ah; guarded matzah) based on the verse in Exodus 12:17, "And you shall guard the matzot."

- The proper thickness of matzah.

  The school of Hillel says that matzah can be up to a hand-breadth thick, which is approximately 4 inches. It's important to note that while the Talmud allows for thicker matzah, later

(continued)

(continued)

> rabbinic authorities have generally recommended thinner matzah to avoid potential issues with leavening during the baking process.
>
> - The procedure of breaking the middle matzah at the seder.
>
>   There are three matzah loaves on the Passover seder table, one on top of each other. The Mishnah in tractate Pesachim (peh-SAKH-eem; Passovers, the plural of Passover) mentions the practice of breaking bread (matzah) at the beginning of the seder.

Rosh Hashanah: It's Not a Party

The first day of the Hebrew month of *Tishri* (TISH-ray) is the Jewish New Year's Day, Rosh Hashanah (Rush Ha-shah-nah). But don't expect a party. Rosh Hashanah is very serious. Observant Jews spend most of the day in prayer and introspection and contemplating *teshuvah* (teh-SHEW-vah; repentance/ return).

Teshuvah, a fundamental concept in Judaism, encompasses the process of recognizing your mistakes, feeling genuine remorse, and taking steps to correct your behavior and return to the right path.

Observant Jews don't limit *teshuvah* to a specific time; The sages encourage it throughout the year. However, it takes on special significance during the High Holy Days, particularly in the period between Rosh Hashanah and Yom Kippur, known as the Ten Days of Repentance.

The Talmud emphasizes that *teshuvah* isn't an abstract concept but a practical process involving internal change, verbal confession, and altered behavior. The sages see it as a powerful tool for spiritual growth and reconciliation.

The concept of *teshuvah* reflects the Jewish belief in human free will and the capacity for moral and spiritual growth. It emphasizes that no matter how far a person strays, they always have an opportunity to return to the right path and restore their relationship with God and fellow human beings.

The Talmud discusses three types of *teshuvah* (teh-shoe-vah; repentance):

>> **Between a person and God:** Repenting for sins committed against God, such as violating religious commandments

>> **Between a person and another person:** Making amends for wrongs done to other people, including seeking forgiveness and providing restitution, when applicable

>> **As a process of self-improvement:** Recognizing one's errors, feeling remorse, confessing, and resolving not to repeat the transgression

According to Jewish teachings, Hell is not a place of fire and brimstone. It's more like a human washing machine, where souls learn what they did wrong and get straightened out and cleansed. The School of Shammai (see Chapter 7 for discussion about the School of Shammai) contributes to the subject. Consider the following passage from the Talmud:

It is taught, Beit Shammai says: "Wholly righteous people will immediately be written and sealed for eternal life. Wholly wicked people will immediately be written and sealed for *Gehenna* [geh-HEN-ah; Hell] because the Talmud states: 'And many of those who sleep in the dust of the earth shall wake, some to eternal life and some to shame and everlasting contempt.'"

Intermediate people will descend to *Gehenna* to be cleansed and to achieve atonement for their sins.

Yom Kippur: Not a Day of Judgment After All

Yom Kippur (YOME key-poor) also known as the Day of Atonement, is the holiest single day in the Jewish calendar. Yom Kippur is a solemn 25-hour period of fasting, prayer, and repentance, during which Jews seek forgiveness for their sins and aim to make amends with both God and fellow humans. The day is marked by abstaining from food, drink, and other physical pleasures, with many spending most of the time in synagogue services focused on themes of repentance and spiritual renewal.

The Talmud says:

> Rabbi Shimon ben Gamliel said: "There were no days as happy for the Jewish people as Yom Kippur. Yom Kippur is a day of joy because it has the elements of pardon and forgiveness."

In fact, the Talmud says that the two happiest days of the year are Yom Kippur and *Tu B'Av* (too buh-ahv) a kind of Jewish Valentine's Day. In ancient times, Tu B'Av was a day when unmarried women would dress in white and dance in the vineyards, while eligible men would come to try to find a bride. In modern times many couples choose to get married on Tu B'Av. (My daughter Malya and her husband William married in Israel on Tu B'Av.) Also, music and dance festivals are often held to mark the occasion.

You can find a passage in a similar spirit elsewhere in the Talmud:

> The *Exilarch* [ex-ill-ark; Jewish community leader] said to Rav Hamnuna: "What is the meaning of that which is written, 'The holy one of God is honored'?"
>
> Rav Hamnuna said to him: "That is Yom Kippur, when there is no eating or drinking, and so the Torah said: 'Honor it with a clean garment.'" In other words, Yom Kippur is a day to honor God, not to feel sad.

Similarly, the Talmud states:

> All are judged on Rosh Hashanah, and their sentence is sealed on Yom Kippur; this is the statement of Rabbi Meir.
>
> Rabbi Yehudah says: "All are judged on Rosh Hashanah, and their sentence is sealed each in its own time": On Passover, the

sentence is sealed concerning grain; on *Shavuot* [shah-voo-oat];
weeks concerning fruits that grow on a tree; on the festival of
Sukkot they are judged concerning water; and mankind is
judged on Rosh Hashanah, and the sentence is sealed on
Yom Kippur.

Why is Yom Kippur considered a happy day? Because people can
assume that they did sufficient meditation on their lives during
the past year. They're hopeful that God will inscribe them in the
Book of Life on Yom Kippur and seal the judgment. The day
allows for deep reflection and self-improvement, which can be a
joyful experience. Yom Kippur frees individuals from the burden
of bad feelings, resentments, and regrets. While it's important
to note that Yom Kippur is primarily a day of atonement and
reflection, the underlying themes of forgiveness, renewal, and
spiritual cleansing contribute to a sense of joy and happiness.

Chapter **11**

On Eating, Praying, and Harmful Speech

E ating, praying, and harmful speech: It sounds like a strange combination for the subject matter of a chapter. But, in fact, just about every topic you can think of is included in the vast Sea of Talmud (a metaphor for the vastness of the Talmud's content). After selecting the topics that I wanted to cover, it occurred to me that eating, praying, and harmful speech actually do have something in common: You do all three with your mouth!

Eating — But Only if It's Kosher

In Judaism, the laws of eating are primarily defined by the Torah, but the Talmud provides the detailed framework for what's considered *kosher* (KOWE-shehr; fit/proper). *Kosher food* is food that complies with these Jewish dietary laws. Although the Torah outlines basic guidelines about clean and unclean animals, the Talmud — particularly in *Masekhta Hullin* (Mah-SEKH-tah KHOO-leen; Tractate Ordinary) — delves deeper into the specifics of what makes food permissible to eat (or not permissible).

These regulations cover everything from the slaughtering process to ensuring that foods remain free from contamination. In the following sections, you can explore the Talmudic teachings surrounding the concept of kosher food and how these ancient rules continue to influence modern Jewish dietary practices.

TECHNICAL STUFF

While I'm on the subject, I want to bust a myth: Rabbis don't bless food to make it kosher. Food is either kosher or it's not kosher, based on adherence to the laws. If you see a rabbi — or any other Jew, for that matter — saying a prayer before eating food, the person is thanking God for the food, not blessing the food or making it kosher.

Sorry, no bacon cheeseburgers

Nowhere in the Torah does a commandment explicitly forbid eating bacon cheeseburgers. But anyone who observes the kosher laws must keep three concerns in mind specifically regarding a cheeseburger:

>> A highly trained individual, known as a *shochet* (SHOW-khet), must slaughter the animal in the proper way, as outlined in the Talmud. This process includes using a surgically sharp knife and a precise, swift incision that minimizes the pain the animal feels. The *shochet* also must do a careful inspection of the animal for defects. The Talmud describes all of these requirements in detail.

>> You can't eat any pork products. All pork products are strictly forbidden according to the kosher laws.

>> Don't mix a dairy product (such as cheese) with a meat product (such as a hamburger).

THE KOSHER LAWS OF JUDAISM

The kosher laws of Judaism are a part of the 613 commandments found in the Torah. According to Jewish tradition, non-Jews don't have to follow the 613 commandments. But all of humanity must follow seven of the commandments.

These commandments, called the *Noahide* (NO-uh-khide) laws or *Sheva Mitzvot B'nei Noach* (SHEH-va MITZ-vote buh-NAY NO-akh; the Seven Laws of Noah), apply to all of humanity because the Torah considers all people descendants of Noah and his sons. In *Masekhta Sanhedrin* (Mah-SEKH-tah San-HEAD-rin; Tractate Supreme Council), the Talmud states: "The sages taught: The descendants of Noah [all of humanity] were commanded to observe seven *mitzvot* [MITZ-vote; commandments designed to connect with God]."

The laws are

- Don't worship idols.

- Don't curse God.

- Don't commit murder.

- Don't engage in sexual immorality.

- Don't steal.

- Don't eat flesh torn from a living animal.

- Establish courts of justice.

In the Jewish faith, God has chosen only Jews to observe the 613 commandments. That's why Jews are called the *chosen people*, not as a sign of seniority or distinction, but because they bear the burden of observing all 613 commandments. For more on the meaning and purpose of this burden, see *Kabbalah For Dummies* (Wiley), which I also wrote.

How was the animal slaughtered?

The Torah doesn't talk about how you must slaughter an animal to make it kosher. But the Talmud goes into enormous detail about the slaughtering process, called *shechita* (sheh–KHEE–tah). The bottom line is that you must slaughter the cow (and all other kosher animals) in the most painless way possible. (I talk about what makes an animal itself kosher in the following section.)

Although the Talmud provides a lot of detail about the accepted method, the basics deal with the knife used (which must be very sharp and perfectly sharpened — with no nicks on the edge of the blade), the place where the knife cuts the animal, and the one — and only one — extremely quick motion needed to slaughter the animal.

Is the animal itself kosher?

To be considered kosher, general rules apply to different types of animals:

>> **Mammals:** Four-legged animals must have split hooves and chew their cud. A cow has both; a pig has split hooves but doesn't chew its cud. So pigs aren't kosher. Period.

What other animals are disqualified? A partial list of non-kosher animals include rabbits, squirrels, bears, dogs, cats, camels, and horses. These animals don't fit the criteria of having split hooves and chewing their cud.

>> **Birds:** No birds of prey or scavengers are kosher, and kosher birds must not be predators.

A few places in the Torah list birds that an observant Jew is forbidden to eat. One of those places is in Leviticus 11:13-19, where the Torah states: "The following you shall abominate among the birds — they shall not be eaten, they are an abomination: the eagle, the vulture, and the black vulture, the kite, falcons of every variety, all varieties of raven, the ostrich, the nighthawk, the sea gull, hawks of every variety, the little owl, the cormorant, and the great owl, the white owl, the pelican, and the bustard, the stork, herons of every variety, the hoopoe, and the bat."

So if a bird doesn't appear in one of these lists, you can assume the bird is permissible to eat. The Talmud includes a discussion about how to identify these birds.

>> **Fish:** Fish must have both fins and scales, which disqualifies catfish and shellfish, such as clams, oysters, and snails.

>> **Reptiles and amphibians:** None of these animals are considered kosher.

>> **Insects:** Most insects aren't kosher — except for certain locusts.

Don't mix dairy with meat

In the Torah, the following line appears three times and is one of the 613 commandments:

Don't cook a kid in its mother's milk.

The Talmud explains that this command means two things:

>> You can't cook milk and meat together.

>> You can't eat a dairy product and a meat product in the same meal, even if they weren't cooked together.

Included in the kosher laws is a discussion about how long a person must wait between eating dairy and eating meat, and you can find a discussion on the topic in the Talmud. The standard practice is to wait six hours after eating meat before consuming dairy, but Jews from certain communities have adopted shorter waiting periods. After eating dairy, neither the Torah nor Talmud offer a mandatory waiting time until you can eat meat, but the general custom is to wait 30 minutes to an hour.

Consult with a qualified rabbi if you need information on kosher foods. My descriptions and explanations in this chapter don't comprise a strict guide on how to keep kosher.

Praying and Blessing

During the time of the First Temple (1000–586 BCE), the Jewish people didn't have any fixed or formal prayers. Individuals who wanted to pray did so spontaneously when they felt the need to talk to God, or to praise God, or to make requests of God.

But at a certain point, *Anshei Knesset HaGedolah* (AHN-sheya kuh-NES-et Ha-gad-OLE; the Men of the Great Assembly), a group of 120 Jewish sages, decided that they needed to compose formal prayers and blessings and integrate them into Jewish life. The process continued to evolve, and the sages finalized the basic prayer framework by the 2nd century CE, following the destruction of the Second Temple (70 CE).

Hello God, it's me

Rabbi Adin Steinsaltz, the renowned Jewish scholar (and my teacher), once said that the essence of prayer is like picking up a phone, calling God, and saying, "Hello God, it's me." Don't think of prayer like some magic formula that can get you what you ask for if you say the right words. In so many synagogues, the faithful mumble prayers at high speed, as though you only need recite the correct formula. But this practice doesn't qualify as prayer; it's magical thinking. Prayer doesn't involve saying "Abracadabra" to make something happen.

The *Anshei Knesset HaGedolah* codified Jewish prayers and blessings, and formalized and standardized the text of prayers and blessings. Their major work regarding prayer involved the construction of the *Amidah* (ah-MEE-dah; Standing), a series of blessings recited while standing, also known as

>> *Shemoneh Esrei* (sheh-MOHW-nah ES-ray; 18 blessings)

>> *hatefillah* (hah teh-FEE-lah; The Prayer)

Saying the Amidah

The sages taught that you need to say the *Amidah* three times a day — morning, afternoon, and evening. It originally consisted of 18 blessings. Under the leadership of Rabban Gamliel II, in the early 2nd century CE, a 19th blessing against heretics was added when sects such as the Sadducees (SAHD-joo-sees) began to threaten the authority of the rabbis. But it's still referred to as *Shemonah Esrei* (18 blessings).

You recite these prayers silently, standing and facing Jerusalem. Jews pray facing Jerusalem for a number of reasons:

>> Jerusalem has been the spiritual center of Judaism for a few thousand years.

>> King Solomon, during the dedication of the First Temple (circa 966 BCE), prayed for God to hear the prayers of the people who faced Jerusalem.

>> Facing Jerusalem helps Jews outside of the Holy Land maintain a connection with their ancestral homeland.

Traditionally, people outside the Holy Land face Israel when they pray, those in Israel face Jerusalem, those in Jerusalem face the Temple Mount, and those on the Temple Mount face the Holy of Holies. The *Holy of Holies* was the innermost and most sacred area of the Temple in Jerusalem. Only the High Priest could enter it, and only once a year on Yom Kippur, to perform rituals for atonement on behalf of the Jewish people.

Synagogues around the world today are built to face Jerusalem to maintain the connection with the holiness of the site.

The Shemonah Esrei, plus one

The structure of the *Amidah* (with its 18 blessings, plus 1) consists of three groupings:

Blessings of praise:

>> Praising God as God of the patriarchs

>> Acknowledging God's power

>> Sanctification of God's name

Blessings that make requests:

>> Wisdom and understanding

>> Repentance

>> Forgiveness

>> Redemption

>> Healing

>> A good year

>> Ingathering of the exiles

>> Restoration of justice

>> Against heretics

>> The righteous

>> Rebuilding of Jerusalem

>> Restoration of the Davidic dynasty

>> Acceptance of prayer

Blessings of gratitude:

>> Restoration of the Temple service

>> Thanksgiving

>> Prayer for peace

Adding blessings to the Amidah

During the morning prayers, in addition to the 19 blessings of the *Amidah*, you must offer additional blessings, which praise God and express gratitude to God for the Divine gifts you receive. Some of these blessings are

>> Who gives me the ability to distinguish day from night

>> Who did not make me a slave

>> Who gives sight to the blind

>> Who clothes the naked

- >> Who releases the bound

- >> Who straightens the bent

- >> Who spreads out the earth upon the waters

- >> Who provides for our needs

- >> Who girds Israel with strength

- >> Who crowns Israel with splendor

- >> Who gives strength to the weary

SEVEN BLESSINGS RECITED AT JEWISH WEDDINGS

At Jewish weddings, a *minyan* (MIN-yahn; a group of ten Jewish men) recites *Sheva Brachot* (SHEH-vah b'ROKH-oat; seven blessings) as part of the wedding procedure. Scholars point out that although these seven blessings probably originated centuries before the Talmud, the Talmud first records them in *Masekhta Ketubot* (Mah-sekh-tah Keh-too-BOAT; Tractate Marriage Contracts):

- Blessed are You, Lord our God, King of the universe, who creates the fruit of the vine.

- Blessed are You, Lord our God, King of the universe, who has created all things for His glory.

- Blessed are You, Lord our God, King of the universe, Creator of man.

- Blessed are You, Lord our God, King of the universe, who created man in His image, in the image [of His] likeness [He fashioned] his from and prepared for him from his own self an everlasting edifice. Blessed are You Lord, Creator of man.

- May the barren one [Jerusalem] rejoice and be happy at the ingathering of her children to her midst in joy. Blessed are You Lord, who gladdens Zion with her children.

(continued)

(continued)

- Grant abundant joy to these loving friends, as You bestowed gladness upon Your created being in the Garden of Eden of old. Blessed are You Lord, who gladdens the groom and bride.

- Blessed are You, Lord our God, King of the universe, who created joy and happiness, groom and bride, gladness, jubilation, cheer and delight, love, friendship, harmony and fellowship. Lord our God, let there speedily be heard in the cities of Judah and in the streets of Jerusalem the sound of joy and the sound of happiness, the sound of a groom and the sound of a bride, the sound of exultation of grooms from under their *chuppah* [KHOO-pah; wedding canopy], and youths from their joyous banquets. Blessed are You Lord, who gladdens the groom with the bride.

Wasteful prayers

In *Masekhta Berakhot* (Mah-sekh-tah Bihr-ah-khot; Tractate Blessings), the discussion of prayers includes the concept of *tefillat shav* (the-FEE-laht shahv; wasteful/vain prayers). The *Mishna* (MISH-nah; repetition; the core text of the Talmud) says, "One who prays about a past event utters a vain prayer." Essentially, you can't change something that already happened by praying about it.

Here are two examples of wasteful prayers, according to the sages of the Talmud:

>> Praying for the gender of a baby whose mother is already pregnant.

>> Praying that the cries of distress heard in a town don't come from your own house.

Blessings for everything (even a trip to the toilet)

Jewish law requires that observers thank God on the occasion of any pleasures they're about to experience. When it comes to eating, the blessings you recite apply specifically to the foods you're about to eat. Blessings are moments of consciousness. The more specific you are in your blessing, the more conscious you can be about what you're receiving.

Before eating

The first part of each blessing is "Blessed are you, Lord our God, King of the Universe. . ."

Here are blessings to be recited before eating:

>> *Hamotzi* (ha moe-tzee; who brings forth): "Blessed are you, Lord our God, King of the Universe, who brings forth bread from the earth."

>> *Borei Pri Hagafen* (bowe-RAY pah-REE Ha GAH-fen; who creates the fruit of the vine): Blessings before drinking wine.

>> *Borei Pri H'Etz* (Bowe-RAY pah-REE ha Aytz; who creates the fruit of the tree): Blessing before eating fruit from a tree, such as an orange or an apple.

>> *Borei Pri Ha'adamah* (bowe-RAY pah-REE-hah-ah-dah-MAH; who creates the fruit of the ground): Blessing before eating something that grows in the ground, such as a potato or a carrot.

>> *Shehakol* (Sheh-ha-COLE; everything): For liquids, meat, and anything not included in the other blessings.

Blessings after eating

Observant Jews say a blessing after eating based on the line in the Torah, "When you have eaten and are satisfied, you shall bless the Lord your God for the good land which He has given you." These are the after-meal blessings:

>> *Birkat Hamazon* (BEER-khat ha-mah-ZONE; blessing of the food): Found in every standard prayer book, recited after eating bread with a meal.

>> *Berakha Me'ayn Shalosh* (Buh-RAKH-ah may-AYIN ha-LOWSH; blessing of the three): Recited after eating foods

made from the seven species mentioned in the Torah — wheat, barley, grape, fig, pomegranates, olive oil, and date honey. The blessing is made up of parts of the first three blessings of the full grace after meals.

>> **Borie Nefashot** (bow-RAY neh-fah-SHOAT; Creator of many souls): A general blessing after eating any food that doesn't require *Birkat Hamazon* or *Berakha Me'ayn Shalosh*.

Blessings of enjoyment and appreciation

The Talmud contains specific blessings of enjoyment, such as appreciating pleasant fragrances, as well as blessings of praise or thanksgiving (such as expressing gratitude, witnessing natural phenomenon, or hearing good news).

A blessing for bad news

The Talmud actually includes a blessing to say when you hear bad news. The Blessing is *Baruch Dayan haEmet* (Bh-RUKH da-YAHN Ha-em-ET; Blessed is the true Judge). The basis for this blessing comes from the teachings of Rabbi Avika and Nachum ish Gamzu (whom I talk about in Chapter 7) — everything that happens occurs because it's God's will. So when a person hears news about a death, the response is *Baruch Dayan haEmet*. With this blessing, the believer acknowledges that God is behind everything that happens.

A successful trip to the bathroom

When you go to the bathroom, you say the blessing *Asher Yatzar* (ah-SHARE yah-TZARE; who has formed). Why would someone say this blessing? Because it thanks God for the healthy functioning of the human body. Here's an English translation of that blessing:

> Blessed are You, Adonai our God, King of the Universe, Who formed man with wisdom and created within him openings and hollows. It is obvious and known in the presence of Your glorious throne that if one of them were ruptured, or if one of them were blocked, it would be impossible to exist and stand in Your Presence.

Reciting 100 blessings a day

In the Talmud, *Masekhta Menachot* (Mah-sekh-tah Meh-nah-khoat; Tractate Meal Offerings) discusses the requirement for saying 100 blessings a day. Rather than just being a silly requirement, these blessings help infuse a person's day with awareness of, knowledge of, and gratitude to God.

The all-purpose blessing

You can use one blessing almost always; known as *Sh'hechiyanu* (sheh-HEKH-ee-AH-new; that we are alive), its English translation is

> Blessed are you, Lord our God, King of the universe, who has kept us alive, sustained us, and permitted us to reach this season.

If you feel grateful for a wonderful and unique experience you're having, if you're wearing a new piece of clothing, if you're eating a seasonal fruit for the first time that year, if you're tasting a new dish of food — you might say the *Sh'hechiyanu* prayer at these moments. Basically, you're saying, "Thank you, God, for I am alive."

Harmful Speech

The mouth plays an active part in life and Jewish tradition through eating (see the section "Eating — But Only if It's Kosher," earlier in this chapter), praying (flip back to the section "Praying and Blessing," earlier in this chapter), and also harmful speech.

The school of Rabbi Yishmael (a high priest at the time of the Second Temple period, about 516 BCE–70 CE) taught: "Anyone who speaks malicious speech increases his sins to the degree that they correspond to the three cardinal transgressions of idol worship, forbidden sexual relations, and bloodshed.

"In the West, the Land of Israel, they say: 'Malicious speech kills three people. It kills the one who speaks, the one who hears the malicious speech, and the one about whom the malicious speech is said.'"

The Talmud explores the variety of ways in which you can engage in harmful speech:

>> **Lashon hara** (la-SHONE ha-RAH; evil speech): Derogatory speech about another person — even if it's true. Observant Jews consider *lashon hara* one of the most serious transgressions in Judaism, compared in severity to the three cardinal sins: murder, idolatry, and sexual immorality. You're also forbidden to listen to *lashon hara*.

>> **Rechilut** (reh-khiy-LOOT; gossip): Spreading information about others, even if that information isn't necessarily negative. The Torah explicitly prohibits this in Leviticus: "You shall not go around as a gossip monger among your people."

>> **Motzi shem ra** (MOE-tzi SHEM-rah; slander): Spreading false negative information about someone; considered worse than *lashon hara*. Judaism forbids speaking negatively about someone, even in jest.

>> **Ona'at devarim** (oh-nah-AHT Deh-vah-REEM; verbal oppression): Any speech that causes emotional pain, embarrassment, or distress to another person, which can include implying or suggesting negative things about a person. Jewish law considers this type of speech equivalent to murder.

Here are what some Talmudic rabbis have to say on the subject:

>> Rabbi Yohanan says in the name of Rabbi Yosei ben Zimra: "Anyone who speaks malicious speech is considered as though he denied the fundamental belief in God."

>> Reish Lakish says: "Anyone who speaks malicious speech increase his sins until the heavens."

>> According to Rav Hisda, Mar Ukva says: "Anyone who speaks malicious speech, it is appropriate to stone him with stones."

» Rabbi Hama, the son of Rabbi Hanina, says: "What is the meaning of that which is written, 'Death and life are in the hand of the tongue' [Proverbs 18:21]? Does the tongue have a hand? The verse comes to tell you that just as a hand can kill, so too a tongue can kill."

» Rav Sheshet said, citing Rabbi Elazar be Azarya: "Anyone who speaks slander, and anyone who accepts and believes the slander he hears, and anyone who testifies falsely about another, it is fitting to throw him to the dogs."

Chapter **12**

Breaking Taboos: The Talmud's Surprising Views on Sex

I f explicit discussions about sex make you uncomfortable, you might want to skip this chapter. The Talmud is a gutsy document, and the Talmudic sages don't get squeamish about life. In the Talmud, you can discuss any topic.

Although the rabbis discussed everything in the Talmud, they often use delicate or symbolic language to do so. For example, instead of saying "sexual intercourse," they often use the phrase "knowing one another" (echoing the biblical usage of "knowing").

In this chapter, I share some major teachings from the Talmud about sex. A good place to start is the Talmudic principle that anything that a couple wants to do sexually is permitted as long as it's consensual.

Note: I focus only on the traditional male/female marriage couple. There are, of course, many other topics discussed in the Talmud on various aspects of human sexuality, including birth control, masturbation, and homosexuality, to name a few.

Sexual Intimacy in the Talmud

According to the teachings of Judaism, sex is considered normal and natural — and contributes to a person's health and wellbeing. Jewish texts give no sense that sex is in any way dirty. The sages of the Talmud are certainly always concerned with issues of modesty, but when a married couple have sexual relations, just about anything goes.

THE HOLY LETTER: A MEDIEVAL PERSPECTIVE ON JEWISH SEXUALITY

In the 12th century, esteemed medieval biblical and Talmudic commentator Nachmanides, also known as the Ramban (not to be confused with Maimonides, the Rambam), wrote a text called *Iggeret HaKodesh* (EE-gehr-et Hah-KOE-desh; The Holy Letter) — or at least, there are historians believe he wrote it. This work, written in the form of a letter, reflects profound Jewish teachings on the sanctity of sexuality and the importance of mutual respect, emotional connection, and divine intention.

One notable passage states:

"When you and your wife are engaged in sexual union, do not behave lightheartedly and regard this act as vain, idle, or improper. Therefore, introduce her into the mood with gentle words that excite her emotion, appease her mind, and delight her with joy. Thus, you unite your mind and intention with hers. Say to her words which in part arouse in her passion, closeness, love, will, and erotic desire, and evoke in her reverence for God, piety, and modesty.

"Never impose yourself upon her nor force her. Any sexual union without an abundance of passion, love, and will is without the Divine Presence. Do not quarrel with her nor act violently whenever coitus is involved. The Talmud says, 'A lion ravishes, and then each has no shame. So acts the brute: He hits and then cohabits and has no shame.' Rather, court and attract her to you first with grace and seduction, as well as refined and gentle words, so that both your intentions be for the sake of God. Do not hurry in arousing passion. Prolong until she is ready and in a passionate mood. Approach her lovingly and passionately so that she reaches her orgasm first."

Getting sex advice from the Talmud

Here are a few instructions and warnings that the Talmud offers about sexual relations:

>> "Three things enfeeble a man's body; namely, to eat standing, to drink standing, and to have marital intercourse in a standing position."

>> "A man is forbidden to compel his wife to have marital relations. Rabbi Joshua ben Levi similarly stated: 'Whosoever compels his wife to have marital relations will have unworthy children.'"

>> "Rabbi Joshua ben Levi said: 'Whosoever knows his wife to be a God-fearing woman and does not duly visit her is called a sinner.'" (To "visit" in this case is one of the euphemisms for having sex.)

>> "Rav Hisda said: 'A man should always be careful about [honoring] his wife because blessings rest on a man's home only on account of his wife.'"

>> "Rav Yehuda said in the name of Shmuel: 'One may not marry someone without first seeing him or her, lest he or she subsequently sees something repulsive and becomes loathsome to the other.'"

>> "You must have close bodily contact during sex. This means that a husband must not treat his wife in the manner of the Persians, who perform their marital duties in their clothes. This provides support for the ruling of Rav Huna who ruled that a husband who says, 'I will not perform my marital duties unless she wears her clothes and I mine' must divorce her and give her also her *ketubah* settlement.'"

Foreplay

Rabbi Yochanan observed, "If the Torah had not been given, we could have learned modesty from the cat, honesty from the ant, chastity from the dove, and good manners from the rooster who first coaxes and then mates."

Here's an excellent example of the symbolic language that the Talmud uses to describe the foreplay between a husband and wife:

"During cohabitation, the husband will hold your pearl in one hand and the kiln in one hand. You, however, should offer them the pearl; but the kiln you should not offer them until they are tormented, and only then should you offer it to them."

Here is how Rashi explains these lines: "When your husband caresses you to arouse your desire for intercourse and holds your breasts at first to increase his passion, do not give him the place of intercourse too soon until his passion increases, and he is in pain with desire."

Control yourself

The Talmudic sages were aware of the power of the sexual urge and the need to keep it in check. The following story illustrates the point:

Once, after ransoming several women from their kidnappers, they were brought to Nahardia to stay at the home of Rabbi Amram. After ushering the women up a huge ladder into his loft, Rabbi Amram asked them to remove the ladder because it took more than ten men to lift it.

That night, while one of the women was walking about on top of the loft, Rabbi Amram caught a glimpse of her in the skylight and was overtaken by her beauty. Singlehandedly, he lifted the huge ladder, which required more than ten men to move, and he began to climb up to the loft.

Halfway up the ladder, he stopped and cried loudly, "Amram's house is on fire!"

The rabbis rushed into the house to extinguish the fire, but when they could not find any, they turned to Rabbi Amram and said, "You caused us great terror for nothing."

Rabbi Amram said, "Far better is it that you were falsely alarmed than you should be rightfully alarmed concerning Amram himself in the World to Come." He then drove the evil inclination from his person, and it went out from him in a pillar of fire. He said to his evil inclination, "I see that you are fire, but I am flesh, yet I am mightier than you."

Another story from the Talmud also illustrates the strength of the sexual urge:

Surely it has been taught: It was said of Rabbi Elazar ben Dordaya that he went to every harlot in the world. Once, on hearing that there was a certain harlot in one of the towns by the sea who accepted a purse of denarii for her hire, he took a purse of denarii and crossed seven rivers for her sake.

While he was with her, she blew forth breath and said: "As this blown breath will not return to its place, so will Elazar ben Dordaya never be received in repentance."

He thereupon went, sat between two hills and mountains, and exclaimed: "O, ye hills and mountains, plead for mercy for me!" They replied: "How shall we pray for thee? We stand in need of it ourselves, for it is said, 'For the mountains shall depart and the hills be removed!'"

So he exclaimed: "Heaven and earth, plead ye for mercy for me!" They, too, replied: "How shall we pray for thee? We stand in need of it ourselves, for it is said, 'For the heavens shall vanish away like smoke, and the earth shall wax old like a garment.'"

He then exclaimed: "Sun and moon, plead ye for mercy for me!" But they also replied: "How shall we pray for thee? We stand in need of it ourselves, for it is said, 'Then the moon shall be confounded and the sun ashamed.'"

He exclaimed: "Ye stars and constellations, plead ye for mercy for me!" Said they: "How shall we pray for thee? We stand in need of it ourselves, for it is said, 'And all the hosts of Heaven shall molder away.'"

Said he: "The matter then depends upon me alone!" Having placed his head between his knees, he wept aloud until his soul departed.

Then a heavenly voice was heard proclaiming: "Rabbi Elazar ben Dordaya is destined for the life of the World to Come!"

Rabbi [on hearing of it] wept and said: "One may acquire eternal life after many years, another in one hour!" Rabbi also said: "Penitents are not only accepted, they're even called 'Rabbi'!"

The rabbis had some advice for people who cannot control their sexual urges:

If a man sees that his evil inclination is conquering him, let him go to a place where he's unknown, wrap himself with black, and do as his heart desires. But let him not publicly profane God's name.

Size doesn't matter

The rabbis in the Talmud often have a great sense of humor. Here's a sample of humor in the sexual realm:

When Rabbi Yishmael, son of Rabbi Yosei, and Rabbi Elazar, son of Rabbi Shimon, would meet each other, it was possible for a pair of oxen to enter and fit between them, under their bellies, without touching them because of their obesity.

> A certain Roman noblewoman once said to them: "Your children aren't really your own because, due to your obesity, it's impossible that you engaged in intercourse with your wives."
>
> They said to her: "Our wives' bellies are larger than ours."
>
> She said to them: "All the more so, you couldn't have had intercourse."
>
> There are those who say that they said this to her: "'For as the man is, so is his strength' [Judges 8:21]; our sexual organs are proportionate to our bellies."
>
> There are others who say that they said to her: "Love presses the flesh." (Meaning, when you love each other, you manage.)

The *Gemara* asks, Why did they respond to her foolish question? After all, it's written: "Answer not a fool according to his folly, lest you also be like him" (Proverbs 26:4). The *Gemara* answers: They answered her in order to "not to cast aspersions on their children's lineage."

Despite the assumption that a wife has a possibly greater desire for sexual intimacy than a husband, one rabbi in the Talmud makes the following observation:

> Rabbi Shimon said: "The sexual urge of men is far more intense than that of women. Rabbi Yochanan asked, "What proof do you bring?" Rabbi Shimon replied, "Look into the marketplace and observe who is seeking the services of whom."

The Talmud also states emphatically, "A man is forbidden to compel his wife to have marital relations." Rabbi Joshua ben Levi similarly stated: "Whosoever compels his wife to have marital relations will have unworthy children."

Iggeret HaKodesh (The Holy Letter), which I discuss in the sidebar "The Holy Letter: A Medieval Perspective on Jewish Sexuality," in this chapter, talks about sex and the human body:

> Neither sex organs nor sexual intercourse are obscene, for how could God create something that contains an obscenity? God created man and woman, and all their organs and functions, with nothing obscene in them. We believe that God created nothing containing either ugliness or obscenity.

Determining sexual requirements based on occupation

According to Jewish law, a man's occupation determined the frequency of sexual intercourse! In fact, a man must seek permission of his wife before changing careers, in part for this reason.

According to an opinion in the Talmud, wives generally prefer physical intimacy more than money. And if a husband wants to change careers, his new job might have an impact on how much strength he has or how available he is for sex. Therefore, a wife has the right to reject a proposed change of jobs.

The Talmud offers some general guidelines as follows:

>> **Men of leisure:** Expected to have sex with their wives every day (if the wives want it)

>> **Laborers:** Twice a week

>> **Donkey drivers:** Once a week

>> **Camel drivers:** Once every 30 days

>> **Sailors:** Once every six months

>> **Torah scholars who are home:** Once a week

   But Torah scholars can leave their homes for two to three years without permission from their wives!

By the way, when is the ideal time for Torah scholars to fulfill their conjugal obligations? Rav Yehuda said that Shmuel said: "The appropriate time for them is from Shabbat eve to Shabbat eve," meaning on Friday nights.

Keeping the evil inclination under control

The Talmud includes a lot of discussion about the *yetzer hara* (YAY-tzair hah-RAH; evil inclination). But the evil inclination isn't always evil. The subject is more subtle than that. The *yetzer hara* takes many forms and generally has to do with temptations. One of the temptations is the sexual urge. The Talmud teaches that the greater the *yetzer hara*, the greater the sexual desire. A famous story about the *yetzer hara* includes this teaching:

> If you kill this evil inclination, the world will be destroyed because, as a result, no one will have the desire to procreate.

> The sages imprisoned the evil inclination for three days. At that time, people searched for a fresh egg throughout all Israel but couldn't find one.

> Abaye, a Babylonian sage said, "It [the *yetzer hara*] provokes Torah scholars more than it provokes anyone else."

Exploring Talmudic Perspectives on Marital Sex

The Talmud offers several guidelines and teachings related to sexual behavior between spouses, emphasizing mutual respect, love, and care.

An important part of the *ketubah* (keh-too-bah; marriage contract) that a couple enter into deals with conjugal rights. In fact, the rabbis in the Talmud have a lot to say about the sexual component of a marriage.

As stipulated in the *ketubah*, a husband has to provide his wife with sexual relations. The *ketubah* specifically states, "I will provide you food, and clothing, and necessities, and your conjugal rights according to accepted custom."

Making love: It's up to the wife

According to the Talmud, "There is the *mitzvah* [mitz-vah; a commandment designed to connect with God] of the enjoyment of conjugal rights." A husband has an obligation to have sexual intercourse with his wife regularly. It's considered a *mitzvah*. The Talmud explicitly states that "a man may not compel his wife to perform the mitzvah of sex."

Rava (a prominent Babylonian sage) goes a step farther and says, "A man is obligated to please his wife through sexual intercourse. He must engage in sexual intercourse with his wife when she so desires. This is a Jewish law." (The section "Determining sexual requirements based on occupation," earlier in this chapter, discusses the rules regarding a man's occupation and frequency of sex.)

Rabbi Yosef taught that a couple having sexual relations with each other must be naked. "He should not treat her as the Persians do, who have conjugal relations in their clothes!" In fact, if a husband insists that they keep their clothes on during sexual relations, it's grounds for divorce. (This, by the way, dispels the myth that Jews have sexual intercourse through a hole in a sheet.)

Keeping a wife happy

A poignant episode recorded in the Talmud explores the matter of a husband's need to be careful of his wife's feelings:

> It is related about Rav Rechumi, who would commonly study before Rava in Mechoza, that he was accustomed to coming back to his home every year on the eve of Yom Kippur.
>
> One day, he was particularly engrossed in the text he was studying, and so he remained in the study hall and did not go home.
>
> His wife was expecting him that day and continually said to herself: "Now he is coming, now he is coming." But in the end, he did not come. She was distressed by this, and a tear fell from her eye.
>
> At that exact moment, Rav Rechumi was sitting on the roof. The roof collapsed under him, and he died.

Rav Rechumi was punished severely for causing anguish to his wife, even inadvertently.

Dealing with a rebellious wife

The *Mishna* (Mish-nah; a compilation of Jewish oral traditions, also known as the Oral Torah), in *Mesekhta Ketubot* (meh-SEKH-tah keh-too-BOAT; Tractate Marriage Contracts), states that a woman who rebels against her husband, refusing to be sexually intimate with him, is fined by reducing the amount of money in the *ketubah* that she would receive upon divorce week by week until there's nothing left. After a year, the husband can divorce her and pay nothing. And during that year, she doesn't receive any financial support from her husband.

But what if a wife finds her husband repulsive? She can divorce him immediately. So what's considered repulsive? If he engages in abusive behavior, physical violence, insults, controlling actions, offensive odor caused by his occupation, or any behavior that violates the wife's dignity and freedom.

REMEMBER

The Talmud isn't a book of law. It's a recording of discussions about the law. You can't quote from the Talmud and assume what you say is the accepted law. In the case of the rebellious wife, however, the sages did make the parameters discussed in this section into law.

Anything goes, as long as no one gets hurt

In the Talmud, the rabbis said, "Whatever a couple wishes to do, they may do." According to Jewish law, they may have sexual intercourse in any manner that they wish. Also, a husband may kiss his wife anywhere on her body. A wife has the same right regarding her husband.

The Talmud states:

> A certain woman came before Rabbi Yehuda HaNasi and said to him, "My teacher, I set him a table, and he turned it over." [A euphemism for the wife presenting herself in the missionary position and the husband flipping her on her stomach or on all fours.]
>
> Rabbi Yehuda HaNasi said, "Any sexual position is acceptable."

The Talmud offers an allegory:

> Sex is like meat that comes from the butcher. If he wants to eat it with salt, he may eat it that way. If he wants to eat it roasted, he may eat it roasted. If he wants to eat it cooked, he may eat it cooked. If he wants to eat it boiled, he may eat it boiled.

HIDING UNDER HIS TEACHER'S BED, A RABBI TAKES NOTES

The Talmud contains a a well-known story about Rabbi Kahane hiding under his teacher, Rav's, bed. The story is self-explanatory. It confirms the Jewish attitude toward the acceptability or even the necessity of sex education. Jewish law doesn't actually permit someone to hide under a bed to see and hear a couple having sexual relations. The law *hezek re'iyah* (he-ZEK reh-ee-YAH; damage by seeing) prohibits visual intrusion into others' private spaces. But the story is exaggerated to make the point that the sages endorse sex ed:

> Rabbi Akiva said to Ben Azzai: "I once entered the bathroom after my teacher Rabbi Yehoshua, and I learned three things from observing his behavior: I learned that you shouldn't defecate while facing east and west, but rather while facing north and south; you shouldn't uncover yourself while standing, but while sitting, in the interest of modesty; and you shouldn't wipe with your right hand, but with your left."
>
> Ben Azzai, a student of Rabbi Akiva, said to him: "Did you dare to take such liberties with your teacher?"
>
> He replied: "It is Torah, and I must learn."
>
> Later, Ben Azzai said to Rabbi Yehuda: "I once entered a bathroom after Rabbi Akiva, and I learned three things from observing his behavior: I learned that you shouldn't defecate while facing east and west, but rather while facing north and south; you shouldn't uncover yourself while standing, but while sitting; and you shouldn't wipe with your right hand, but with your left."

> Rabbi Yehuda said to him: "Did you dare to take such liberties with your teacher?"
>
> He replied: "It is Torah, and I must learn."

On a similar note, the *Gemara* then relates that

> Rav Kahana entered and lay beneath Rav's bed. He heard Rav chatting and laughing with his wife and having relations with her. Rav Kahana said to Rav: "The mouth of Abba [Rav] is like one who has never eaten a cooked dish [meaning his behavior was lustful]."
>
> Rav said to him: "Kahana, you're here? Leave; this is an undesirable behavior." Rav Kahana said to him: "It is Torah, and I must learn."

Chapter **13**

Litigating the Talmudic Way

I n this chapter, I describe Jewish civil and criminal law, as well as the court system as described in the Talmud.

Jewish law includes a principle called *dina malkhuta dina* (dee-nah mal-khoot-ah dee-nah) which means "the law of the land is the law." In other words, Jewish law states that Jews should follow the laws of the country in which they reside. But Jewish tradition, as recorded in the Talmud, has its own slant on criminal and civil law and the court system.

Jewish Courts

The Talmud describes three main types of courts:

» **Beit Din** (Bait Din; House of Justice): Consisting of three judges, these courts deal with civil and monetary cases in smaller communities.

- >> **Lesser *Sanhedrin*** (san-head-rihn; legislative assembly): Comprising 23 members, these courts existed in towns that had populations of at least 120 households. They handled cases, for example, involving capital punishment. No lesser *Sanhedrins* exist today.

- >> **Great *Sanhedrin*:** The highest court, which had 71 members, convened daily in the Temple from 516 BCE to 425 CE. After the destruction of the Temple in 70 CE it moved to Yavne and then to various places. It had jurisdiction over national and public matters and acted as a Court of Appeals. There is no Sanhedrin functioning today.

The Sanhedrin tractate serves as the primary source in the Talmud for understanding the structure and function of these ancient Jewish courts.

The word *Sanhedrin* is derived from the Greek term *synedrion*, which means "assembly" or "council."

The earliest references to the three-judge court (*Beit Din*), the lesser *Sanhedrin*, and the Great *Sanhedrin* appear in the opening words of the first *Mishna* (mish-na; the systematic compilation of Jewish legal traditions, completed in the early 3rd century CE by Rabbi Judah ha-Nasi.) of *Masekhta* (mah-SEKH-tah; Tractate) *Sanhedrin* in the Talmud. The first line reads:

> Cases concerning monetary law are adjudicated by three judges. Cases concerning robbery and personal injury are adjudicated by three judges.

The Beit Din

A three-person *Beit Din*, which convenes only as necessary, has a number of important functions:

- >> Handles general civil cases, including monetary disputes and property issues

- >> Has the authority to impose fines

- >> Often functions as an arbitrator to help resolve disputes in an amicable fashion

- >> Administers divorce proceedings and grants divorces

A *Beit Din* doesn't have any authority over capital cases.

Beis Din exist today in various forms across Jewish communities worldwide. These rabbinical courts serve several important functions in modern Jewish life:

Ancient Jewish tradition as recorded in the Talmud set the number of Judges at three to make sure that every decision would have a majority. Usually, one rabbi participates among the three-person panel of judges.

The qualifications to sit on a beit din are extensive and cover various aspects of character, knowledge, and personal qualities. They are discussed in the Talmud as well as in the *Code of Jewish Law*, and Maimonides *Mishneh Torah*. It is understood that a local Beit Din cannot always find candidates who have all of these requirements. It's important to note that while these are the ideal qualifications, the specific requirements may vary depending on the type of case and the community. These qualifications also apply to people who sit on the lesser *Sanhedrin* and the Great *Sanhedrin*. Here are the ideal qualifications:

>> Distinguished in Torah knowledge

>> Learned in Jewish law

>> Versed in other branches of learning, including medicine, mathematics, astronomy, and even knowledge of idolatry and occult practices

>> The ability to adapt Torah law to various situations

>> Wisdom and understanding

>> Humility

>> Fear of God

>> Indifference to monetary gain

>> Love of truth

>> Love of fellow man

>> A good reputation

>> Patience and respect for others

>> Mature age (preferably at least 40 years old)

- >> Good appearance
- >> Ability to express views clearly
- >> Conversant in multiple languages
- >> Free from suspicion regarding conduct
- >> Not involved in gambling, usury, or other disqualifying activities
- >> Preferably not childless

In some cases, particularly for smaller communities, qualified laymen who meet certain standards of observance and knowledge may serve on a Beis Din.

The disputing parties or the community often choose the judges, with an emphasis put on fairness and expertise. Both parties are treated equally, with no lawyers involved. The judges investigate and deliberate before voting on a decision.

What happens if one of the parties doesn't follow the dictates and decisions of the court or refuses to appear as summoned. A *Beit Din* often issues a public declaration of contempt in such cases. This declaration can lead to social and religious sanctions, such as being denied honors in the synagogue or various social interactions within the community.

RELEASE FROM A VOW

Once, I took part in a Beit Din. I was one of the three judges. Someone vowed that he would never charge money for lectures on the Holocaust. He gave a lot of lectures on different subjects, and he was paid for these lectures. But for lectures on the Holocaust, he made an exception. After a few years, he noticed that he didn't receive many invitations to give lectures on subjects other than the Holocaust. He asked that a *Beit Din* void his vow to not charge for lectures on the Holocaust because he found that he needed the money for his livelihood. The Beit Din released him from his vow.

The lesser Sanhedrin

Every city in ancient Israel that had a minimum count of 120 households had a lesser *Sanhedrin* made up of 23 members. The lesser *Sanhedrin* courts were responsible for

>> Local legal matters, similar to a municipal court in the United States today.

>> Local criminal cases that were deemed unnecessary for the Great *Sanhedrin* to handle.

The division of cases was generally predetermined by law and tradition. However, if a lesser *Sanhedrin* failed to reach a conclusive verdict, the case would be referred to the greater Sanhedrin. (See the following section for information about the Great *Sanhedrin*, which dealt with complex cases.)

>> Some local capital cases.

>> Any community issues and disputes.

>> Religious matters that affected the community.

>> Legal rulings were consistent with Jewish law across different regions.

Candidates for membership of a lesser *Sanhedrin* had to meet certain requirements:

>> **Wisdom and piety:**

>> **Moral and physical blamelessness:** So that they can command respect from the people

>> **Leadership experience:** Especially experience as a judge and/or community leader

>> The capacity to oversee legal and religious matters

>> **Learning:** In both divine law and secular sciences, such as medicine and astronomy

>> **Language proficiency:** In several languages so that they don't have to depend on interpreters

>> **Proof of lineage:** As a priest, as well as either a Levite or an Israelite

The Great Sanhedrin

The Great *Sanhedrin* functioned as the Supreme Court of ancient Israel. The Great *Sanhedrin* had similar requirements for candidacy to those of the lesser *Sanhedrin* (see the preceding section); but the Great *Sanhedrin*'s 71-member court had more responsibilities. These responsibilities included

>> Overseeing Temple rituals

>> Overseeing religious law

>> Preparing Torah scrolls for the current king of the Israelites and the Temple. It's important to note that the establishment of the monarchy was seen as a rejection of God's direct rule over Israel. God warned the Israelites through Samuel about the potential dangers of having a human king but ultimately granted their request.

>> Acting as supreme court for criminal matters, including most capital crimes and cases involving false prophets

>> Enacting laws and interpreting the Oral Torah

>> Making decisions that all religious courts had to abide by

>> Declaring war

>> Appointing kings and high priests

>> Regulating the calendar

>> Supervising local lesser *Sanhedrins*

>> Hearing and deciding appeals

>> Making resolutions on ritual laws

>> Managing national crises

>> Managing international relations

>> Overseeing religious education

Understanding Jewish Law

The Ten Commandments (which God gave to Moses on Mount Sinai, according to the Torah, the Five Books of Moses) provide the foundation of all Jewish teachings and laws. When someone breaks one of the Ten Commandments between humans (versus against God), the Jewish courts usually identify the crime as either the breaking of a civil law or a criminal law. The Talmud is profoundly concerned with both.

The Ten Commandments

The Ten Commandments continue to hold timeless significance. They serve as a moral and spiritual guide, shaping the ethical beliefs of Judaism.

Some of the commandments deal with the relationship between humans and God, and some deal with behavior among people. Of course, commandments that focus on how people treat each other always have God implied within them. In Judaism, everything ultimately derives from God.

The Commandments are:

1. I am the Lord your God who brought you out of Egypt.

2. You shall have no other gods before Me; do not make idols.

3. Don't take the name of the Lord in vain.

4. Remember the Sabbath day to keep it holy.

5. Honor your father and mother.

6. You shall not murder.

7. You shall not commit adultery.

8. You shall not steal.

9. You shall not bear false witness against your neighbor.

10. You shall not covet anything that belongs to your neighbor.

Jewish civil laws

Jewish civil laws are concerned with issues such as the following:

>> **Social welfare:** Obligations to provide for children, educate them, and train them for a profession.

>> **Torts:** A *tort* is a wrongful act that causes injury to another person or their property. Jewish law requires compensation for damages caused by a person or their property (interpreting the phrase "an eye for an eye," from Torah as financial compensation). In the section "'An eye for an eye?' Not literally!" later in this chapter, you can examine the Talmudic interpretation of this phrase.

>> **Family law:** Regulations concerning marriage and divorce.

>> **Financial law:** Laws that deal with contracts and partnerships.

>> **Inheritance:** The fate of an estate.

>> **Agency:** The relationship between an agent (someone doing something on the behest of someone else) and who they represent.

>> **Property rights:** Rules on property claims and ownership.

>> **Labor relations:** Regulations on employment terms, rents, and leases.

>> **Bailment:** *Bailment* involves taking possession of something without taking ownership of it. These rules govern the safekeeping of another's property.

>> **Contractual obligations:** Legal procedures for forming and enforcing contracts.

Jewish criminal laws

Many rules and principles, all of which appear in the Talmud, govern crimes. Some of them are

>> **Equality before the law:** The law treats all parties equally, without preference based on status or wealth.

>> **Intent:** The legal term in secular law is *mens rea* (mens ray-ah), which is Latin for "guilty mind." In Jewish law, you must figure out intent to determine guilt; it distinguishes between intentional and unintentional transgressions.

>> **Bias toward acquittal:** The system favors acquittal in order to avoid wrongful convictions, with rigorous standards for evidence and testimony.

» **Witness reliability:** The Jewish courts must thoroughly examine witnesses, and the witnesses' testimonies must be consistent; any contradiction can invalidate their evidence.

» **Daytime trials:** The Jewish courts must conduct trials during the day to help ensure transparency and fairness. The Mishnah states: "In capital cases, they hold the trial during the daytime and the verdict must also be reached during the daytime." Daylight allows for better observation of witnesses, evidence, and the demeanor of those involved in the proceedings. Conducting trials during daylight hours symbolizes the pursuit of truth and transparency in the judicial process. Night trials might lead to rushed judgments due to fatigue or a desire to conclude quickly. Daylight proceedings reduce the risk of mistakes that might occur in dimly lit conditions. Daytime trials are more accessible to the public, promoting openness and community involvement. This ensured that life-and-death decisions were made with utmost care and consideration.

» **No self-incrimination:** The Jewish courts can't admit confessions into evidence; they consider only witness testimony as valid evidence.

» **Judicial integrity:** Judges must be impartial, knowledgeable, and of good character, ensuring fair trials.

» **Capital punishment:** Four types of sanctioned execution exist — stoning, burning, beheading, and strangling. But the Jewish courts rarely convicted someone of a capital crime because of stringent requirements. (See the section "Capital punishment: No way (almost)!" later in this chapter.)

Justice in the Talmud

The Talmudic system of justice is so thorough that it provides us with precise punishments to fit each crime. The punishments are not always given — in fact when it comes to capital crimes the punishments are almost never given — but looking closely at them gives one a sense of the severity of the crime as perceived by the sages.

Types of civil damages

At one time, the Talmud included an extremely large *masekhta* (tractate) of the Talmud called *Nezikin* (Neh-zee-keen; Damages). It was so large that the sages divided it into three parts, with each part focusing on a different aspect of civil law:

>> *Bava Kamma* (Bah-vah kah-mah; The First Gate): Deals primarily with damages and the responsibilities that individuals have when their property or actions cause harm to others.

>> *Bava Metzia* (bah-vah-met-tziah; The Middle Gate): Addresses disputes related to monetary matters, employment agreements, and the recovery of lost objects.

>> *Bava Batra* (bah-vah baht-rah; The Last Gate): Focuses on partnerships, inheritance, and loans.

Together, these tractates form the foundation of Jewish civil law, emphasizing ethical obligations and justice in interpersonal dealings.

Another *masekhta* in the Talmud, *Sanhedrin* (legislative assembly) focuses on discussions about criminal law. A related discussion appears in *Masekhta Makkot* (mah-coat; lashes), which primarily deals with topics such as colluding witnesses and punishments, including lashes. (The singular form of *makkot* is *makka* [mah-kah].)

The Talmud delves deeply into various types of *nezikin*, exploring the complexities of human responsibility and accountability. These practical categories often bear symbolic names, reflecting the underlying principles of justice and fairness. By analyzing specific scenarios, the Talmud sets out guidelines for resolving disputes and ensuring ethical conduct in society. Among the most notable categories of damages are

>> **Horn:** Damage caused by an ox or another animal attacking an animal or a person

>> **Pit:** Harm resulting from an uncovered pit that causes injury

>> **Fire:** Damage caused by fire spreading to another's property

>> **Theft:** Compensation required for stolen goods

>> **Assault:** Damages for personal injury, including medical expenses and loss of income

>> **False witness:** Liability for damages caused by false testimony

>> **Property damage:** Compensation for damage to another's property

>> **Negligence:** Liability for harm caused by negligent actions or inactions

Punishments for non-capital crimes

The punishments as stated in the Talmud for non-capital crimes include:

Crime	Punishment
Theft	Returning the stolen item and paying a fine, often double the value of the stolen article
Assault	Compensation for medical expenses, loss of income, pain, and humiliation
Perjury	The same penalty that would have been imposed on the accused if convicted
False weights and measures (This includes: Using inaccurate scales or balances, employing different sized weights for buying and selling, or possessing imprecise measuring devices.)	Fines and public shaming
Damage to property	Compensation for the damage caused
Slander	Fines and public apology

Crime	Punishment
Breaking an oath	Atonement and sometimes monetary compensation
Injury to animals	Compensation to the owner for loss or harm
Usury (charging interest on loans)	Returning the interest charged, with possible additional fines
Eating non-kosher food	Typically requires ritual atonement, rather than a legal penalty

Capital punishment: No way (almost)!

The Torah indicates that people who commit certain acts or crimes should receive capital punishment. In other words, they should be executed.

In reality, however, in Talmudic times (and later, as well), capital punishment was almost never done. Jewish law and belief put such a strong value on the sacredness of human life that the sages enacted requirements that make convicting someone of a capital crime almost impossible:

>> You must have two qualified witnesses who actually saw the crime.

>> Those witnesses needed to warn the perpetrator of the severity and illegality of that act before it took place.

>> In capital cases, a lesser *Sanhedrin* (judicial assembly) of 23 judges must have a majority vote.

The sages so opposed capital punishment that the *Mishna* (the written collection of Jewish oral traditions, also known as the Oral Torah; it was compiled and redacted by Rabbi Yehudah ha-Nasi in the early 3rd century CE.) itself states, "If a *Sanhedrin* executed one person in 70 years, it was called 'bloodthirsty.'"

But according to Jewish law, a murderer who kills someone without witnesses would not necessarily go free. There were other ways to deal with suspected murderers when direct evidence was lacking. For example, the court could imprison the suspect indefinitely.

Talmudic law says that if all 23 judges in a lesser *Sanhedrin* vote guilty, the person on trial is acquitted. A unanimous guilty decision implied, according to the sages, that the accused couldn't sufficiently defend themselves. At least one judge needed to have some doubt that the accused was guilty.

Here are some capital crimes and their stated punishment, as described in the Talmud:

Crime	Punishment
Murder	Decapitation
Idolatry	Stoning
Adultery	Strangulation
Kidnapping	Strangulation
Blasphemy	Stoning
Sabbath violation	Stoning
False testimony in capital cases	Potentially punishable by the same penalty intended for the accused
Incest	Either burning or strangulation, depending on the relationship involved
Bestiality	Stoning
Rebellious son	Stoning

"An eye for an eye"? Not literally!

I'm pleased to have this opportunity to clarify the meaning of the famous words in the Torah "an eye for an eye, and a tooth for a tooth." Many people misunderstand this quote, and I want to clear things up.

NO SUCH THINGS AS A LAWYER

One day, I had an opportunity to introduce my father to my teacher, Rabbi Adin Steinsaltz. My father, who was always filled with questions, said to Rabbi Steinsaltz, "According to Jewish law, is an attorney allowed to lie for his client?" Rabbi Steinsaltz replied, "According to Jewish law, there is no such thing as a lawyer." The parties involved present their cases before the judges, and the judges question each of the parties. The judges then make their decision.

Jewish law doesn't take this phrase literally at all. I can understand people's confusion because, after all, it says what it says — and that's what it says. But anyone who knows how the great sages read the Torah know that you can never read a verse and assume that the literal meaning is what it's all about. Jews simply don't look at the Torah only literally. In this case, the principle regarding injuries and Jewish law is the requirement of monetary compensation.

There's a famous saying regarding Talmud study: "He who believes that the ox in the Talmud is a real ox has not even begun to understand the Talmud." Don't take Torah verses at face value because they often contain deeper moral, ethical, or legal lessons beyond their literal meaning.

The sages state that you shouldn't take "an eye for an eye" literally for several reasons. The sages discuss these reasons in *Masekhta Bava Kamma* (Tractate The First Gate):

>> **Avoiding inherent inequality:** If a blind person injures another person who isn't blind, they couldn't fulfill "an eye for an eye" in an equal way. Rabbi Shimon argues that if taken literally, the principle could lead to unjust outcomes. What if one person who has a larger eye injures someone who has a smaller eye?

>> **Turning to other verses:** The Talmud points out that other biblical verses discuss damages in terms of monetary compensation. For example, Exodus states, "This is the law when two men fight, and one hits the other with a stone or with his fist. If the victim does not die but rather becomes bedridden and then gets up and can walk under his own

power, the one who struck him shall be acquitted. Still, he must pay for the victim's loss of work and must provide for his complete cure."

>> **Meditating on the act:** In the Talmud, the sages argue that the language of "an eye for an eye" should inspire us not to retaliate literally, but rather to meditate on the seriousness of the injurious act.

>> **Looking to history:** No historical record or evidence exists that anyone enacted this kind of literal retaliation in Jewish life. The long-standing Jewish tradition involves seeking justice through compensation, not physical harm; fairness, rather than revenge.

Following the Laws

Laws play a crucial role in maintaining order within a community, guiding ethical behavior, and ensuring fairness. One way to understand the significance of following laws, and the diligence that is practiced in doing so, is by examining a specific example: the responsibility of returning lost objects.

The section of the Talmud called *Bava Metzia* (The Middle Gate) deals, among other things, with an aspect of Jewish civil law related to lost and found objects. In any community, you have to deal with the issues that relate to lost objects. If you find a lost object, what do you do with it? What's your responsibility? Simply put: You have a responsibility to try to locate the owner of a lost object if you find one.

Finding lost objects

In the following, I'll first provide you with a Mishna that deals with an aspect of the topic. Then, I'll repeat that same text but with a commentary (by Rabbi Adin Steinsaltz) that will help us to understand what the Mishna is actually saying. After that, I'll discuss the implications of the Mishna and tell you how this Mishna is discussed in the Talmud. Finally, I'll apply the discussion to real life.

Turning to the Mishna on lost objects

Bava Metzia contains the following *Mishna*:

> Found scrolls, he reads them once in 30 days. And if he doesn't know to read, he rolls them. But he shall not study in them for the first time. And another shall not read with him.
>
> Found a garment, he shakes it once in 30 days, and he spreads it for its sake, but not for his prestige.
>
> Silver vessels or copper vessels, may use them for their sake but not erode them. Gold vessels or glass vessels, he may not touch them until Elijah will come. (Elijah heralds the Messiah.)
>
> Found a sack, or a basket, or any item that's not his manner to take he doesn't take.

Rabbi Yehuda HaNasi wrote the *Mishna* in as concise a way as possible. It contains few complete sentences. A commentator such as Rashi or Rabbi Steinsaltz can step in and clarify the meaning of what the *Mishna* says. As a new student of the Talmud, you might make out the meaning of a few phrases, but you need a student who has studied the Talmud for a sufficient amount of time to fill in the blanks in order to get a better understanding of the text.

Now, here's the same *Mishna*, but this time including the commentary of Rabbi Steinsaltz:

> If one found scrolls, he reads them once in 30 days in order to ventilate them and prevent mold. And if he doesn't know how to read, he rolls and unrolls them in order to ventilate them. But he shall not study passages in them for the first time because he would leave the scroll exposed to the air for a lengthy period, thereby causing damage. And another person shall not read the scroll with him because each might pull it closer to improve his vantage point, which could cause the scroll to tear.
>
> If one found a garment, he shakes it once in 30 days, and he spreads it out for its sake, to ventilate it; but he may not use it as a decoration for his own prestige.
>
> If one found silver vessels or copper vessels, he may use them for their own sake to prevent tarnish and rust, but he may not

use them to the extent that he will erode them. If he finds gold vessels or glass vessels, which aren't ruined by neglect, he may not touch them until Elijah will come and identify the owner.

If a person found a sack, or a basket, or any other item that it's not his typical manner to take and carry because it's beneath his dignity, he shall not take it because one need not demean himself in order to return a lost item.

Getting clarification with the *Gemara*

The *Gemara* (geh-mah-ra; a component of the Talmud, providing commentary and analysis on the Mishnah) that follows the *Mishna* explores the concepts in the *Mishna* and expands upon them. Here are some of the points made in the *Gemara*:

>> If you find an inexpensive mass-produced item (not a handwritten scroll), you can sell the item. If you find the owner, you can give the money from the sale to them.

>> If you borrow a Torah scroll or lease it (or any other item that you rent), you must not lend or rent it to someone else. And don't consider that a third party might need a Torah: If you found it, you must hold onto it.

>> If you find a lost object, you must learn the proper way to take care of it. The *Gemara* goes into detail about how to best take care of a Torah scroll. Whatever you find that seems lost, you must figure out how to take good care of it until you find the owner.

>> If two people are reading from the same Torah scroll at the same time, it might get ripped.

>> If you want to use the Torah scroll for yourself, don't study a passage that you never studied before. Because of the excitement of the reader or the frequency with which the reader studies the passage, the scroll could get damaged.

>> Take care of items such as silver, copper, and wooden vessels.

>> A person can be exempt from holding a lost object if having that object is contrary to the social status of the finder.

For example, imagine that a distinguished and elderly rabbi finds a pile of magazines bound by some cord. He thinks perhaps someone dropped the pile of periodicals inadvertently. He then notices that the magazines have naked women on their covers. It's surely not appropriate for him to carry these publications. The person who found them doesn't have to return them to the owner.

The *Gemara* also offers a few teachings not directly related to the text. The *Gemara* is frequently saying things such as "While we're on the subject" or "Now that we've read a teaching from a specific sage, this reminds me that. . ." The Talmud was written in the language of thought, as Rabbi Steinsaltz put it. The text often goes in another direction entirely and then comes back to the original subject.

Seeking advice from the Talmud

If you find what seems to be a lost object, the Talmud asks that you ask yourself, "Would the owner of the lost object feel despair and give up hope of ever finding it?" If you think that the owner is still holding on to hope of finding the object, you must continue to try to locate the one who lost the item. For example, if I find a 99-cent pen in the middle of the highway, I think I can assume that the owner has lost all hope or doesn't care much about the pen, and therefore I can give up efforts to locate the owner. On the other hand, if I find a gold bracelet, the rightful owner likely wants it back and won't give up on it.

The finder's responsibility includes

>> Making a public proclamation and telling neighbors

>> Announcing in study halls and synagogues

>> Taking care of the item

>> Selling perishable goods found and setting aside the money earned to give to the owner if they appear

So, in essence:

>> **From the Torah:** Returning lost objects has a Torah basis; it instructs people not to ignore lost items, but to return them to their owners.

- >> **Identification marks:** The Talmud stresses that if an item has distinctive aspects, the finder has to announce repeatedly the item's recovery and its unique marks until they locate the owner.

- >> **Finder's responsibility:** The finder must keep the item safe and can't use it for personal benefit. They should make reasonable efforts to return it, including public announcements or posting notices.

- >> **Ownership:** The Talmud explores when you can assume that an object no longer belongs to its owner.

- >> **Psychological factors:** The concept of *ye'ush* (yeh-oosh; despair) applies; if an owner gives up hope of recovering their lost item, you can consider it *hefker* (hef-kehr; ownerless) and keep it.

Taking an oath is a big deal — I swear!

In the Talmud, an oath, known as a *shevu'ah* (sheh-voo-ah), is a solemn declaration that invokes God as a witness to the truth of a statement or the fulfillment of a promise. In the Talmud, the sages consider oaths serious and binding: After all, God is serving as the witness.

APPLYING THE RULES OF FOUND OBJECTS

My wife and I were in the local park one evening at a time when no one else was there. We noticed a woman's sweater left on a bench. We wondered what to do. There was no "lost and found" in the park. My wife wondered if we should take the sweater and hold on to it for safekeeping, planning to go back the next morning to look for the owner. I suggested that the owner of the sweater might come back that evening to look for the sweater at the place where they left it. Had we taken the sweater with us, the person might think that the sweater was lost forever. We decided to leave the sweater where it was with the hope that it would still be there if the owner came looking for it.

In a Jewish court, a judge or a court official administers an oath. Some oaths refer to an event that happened in the past, affirming a person's past actions. An oath can also declare a commitment to an event in the future. Many Jews have the practice of saying, "*B'li neder*" (buh-lee neh-dehr; without a vow) when they promise to do something but don't want anyone to consider the promise an oath.

A claimant often use oaths to resolve claims when he or she doesn't have enough evidence.

A false oath has serious spiritual repercussions. But, if necessary, a local Jewish court of three people (a *Beit Din*, which I talk about earlier in this chapter) can release a person who took an oath if the case meets certain requirements.

The Talmud teaches that, in a Jewish court, the person taking an oath must

>> Stand

>> Hold a Torah scroll or another sacred object

>> Take the oath in the name of God

>> Articulate the vow clearly that they will swear truthfully

>> Speak the oath orally

The Part of Tens

Uncover ten essential Talmudic concepts that every learner should know.

Get to know ten influential sages who helped shape the Talmud.

Find recommendations for further reading to deepen your Talmudic study.

IN THIS CHAPTER

» Understanding the role of concepts
to the Talmud

» Getting to know some of the most
important principles for
understanding the Talmud

Chapter **14**

Grasping Ten Important Talmudic Concepts

I n the study of the Talmud, concepts serve as the building blocks for understanding the complex layers of Jewish law, ethics, and philosophy. These concepts reflect deep discussions, debates, and interpretations that have been developed over centuries by scholars and rabbis. They provide insight into the moral, legal, and spiritual aspects of Jewish life.

Although the many Talmudic concepts could fill a book (and have filled many of them, in fact), this chapter offers a sampling of ten of them.

One of the stumbling blocks to the study of the Talmud is that there are literally thousands of terms and concepts that are discussed but not always defined. In order to study the Talmud effectively it is best to know the definition of these concepts before studying the text. This could, of course, take a lifetime. But don't despair! You will certainly be able to study the Talmud with the help of Rabbi Adin Steinsaltz who devoted his life to writing and publishing tools to aid in the study of the Talmud.

Two major tools here that will help both the advanced student as well as beginners: *Reference Guide to the Talmud* by Rabbi Adin Steinsaltz (nearly half of its pages are devoted to Talmudic concepts) and *The Essential Talmud* by Rabbi Adin Steinsaltz (this book describes, in broad strokes, many of the categories of Talmudic Concepts found in the Talmud.)

For this chapter, I have gone through the Rabbi's reference guide, and I have selected ten concepts that I feel are among the more important ones in Jewish life.

Eilu v'Eilu

Eilu v'eilu (AY-loo vuh-AY-loo; *these and those) are the words of the living God.* This principle indicates that multiple interpretations are valid in Jewish law, even if they seem to contradict each other. An example of this is the well-known Talmudic debate between Shammai and Hillel about how to light Chanukah candles (see Chapter 7), where the anonymous voice of the Talmud believes that both sides expressed truth, even though the law generally followed Bet Hillel. (In addition to thousands of quotations identified by whose words they are, there is also an anonymous voice of the Talmud itself and it is called Stam (stahm; anonymous.) The basic principle here suggests that multiple interpretations can be valid within the framework of Jewish law. This concept recognizes that different perspectives can each contain elements of truth, even if they seem contradictory. Multiple interpretations can be valid within the framework of Jewish law.

Siyag L'Torah

Siyag l'Torah (see-YAHG luh-TOE-rah; *a fence around the Torah*) is the rabbinic practice of issuing additional laws to prevent people from violating the Torah's commandments by mistake.

The *fences* are protective measures to make sure people follow the commandments by keeping observant Jews away from possible transgressions. This teaching came from the Great Assembly, the ancient group of sages who made decisions of communal importance. and is an essential part of Jewish law and tradition.

The Great Assembly, known in Hebrew as *Anshei Knesset HaGedolah* (AHN-shay K'NES-eht Hah-Geh-DOLE-ah), which translates to "Men of the Great Assembly," was a significant institution in Jewish history that played a crucial role in shaping Jewish law and tradition during the early Second Temple period. The Great Assembly consisted of 120 members, including scribes, sages, and prophets. The Great Assembly served several important functions in Jewish history:

>> Transmission of Torah: They formed a link in the chain of Torah transmission, receiving it from the Prophets and passing it on to subsequent generations.

>> Canonization: They are credited with redacting and canonizing several books of the Hebrew Bible.

>> Liturgical Contributions: They formalized the text of many prayers and blessings.

>> Educational Reforms: The Great Assembly initiated a democratization of Jewish education, making Torah knowledge accessible to all.

An example of *siyag l'Torah* is the rabbinic prohibition against handling money on Shabbat. The Torah prohibits work on Shabbat. To prevent people from inadvertently performing work-related activities, the rabbis extended this prohibition to include handling money, which could lead to business transactions. This additional rule acts as a fence to protect the sanctity of Shabbat by keeping people away from activities that might lead to violating the laws and commandments.

Makhloket

Students of the Talmud often see *makhloket* (mahkh-LOW-khet) meaning division, dispute, or disagreement, between different opinions, especially regarding Jewish teachings and laws, as a constructive element when done *l'shem shamayim* (luh-SHAME shah-MAH-yeem; for the sake of Heaven), meaning the disagreement aims to uncover truth and enhance understanding. The Talmud values such debates, and they contribute to the depth of Jewish legal discourse.

D'oraita and D'rabanan

D'oraita (duh-or-AIY-tah), meaning law from the Torah, are laws and commandments that come from the Written Torah (*d'oraita* is Aramaic for "from the Torah"). These laws and commandments are more authoritative than rabbinic laws, known as *D'rabbanan* (duh-rah-bun-AHN; from the rabbis). Laws from the Torah take precedence when the two are in conflict. *D'rabbanan* are obligatory, but they don't have the status that Torah laws (*d'oraita*) do.

An example of *d'oraita* is the commandment to observe the Sabbath, which is explicitly stated in the Torah. In contrast, an example of *d'rabbanan* is the prohibition against eating chicken with milk. Although the Torah prohibits cooking a "kid in its mother's milk," the extension of this rule to include poultry is a rabbinic enactment. (See Chapter 11 for more about cooking a "kid in its mother's milk.")

Tza'ar Ba'alei Chayim

Tza'ar ba'alei chayim (tzah-ARE bah-ah-LAY khah-YEEM; the suffering of living creatures) outlines a fundamental Jewish ethical principle that prohibits causing unnecessary pain to animals. It's not a specific commandment from the Torah. It comes from various Torah verses and rabbinic interpretations stressing compassion for animals in Jewish law.

Kal Vakhomer

Kal vakhomer (kal vah-KHOH-mare; light and heavy) is one of the 13 hermeneutical rules used to interpret the Torah. It refers to deriving one point of view from another, a Talmudic principle used by the sages as part of their legal reasoning. It states that a rabbinic scholar who consults the Talmud can draw a conclusion about a more significant case based on what was already accepted in a lesser case. Basically, if a rule applies in a less important situation, it should apply in a more important one. It's similar to the English expression "all the more so."

For example, when God tells Moses to speak to Pharaoh, Moses argues using a *kal vakhomer*: If the Israelites, who would benefit from the message of Moses, didn't listen to him, then surely Pharaoh, who wouldn't benefit, would be even less likely to listen. Kal vakhomer is widely used throughout the Talmud and continues to be an essential tool in Jewish legal reasoning and Torah interpretation.

Pikuach Nefesh

Pikuach nefesh (peh-KOO-akh NEH-fehsh; "saving a life") means that saving a life trumps almost all other commandments. A fundamental principle in Jewish law says that saving a human life is more important than almost all other laws, so observant Jews can violate most laws, if they need to, in order to preserve life. The sanctity and value of human life is primary. Exceptions to this allowance include prohibitions against murder, idolatry, and certain sexual transgressions.

In some ways the concept of saving a life is related to the notion of a pious fool, known in Hebrew and explained in the Talmud as as *chassid shoteh* (KHAH-sid SHOW-teh; a pious fool). A pious fool refers to someone whose misguided or excessive piety leads to harmful or foolish actions. The most well-known example of a pious fool in the Talmud is that of a man who sees a woman drowning but refuses to save her because he believes it would be immodest to look at or touch her. A related example, also in the Talmud, is someone who removes their *tefillin* (teh-FIL-in), which are phylacteries, small leather boxes containing Hebrew texts worn by Jews at morning prayer as a reminder to observe the Torah laws, before jumping into water to save a drowning child, potentially causing a fatal delay. Still another example is of someone who gives away all their money to charity, leaving themselves impoverished.

Bediavad

Bediavad (beh-dee-ah-VAHD; *extenuating circumstances*) is a term used in Jewish law to describe a situation that's less than ideal but still acceptable after the fact. It implies leniency in extenuating circumstance and refers to those circumstances that a person or a court considers, although not preferable, at least valid after a person completes them. The concept usually applies to situations where someone can't meet the ideal conditions, and so deems the action acceptable under the circumstances. It's similar to the Latin term *ex post facto* (after the fact).

An example of *bediavad* is if someone hears the Scroll of Esther on Purim without the required *minyan* (MIN-yahn; a quorum of ten people). Ideally, during Purim, you should hear the Scroll of Esther with a *minyan* but if you hear it without the *minyan,* in other words without ten people present, the participant still considers the obligation fulfilled.

Kinyan

Kinyan (kin-yahn; acquisition) is a method of legally acquiring ownership in Jewish law. It refers to the legal, symbolic act of acquiring rights or ownership over an item or property. The concept is used in various situations, such as the acceptance of a *ketubah* (keh-TOO-bah; marriage contract) by a groom. For example, a *kinyan* could involve the exchange of an object to indicate two parties have reached an agreement, such as a groom receiving a handkerchief from the rabbi to symbolize his legal acquisition of marital obligations.

Hefker

Hefker (hef-kehr; ownerless property) means declaring something ownerless and permitting anyone to claim it. It specifies that a property has been abandoned by its owner, either intentionally or because the owner has given up hope of recovering it. After a court or person in authority designates a property as *hefker*, the first person who takes possession of the property can legally acquire it. For example, a teacher can announce that any items left behind in a classroom at the end of the school term are declared *hefker* (ownerless), so anyone can take them.

Chapter **15**

Ten Books for Your Talmud Library

When I study the Talmud, which happens just about every day, I have a lot of companion books within arm's reach, reference books that I've gathered over the years. This chapter talks about some of those books. I've also included versions of the complete Talmud itself that you can use to study.

Koren Talmud Bavli

If you want to study Talmud, consider investing in the *Koren Talmud Bavli* (BAHV-li; Babylonian) with commentary by Rabbi Adin Even-Israel Steinsaltz (Koren Publishers). It's a bilingual (Hebrew and English) set of 42 volumes, based on Rabbi Steinsaltz's original Hebrew commentary. It took Rabbi Steinsaltz 45 years to complete this project.

The volumes were published over several years and completed in 2019. The text of the Talmud is accompanied by the Rabbi's brilliant commentary. It includes many other elements as well, such as background notes and illustrations to help clarify the text, biographies of major personalities in the Talmud, and the *halakhot* (ha-la-KHOAT; laws) that grow out of the Talmudic discussions. The Steinsaltz Talmud, as it is generally called, aims to make the Talmud more accessible to a wider audience, continuing Rabbi Steinsaltz's lifelong mission of making Jewish texts available to all.

Talmudic scholars consider the *Koren Talmud Bavli* a work of genius, in part because of its profound content, as well as the fact that it speaks to both the beginner and the more experienced student of the Talmud. Nobody has ever made more of an impact on the popularization of Talmud study than Rabbi Steinsaltz.

In the spirit of full disclosure, I was a private student of Rabbi Steinsaltz's for 30 years. I wrote a memoir about our time together called *On the Road with Rabbi Steinsaltz: 25 Years of Pre-Dawn Car Trips, Mind-Blowing Encounters and Inspiring Conversations with a Man of Wisdom* (Jossey-Bass, Inc.).

Talmud Bavli: The Schottenstein Edition

Another English translation of the Talmud that has been published (and completed in 2015) is *Talmud Bavli: The Schottenstein Edition* (ArtScroll/Mesorah). The Schottenstein edition was compiled by a large team of scholars. This $20 million project involved up to 80 scholars working simultaneously on the more than 35,000 pages. It consists of 72 volumes.

The Schottenstein edition is jam-packed with extensive footnotes. Many of the footnotes in the Schottenstein edition may be over the heads of most beginners but reading them becomes an education in itself.

I want you to know that I have both editions. While I study using the Steinsaltz edition, I often refer to the Schottenstein edition as well, mostly to compare the translations. Basically, in my opinion, the Steinsaltz edition teaches you how to think about the contents of the Talmud, while the Schottenstein edition teaches you what to think.

WARNING

THE SONCINO ENGLISH TALMUD

The *Soncino English Talmud* was originally published in 1935 and completed in 1952. In 1978 Soncino Press issued a new 18 volume edition. For decades the *Soncino English Talmud* was the only source for the student who couldn't navigate the original classic edition of the Talmud — which is written in Aramaic and Hebrew.

But the *Soncino English Talmud* does have a bunch of drawbacks:

- Contains no commentary; it's strictly a literal translation of the Talmud, with occasional footnotes (which, frankly, often, in my opinion, confuse the reader more than clarifies).

- A British translation; and British English can differ significantly from American English.

- Cleans up the text in a kind of prudish way. As I point out throughout this book, the sages of the Talmud weren't prudes. They treated all subjects openly and honestly. The editors of the Soncino Talmud, however, often used euphemisms instead of translating the text literally.

For example, on page 17a of *masekhta* (mah-SEHK-tah; tractate) *Avodah Zara* (Ah-vowe-DA Zah-RAH; Strange Worship) whereas in the Soncino edition says, "She (the prostitute) blew forth breath and said: As this blown breath will not return to its place, so will Elazar b. Dordia never be received in repentance," the Steinsaltz edition (with a more accurate translation) says, "She passed wind and said: Just as this passed wind will not return to its place, so too Elazar ben Dordia will not be accepted in repentance." Commentaries make it clear: She flatulated!

Because we have the Steinsaltz and Schottenstein English editions of the Talmud, you don't really have a reason to invest in a copy of the Soncino edition. But you can find the Soncino edition online in several places, such as the website Halakhah.com by Tzvee Zahavy (www.halakhah.com).

William Davidson Talmud

Sefaria (www.sefaria.org), a website that offers free access to texts related to the Torah, includes an online version of the Talmud called the *William Davidson Talmud*. The *William Davidson Talmud* includes Rabbi Adin Even-Israel Steinsaltz's complete modern English translation and commentary of the Talmud. But it doesn't include any of the many other items found in the complete *Koren Talmud Bavli*, such as margin notes, brief biographies of the rabbis and sages in the text, illustrations, and further explanations. (see the section "Koren Talmud Bavli," earlier in this chapter).

Reference Guide to the Talmud

The *Reference Guide to the Talmud* (Koren Publishers), by Rabbi Adin Steinsaltz, can help Talmud students who want to sink their teeth into the Talmud as a whole, including its history and background information.

The book is divided into four parts:

>> Historical Background

>> Study of the Talmud

>> *Halakha* (ha-la-KHAH; Jewish law)

>> Additional Resources for the Study of the Talmud

The *Guide* includes a glossary of basic words, Talmudic terminology, Talmudic concepts and terms, Talmudic weights and measures, Rashi script (which you can read about in Chapter 2), principles governing the Talmud, and much more.

Introduction to the Talmud

This excellent volume, titled *Introduction to the Talmud: History, Personalities, and Background* (ArtScroll Mesorah Publications), by a team of Torah scholars, includes a sizable amount of background information on the Talmud. Although the publisher presents this book as a companion volume to *Talmud Bavli: The Schottenstein Edition* (see the section "Talmud Bavli: The Schottenstein Edition, earlier in this chapter), it provides a valuable resource for anyone who wants to dive deeply into the Talmud and its history.

It includes a lengthy section on the history of the Talmudic Era (from 10 BCE to 500 CE) and details about all the major personalities in the Talmud. In addition, the book includes an English translation of *Introduction to the Mishnah*, by Maimonides (the illustrious rabbi/philosopher who lived 1138–1204), and translations of other works by Maimonides. Although this book wasn't designed specifically for beginners, beginners can get a lot of valuable insight into the Talmud just by flipping through its pages.

The Essential Talmud

The Essential Talmud (Basic Books), by Rabbi Adin Even-Israel Steinsaltz, provides a one-volume overview and introduction to the beliefs, attitudes, and methods of the Talmud, written by one of the foremost experts on the Talmud. The book is divided into three parts:

>> History

>> Structure and Content

>> Method

Ein Yaakov

Ein Yaakov: The Ethical and Inspirational Teachings of the Talmud, translated with commentary by Avraham Yaakov Finkel (Jason Aronson, Inc.) is a translation of *Ein Yaakov (Ayn YAH-Ah-kove; The Well of Jacob)*, compiled in the 16th century by Rabbi Yaakov ibn Chaviv.

Ein Yaakov (the Well of Jacob), is a collection of the Aggadic (ah-GAH-dik non-legal narratives) material found in the Talmud (see Chapter 6 for more about the Aggadah). In addition to the translation, which makes up the bulk of the book, Ein Yaakov includes an extremely valuable translation of "The Aggadot of the Talmud," by Rabbi Avraham, the son of Maimonides, written in the early 13th century, which explains the profound importance in studying the Aggadic parts of the Talmud.

This edition of Ein Yaakov is 824 oversized pages and consists of a translation of the original material in its entirety. Rabbi Yaakov ibn Chaviv originally wrote his version for the masses, so non-scholars who didn't understand or had no interest in the legal parts of the Talmud could focus on the stories interspersed throughout the Talmud. The book is organized by the masekhtot (mah-SEKH-tote; tractates) of the Talmud and includes several hundred stories.

Who's Who in the Talmud

Who's Who in the Talmud (Jason Aronson, Inc.), by Shulamis Frieman, includes entries of every single rabbi in the Talmud (over 1,000), from Rav Abba to Rav Zutra. Each entry includes the date of birth or era in which the rabbi lived, place of birth, the names of their teachers, major students and colleagues, places in the vast Talmud where the rabbi is mentioned, and a sampling of stories about the rabbi. The book also includes a lengthy introduction to the Talmud itself.

When studying Talmud, I often come across the name of a rabbi or sage I may not know. Who's Who in the Talmud is my go-to source for basic, useful information about the people in the Talmud.

Talmudic Images

In Talmudic Images (Maggid), Rabbi Adin Steinsaltz has selected 13 of the most well-known sages from the Talmud's pages and offers us a verbal sketch of each. Most of what we know about the sages comes from small pieces of information scattered throughout the Talmud. Rabbi Steinsaltz brings together information about each Talmudic sage to give a vivid sense not only of their activities, but also their personalities.

As he writes in the introduction to the book, "[T]he volume does not attempt to provide a history of the sages, nor to describe their different schools of thought. It is intended to give a certain impression, a sketch of personalities, not only as thinkers and scholars, but also as human beings, whom we ourselves — as have others throughout the generations — can see standing before us, alive."

The Talmudic Anthology

Sometimes, I'm looking for a quotation that I can use in a note or an e-mail to someone, and the 570-page book *The Talmudic Anthology: Tales and Teachings of the Rabbis* (Behrman House), edited by Louis Newman, helps me find just what I'm looking for. The book is organized topically: From Abstinence to Zion and a few hundred other topics in between, this compendium includes all kinds of content from the Talmud, including stories, sayings, and interpretations. The compiler, Louis Newman, also edited the superb *Hasidic Anthology* (Jason Aronson, Inc.), which is a compilation of quotations, organized by topic, taken from the writings of the great Hasidic (khah-SID-ik) masters — the leaders of Hasidism, the Jewish religious movement that focuses on joy and Jewish mysticism that emerged in 18th-century Eastern Europe.

Some Additional Books on My Talmud Bookshelf

The following books can be valuable additions to your library. They are not essential like the 10 books mentioned above— which can become the core books in your Talmud library, but they all serve to provide interesting background for a more complete understanding of the Talmud.

» *The Talmud Treasury: An Index of Fascinating Facts and Stories* (Mosaica Press), by Rabbi Zvi Zimmerman

» *The Talmud: A Biography* (Princeton University Press), by Barry Scott Wimpfheimer

» *The Jewish Woman in Rabbinic Literature: Psychohistorical Perspective* (Ktav Publishing House), by Menachem M. Brayer

» *The Formation of the Babylonian Talmud* (Oxford University Press), by David Weiss Halivni

» *Why Do I Need to Learn Gemara?* (Philipp Feldheim), by Chaim Rosenblatt

» *Swimming in the Sea of Talmud: Lessons for Everyday Living* (Jewish Publication Society), by Michael Katz and Gershon Schwartz

» *Women and Jewish Law: The Essential Texts, Their History, and Their Relevance for Today* (Knopf Doubleday Publishing Group), by Rachel Biale

» *Find It in the Talmud: An Encyclopedia of Jewish Ethics and Conduct* (Urim Publications), by Mordechai Judovits

» *Sages of the Talmud: The Lives, Sayings, and Stories of 400 Rabbinic Masters* (Urim Publications), by Mordechai Judovits

» *Everyman's Talmud: The Major Teachings of the Rabbinic Sages* (Schocken), by Abraham Cohen

» *The Wisdom of the Talmud: A Thousand Years of Jewish Thought* (Citadel), by Ben Zion Bokser

» *Introduction to the Talmud and Midrash* (Fortress Press), by Hermann L. Strack and others

Appendix

The 63 Books of the Babylonian Talmud

I hate to complicate things, but there are two Talmuds — the Jerusalem Talmud and the Babylonian Talmud.

The Jerusalem Talmud, known as the *Yerushalmi* (yeh-roo-SHAHL; of Jerusalem) was compiled in the Land of Israel around the 4th century CE. Roman oppression interrupted its *redaction* (in this usage, meaning organizing and editing) because many scholars had to flee to Babylon. Because of this interruption, Talmudic scholars see the *Yerushalmi* as a less complete text, fragmentary and difficult to read.

The Babylonian Talmud, known as the *Bavli* (BAHV-lee; of Babylonia) was compiled in Babylonia between the 3rd and 6th centuries CE. It benefited from a more thorough redaction process over a longer period than the *Yerushalmi* received, resulting in a more comprehensive and systematic presentation of discussions. Scholars consider this Talmud more authoritative, and I discuss the *Bavli* Talmud in this entire book.

When Jewish literature and scholarship uses the term *Talmud*, it refers to the Babylonian Talmud. Otherwise, when referring to the Jerusalem Talmud, it is either called *the Jerusalem Talmud* or *the Yerushalmi*.

Around 200 CE, Rabbi Yehudah HaNasi organized the *Mishna* (MISH-nah; Repetition), the foundational part of the Talmud that represents a comprehensive written collection of Jewish oral laws and traditions. See Chapter 1 for more about the *Mishna*. Rabbi HaNasi divided the *Mishna* into six *sedarim* (she-DAHR-eem; orders) (singular, *seder*, SAY-dehr). In subsequent generations, various scholars divided those six *sedarim* into 63 *masekhtot* (mah-SEKH-tote; tractates) (singular, *masekhta*, Mah-sekh-tah). This appendix provides a list of those *masekhtot* separated by *seder*, along with a brief explanation of the general themes of each *masekhta*.

Seder Zeraim (Seeds)

Seder Zeraim (Zeh-AYE-eem; Order Seeds) contains *masekhtot* (tractates) that deal with prayers, blessings, *tithes* (a system of agricultural taxes mandated in ancient Israel), and agricultural laws:

>> *Berakhot* (Behr-ah-KHOTE; Blessings): Blessings and prayers; in other words, liturgical rules.

>> *Peah* (PAY-ah; Corner): Corners of fields and gleanings left for the poor. The commandment to leave the corners of one's field unharvested appears in Leviticus 19:9-10 and Leviticus 23:22. This practice was instituted as a form of agricultural charity, allowing the poor, the stranger, the widow, and the orphan to gather food for themselves.

>> *Demai* (Deh-MY; Doubtful): Produce bought from a person whose tithings are suspect.

>> *Kilayim* (Kih-LIE-eem; Prohibition): Forbidden mixtures of plants, animals, and clothing refers to several prohibitions in Jewish law against combining certain species or materials. The main categories of forbidden mixtures include planting mixed seeds (sowing different types of seeds together in the same field,) grafting trees of different species together, crossbreeding animals, mixed animal labor (using animals of different species together for work, such as plowing), and wearing garments made of a mixture of wool and linen.

>> *Sheviit* (She-VEE-it; Seventh): The Sabbatical Year. Every seventh year, the land in Israel is commanded to lie fallow. During this year, no one can sow or harvest the fields or prune the vineyards, and Jewish law considers any produce that grows naturally ownerless and available to all.

- **Terumah** (Teh-ROO-mah; Heave Offerings): Portions of agricultural produce that the farmer separates and gives to the *Kohanim* (koh-HA-neem; priests in the Temple). The term *heave* refers to an upward motion used when presenting an offering. The priest lifts (heaves) the sacrifice toward the altar in an up-and-down movement.

- **Ma'aserot** (Mah-ah-SEH-rote; Tithes): Given to the Levites, descendants of Levi (one of the 12 sons of Jacob) who were set apart for divine service. The Levites served as assistants to the *Kohanim*.

- **Ma'aser Sheni** (Mah-ah-SAYR shay-NEE; Second Tithe): A specific type of tithe separated from the initial tithe on agricultural produce; this second tithe comes from the produce after the first tithe and *terumah* have been separated. It must be eaten in Jerusalem.

- **Challah** (CHAH-la; Bread): The laws related to the *mitzvah* (MITZ-vah; Divine commandment) of separating challah, which is a portion of dough set aside as a gift for the *Kohanim*.

- **Orlah** (OR-la; Uncircumcised): Refers to the biblical prohibition against using fruits from newly planted trees during their first three years of growth. This concept is based on Leviticus 19:23-25.

- **Bikkurim** (Be-kur-EEM; First Fruits): Sacrificial offerings brought to the *Beit Hamikdash* (Bate ha MIG-dahsh; House of Holiness, the holy temple in Jerusalem)

Seder Moed (Festival)

The *masekhtot* (tractates) of *Seder Moed* (SAY-dehr MOE-ed; Order Festival) discuss the laws of the Sabbath and other Jewish festivals:

- **Shabbat** (Shah-BAHT; Sabbath): The 39 forbidden labors of the Sabbath. (See Chapter 10 for a list of the 39 forbidden labors.)

- **Eruvin** (Eh-voo-EEN; Mixtures): A set of rabbinic enactments that allow Jews to carry objects and travel more freely on Shabbat and holidays.

>> **Pesachim** (Peh-SAKH-eem; Passover Festivals): Laws regarding observance of *Pesach* (singular of *Pesachim*).

>> **Shekalim** (Sheh-kah-LEEM; Shekels): The annual head tax paid to the Holy Temple of half a shekel (a *shekel* was an ancient coin).

>> **Yoma** (YO-ma; The Day): Observance of the holiday *Yom Kippur* (Yome key-POOR; Day of Atonement). Primarily focuses on the laws and rituals of Yom Kippur, the Day of Atonement, as observed in Temple times.

>> **Sukkah** (Sue-KAH; Hut/Booth): Observance of the holiday of *Sukkot*, (Booths). A *sukkah* is a temporary structure constructed for the Jewish festival of *Sukkot*, which commemorates the Israelites' wandering in the desert after their exodus from Egypt. During *Sukkot*, Jews eat, sleep, and spend time in the *sukkah*, treating it as a temporary home for the duration of the holiday. See Chapter 10 for more on the *sukkah* and the holiday of *Sukkot*.

>> **Beitzah** (BAY tzah; Egg): Primarily deals with the laws and regulations concerning Jewish holidays. The *masekhta* is named *Beitzah* because it begins with a discussion about whether you can eat an egg laid on a holiday on that day.

>> **Rosh Hashanah** (Rowsh ha-SHAH-nah; Head of the Year): Observance of the Jewish New Year.

>> **Ta'anit** (TAH-ahn-eet; Fast): Primarily deals with the laws and customs related to fasting in Judaism, particularly public fasts decreed in times of distress.

>> **Megillah** (Meh-GILL-ah; Scroll): Primarily focused on explaining the laws and customs related to the Jewish holiday of Purim. It also deals with the sanctity of synagogues and Torah scrolls, the treatment of sacred objects, and rules for public Torah reading.

>> **Moed Katan** (Moe-ed kah TAHN; Minor Festivals): The term *Chol Hamoed* (khol Ha-MOE-ehd; secular/mundane festival days) refers to the days that fall between the first and last days of the week-long Jewish festivals of Passover and *Sukkot*, and these days have a unique status in Jewish observance. The word *chol* means "secular" or "mundane," and *moed* means "appointed time" or "festival."

>> **Chagigah** (Khah-GEE-gah; Festival Offering): Sacrificial offerings during the three pilgrimage festivals of *Sukkot, Pesach,* and *Shavuot* (Shah-voo-OAT; Weeks). The festival of Shavuot doesn't not have its own tractate, so most discussion about it occurs in this tractate, *Masekhta Chagigah.* It commemorates the giving of the Torah to the Israelites at Mount Sinai and celebrates the covenant between God and the Jewish people.

Seder Nashim (Women)

Marriage, divorce, some forms of oaths, and laws of the *Nazirite* (people who vow abstinence and dedication to God) appear in the *masekhtot* (tractates) of *Seder Nashim* (nah–SHEEM; Order Women):

>> **Yevamot** (Yh-vah-MOAT; Levirate Widows): Refers to women who are subject to the laws of *levirate marriage,* the practice of a man marrying his deceased brother's childless widow in Jewish tradition. The tractate also deals with the concepts of *chalitzah* (khah-LEE-tzah; removal) and *agunot* (ah-goo-note; chained/anchored). *Chalitzah* is a Jewish ceremony that releases a childless widow from the obligation of levirate marriage and allows her to marry someone else.

In the context of Jewish law, an *agunah* refers to a woman who can't legally remarry because of specific circumstances. One major issue is the question of what constitutes sufficient evidence of a husband's death to allow remarriage. The issue of *agunot* remains a significant concern in modern Jewish law and practice, with ongoing efforts to find solutions that balance traditional *halakhic* (ha-LAH-khik; Jewish legal) requirements with the need to prevent women from being trapped in unwanted or non-existent marriages.

>> **Ketubot** (Keh-too-BOAT; Marriage Contracts): Marriage contracts, financial obligations, and the mutual rights and duties of husband and wife.

>> **Nedarim** (Neh-DAHR-eem; Vows): The making and annulment of vows and oaths.

>> **Nazir** (NAH-zear; Separate/Abstain): Refers to a person who has taken a special vow of abstinence and dedication to God, known as a Nazirite vow. A Nazirite abstains from all grape products, including wine and vinegar, refrains from cutting his hair, and avoids contact with dead bodies, even close relatives. Samson is probably the most famous Nazirite in the Bible.

>> **Sotah** (SOW-tah; Wife Suspected of Adultery): Primarily deals with the biblical ritual described in Numbers 5:11-31, known as the ordeal of the bitter water. This ritual was performed when a husband suspected his wife of adultery but had no proof.

>> **Gittin** (GIT-ten; Divorce Documents): Laws and procedures of divorce and the annulment of marriage.

>> **Kiddushin** (Kid-DOO-shin; Betrothal): The first of two stages in the traditional Jewish marriage process. This stage legally binds the couple together as husband and wife, even though they don't yet live together. *Kiddushin* creates a legally binding marital status, unlike an engagement, which has no legal standing. After *kiddushin* is performed, Jewish law considers the woman married and forbidden to all other men.

The Talmud outlines three ways that the couple can effect *kiddushin*: exchange money or an object of value, sign a document, or have sexual intercourse with the intent of marriage.

Seder Nezikin (Damages)

Seder Nezikin (Neh-ZEE-keen; Order Damages) contains *masekhtot* (tractates) that talk about civil and criminal law, courts and oaths.

A very large *masekhta* (tractate) was divided into the first three *masekhtot*, hence the names referencing gates:

>> **Bava Kamma** (Bah-vah KAH-mah; The First Gate): Damage to person and property, loans and interest, stolen goods

>> **Bava Metzia** (Bah-vah-met-TZEE-ah; The Middle Gate): Lost and found property, embezzlement, fraud, *usury* (the practice of lending money at unreasonably high interest rates), sales, rentals, rights of hired laborers

>> **Bava Batra** (Bah-vah-BAHT-Rah; The Last Gate): Real estate, possessions, inheritance, partnership, evidence, testimony

The remainder of the *masekhtot* in this *seder* focus on specific aspects of the law:

>> **Sanhedrin** (Sahn-HEAD-rin; Supreme Council): The system of courts, judicial procedure, and capital punishment.

>> **Makkot** (MAH-coat; Lashes): False witnesses, cities of refuge, and corporal punishment.

A *city of refuge* was a designated place of asylum in ancient Israel for those who had committed unintentional manslaughter. These cities provided protection for individuals who had accidentally killed someone, allowing them to flee there to escape blood vengeance from the victim's family.

>> **Shevuot** (Sheh-voo-OAT; Oaths): The laws and regulations concerning *oaths* (sworn statements) in Jewish law.

>> **Eduyyot** (Aye-doo-YOTE; Testimonies): A collection of individual testimonies and statements made by various rabbis, often presenting minority opinions on various *halakhic* (Jewish legal) matters. The tractate serves to preserve important legal opinions that might otherwise have been forgotten or overlooked, ensuring a comprehensive record of rabbinic discussions and ruling. Unlike other *masekhtot* that focus on specific themes or laws, *Eduyyot* covers a wide range of topics from various areas of Jewish law and practice.

>> **Avodah Zara** (Ah-vowe-DAH zah-RAH; Strange Worship): Refers to idolatry or the worship of deities other than the God of Israel. *Masekhta Avodah Zara* in the Talmud deals with laws pertaining to Jews living among Gentiles and regulations concerning interactions between Jews and idolaters.

>> **Avot** (Ah-VOTE; Ancestors): Also known as *Pirkei Avot* (PEER-kay ah-VOTE; Chapters of the Fathers), this unique section of the *Mishna* focuses on ethical teachings and moral wisdom, rather than legal discussions. The *masekhta* is divided into six *perakim* (peh-rah-KEEM; chapters), each presenting various teachings attributed to different rabbis.

>> **Horayot** (Hoar-eye-YOTE; Decisions): Deals with erroneous rulings and decisions made by Jewish religious authorities, including erroneous rulings by the *Sanhedrin* (high court); mistaken decisions by the high priest; inadvertent sins committed by leaders, including the king; and sacrificial offerings required for atonement of these errors.

Seder Kodashim (Holy Things)

The *Seder Kodashim* (Koh–dah–SHEEM; Order Holy Things) has *masekhtot* (tractates) that deal with sacrificial rites, the Temple, and dietary laws:

>> **Zevachim** (Zeh-Vah-KHEEM; Sacrifices): Laws and regulations concerning animal sacrifices in the Temple in Jerusalem.

>> **Menachot** (Meh-nah-KHOAT; Meal Offerings): Laws and regulations concerning flour-based offerings brought to the Temple in Jerusalem, as well as oil and wine *libations* (a ritual pouring of liquid as an offering).

>> **Chullin** (KHOO-leen; Ordinary): Kosher slaughter and the dietary regulations of non-sacrificial animals.

>> **Bechorot** (Beh-KHOAR-oat; Firstborns): Firstborn animals and sons in Jewish tradition; explores the ritual of *Pidyon HaBen* (PID-yon ha-BEN; Redemption of the Son) where a father symbolically redeems his firstborn son from priestly service.

>> **Arachin** (Ah-rah-KHEEN; Valuations): Based on the biblical passages in Leviticus 27 that outline the concept of vowing a person's value to the Temple. It expands on these laws, providing detailed interpretations and applications of the

rules for determining the monetary value of individuals when someone pledges to donate a person's worth to the Temple.

>> **Temurah** (Teh-moo-RAH; Exchange): The substitution of animals designated for sacrifice in the Temple, based on prohibitions found in Leviticus 27:10 and 27:33 against substituting a non-consecrated animal for one already consecrated for sacrifice.

>> **Keritot** (Keh-ree-TOAT; Excisions): Sins punishable by *karet* (KAH-ret; cutting off), a divine punishment of removal from the Jewish people. This *masekhta* lists 36 transgressions that, if committed intentionally, qualify you for punishment by *karet*.

>> **Me'ila** (Meh-EE-la; Trespass/Sacrilegious Treatment): Rooted in Leviticus 5:15-16, which outlines the consequences of unintentionally misusing sacred items.

>> **Tamid** (Tah-MEED; Daily): The daily Temple service, focusing on the morning and evening burnt offerings.

>> **Middot** (MEE-dote; Measurements): Detailed description of the Second Temple in Jerusalem, providing a comprehensive account of the Temple's architecture, layout, and dimensions.

>> **Kinnim** (Key-NEEM; Nests):The sacrificial procedures for birds, typically doves or pigeons, which those who couldn't afford larger animal offerings would bring to the Temple.

Seder Tohorot (Purities)

Laws of ritual purity and impurity of the dead, food, and body appear in the *masekhtot* (tractates) of *Seder Tohorot* (Toe-hohr-OAT; Order Purities). Discussions of cleanliness, purity, and impurity in this *seder* refer to spiritual cleanliness, not the contemporary use of the word (meaning physically soiled):

>> **Kelim** (KAY-leem; Vessels): Ritual uncleanness of utensils and garments.

>> **Oholot** (Oh-ho-LOAT; Tents): The defilement caused by a corpse to houses.

>> *Negaim* (Neh-gah-YEEM; Afflictions): Rooted in Leviticus chapters 13 and 14, which describe various skin afflictions and their ritual implications. The complex laws of *tzaraat* (tzah-RAHT; skin disease), often mistranslated as "leprosy," refers to a broad range of skin afflictions. *Tzaraat* can appear on human skin, clothing, or even the walls of houses; and Jewish law often interprets it as a divine punishment for sins, particularly evil speech.

>> *Parah* (Pah-RAH; Heifer): Laws and rituals surrounding the red heifer, which is based on the biblical commandment described in Numbers 19:1-22. It details the process of selecting, preparing, and sacrificing the red heifer.

>> *Tohorot* (Toe-hor-OAT; Purities): Specifically deals with the laws of ritual purity and impurity in Judaism. It discusses various degrees of ritual impurity and the processes for purification; it also provides insights into the complex system of ritual purity in ancient Jewish life, reflecting the importance placed on maintaining a state of spiritual readiness in daily activities.

>> *Mikvaot* (Mick-vah-OAT; Pools of Water): The construction and maintenance of a *mikvah* (MIK-vah; a Jewish ritual bath).

>> *Niddah* (NEE-dah; Menstruating Woman): Outlines the laws requiring physical separation between husband and wife during the menstrual period and for a specified time afterward.

>> *Machshirin* (Makh she-reen; Things Rendered Fit): Liquids and foods that are susceptible to ritual uncleanness.

>> *Zavim* (Zah-VEEM; Seminal Emissions): Secretions that render a person unclean.

>> *Tevul Yom* (Teh-vool YOME; Immersed on That Day): Derived from Leviticus 22:6-7, which states that a person who has become ritually impure remains in that state until evening, even after immersion in a *mikvah*.

>> *Yadayim* (Yah-DIE-eem; Hands): The defilement of the hands and their purification.

>> *Uktzin* (Ook-TZEEN; Stems): Fruits and plants susceptible to uncleanness.

Index

Dedication

Rabbi Adin Steinsaltz z'l. I called you my Teacher; you called me your friend.

"The righteous, even after death, are called living." (Talmud, Masekhta Berachot.)

Acknowledgments

Heartfelt gratitude to: Tracy Brown Hamilton, Project and Development Editor. I was "pregnant" with this book, and you were my extraordinary "midwife." Laura Miller, Copy Editor. You dazzled me every step of the way. Laura, you are brilliant and amazing. Shannon Kucaj, Acquisitions Editor. With the sincerest gratitude for your kindness, enthusiasm, and your belief in me.

Danny Siegel, my first Talmud teacher. It has been almost 50 years since you introduced me to Rabbi Akiva. You changed my life. Rick Blum, friend and *chavrusa*. Ken Kurzweil, for your patience, support, and computer expertise. Malya, Miriam, and Moshe, "for the fruit." Bobby Kurzweil, my wife, my inspiration, my partner.

Author Biography

Arthur Kurzweil is a writer, teacher, and magician. He's the author of several books, including *The Torah for Dummies* (Wiley), *Kabbalah for Dummies* (Wiley), *On the Road with Rabbi Steinsaltz* (Ben Yehuda Press), *Pebbles of Wisdom from Rabbi Adin Steinsaltz* (Jossey-Bass), and *From Generation to Generation: How to Trace Your Jewish Family History and Genealogy* (Jossey-Bass).

As a member of both the Society of Magicians and the International Brotherhood of Magicians (Order of Merlin), he often performs his one-man show, "Searching for God in a Magic Shop." He has received the Distinguished Humanitarian Award from The Melton Center for Jewish Studies at The Ohio State

University for his unique contributions to Jewish education; a membership in Beta Phi Mu, the International Honor Society for Library and Information Science; and a lifetime achievement award from the International Association of Jewish Genealogical Societies.

He and his wife, Bobby, share 8 children and 13 grandchildren.

Publisher's Acknowledgments

Acquisitions Editor: Tracy Boggier

Senior Project Editor:
Tracy Brown Hamilton

Copy Editor: Digital Quills LLC

Tech Reviewer: Dr. Rick Blum

Production Editor:
Saikarthick Kumarasamy

Cover Image:
© TSViPhoto/stock.adobe.com